Teaching and Language Corpora

APPLIED LINGUISTICS AND LANGUAGE STUDY

GENERAL EDITOR

PROFESSOR CHRISTOPHER N. CANDLIN,
Macquarie University, Sydney

For a complete list of books in this series see pages v–vi

Teaching and Language Corpora

Edited by

Anne Wichmann
Steven Fligelstone
Tony McEnery
Gerry Knowles

Longman
London and New York

Addison Wesley Longman Limited
Edinburgh Gate
Harlow, Essex CM20 2JE
England

and Associated Companies throughout the world

*Published in the United States of America
by Addison Wesley Longman Inc., New York*

First published 1997

ISBN 0 582 27609-8 Paper

British Library Cataloguing-in-Publication Data
A catalogue record for this book is
available from the British Library

Library of Congress Cataloging-in-Publication Data
A catalog entry for this title is available from the
Library of Congress

Set by 35 in 10/12 pt New Baskerville
Produced through Longman Malaysia,

APPLIED LINGUISTICS AND LANGUAGE STUDY

GENERAL EDITOR

PROFESSOR CHRISTOPHER N. CANDLIN,

Macquarie University, Sydney

Language and Development:
Teachers in a Changing World
BRIAN KENNY *and*
WILLIAM SAVAGE (EDS)

Autonomy and Independence in
Language Learning
PHIL BENSON *and* PETER VOLLER (EDS)

Literacy in Society
RUQAIYA HASAN *and*
GEOFFREY WILLIAMS (EDS)

Phonology in English Language
Teaching: An International Approach
MARTHA C. PENNINGTON

From Testing to Assessment:
English as an International Language
CLIFFORD HILL *and* KATE PARRY
(EDS)

Language as Discourse:
Perspectives for Language Teaching
MICHAEL MACCARTHY *and*
RONALD CARTER

Language and Discrimination:
A Study of Communication in
Multi-Ethnic Workplaces
CELIA ROBERTS, EVELYN DAVIES *and*
TOM JUPP

Translation and Translating:
Theory and Practice
ROBERT T. BELL

Language, Literature and the Learner:
Creative Classroom Practice
RONALD CARTER *and*
JOHN MCRAE (EDS)

Theory and Practice of Writing:
An Applied Linguistic Perspective
WILLIAM GRABE *and* ROBERT B. KAPLAN

Measuring Second Language
Performance
TIM MCNAMARA

Interaction in the Language
Curriculum: Awareness, Autonomy
and Authenticity
LEO VAN LIER

Second Language Learning:
Theoretical Foundations
MICHAEL SHARWOOD SMITH

Analysing Genre – Language Use in
Professional Settings
V.K. BHATIA

Rediscovering Interlanguage
LARRY SELINKER

Language Awareness in the Classroom
CARL JAMES *and* PETER GARRETT (EDS)

Process and Experience in the
Language Classroom
MICHAEL LEGUTKE *and*
HOWARD THOMAS

An Introduction to Second
Language Acquisition Research
DIANE LARSEN-FREEMAN *and*
MICHAEL H. LONG

Listening in Language Learning
MICHAEL ROST

The Classroom and the Language
Learner: Ethnography and Second-
Language Classroom Research
LEO VAN LIER

Second Language Grammar:
Learning and Teaching
WILLIAM E. RUTHERFORD

Contents

Preface

Most of the chapters in this volume were first presented at the conference on Teaching and Language Corpora (TALC) at Lancaster University in the Spring of 1994. The idea for the conference, and hence the book, arose from discussions among members of ICAME (International Computer Archive of Modern English), and in particular as a result of a session initiated and led by Steve Fligelstone.

ICAME meets annually to report on research based on computer corpora of English, and more recently other languages. Many of the members are also teachers, and it became increasingly clear in recent years that they were not only engaged in research into corpora, but were using corpora, or corpus-derived data, to inform their teaching and to drive the learning process.

This was clearly by no means a secondary activity, and many of them responded to our call for articles dealing with the pedagogical aspect of corpus exploitation. We were delighted at the interest shown and hope that, by bringing together in one volume some of these contributions, many more teachers will find inspiration and encouragement to embark on similar activities.

The Editors

Editors' acknowledgements

This book reflects the innovative work and commitment of a large number of teachers. Our thanks go first to them, and then to the many researchers, teachers and computer specialists whose work has provided the foundations on which these chapters build. In particular we would like to thank the members of ICAME who provide a supportive framework in which new ideas can be conceived, developed and, above all, shared.

Publishers' acknowledgements

We are grateful to the following for permission to reproduce copyright material:

Faber & Faber Ltd and Farrar, Straus & Giroux, Inc for extracts from the poems 'Send No Money' from *The Whitsun Weddings* (UK Title)/*Collected Poems* (US Title) by Philip Larkin. Copyright © 1988, 1989 by the Estate of Philip Larkin, and 'Elvis Presley' from *The Sense of Movement* (UK Title)/*Collected Poems* (US Title) by Thom Gunn. Copyright © 1994 by Thom Gunn; Newspaper Publishing Plc for the article 'Restrictions on young drivers considered' by Christian Wolmar from *The Independent* 26.1.93 and an extract from the article 'For church and state it's divorce – Italian style' by Michael Sheridan from *The Independent* 2.10.89; A.P. Watt Ltd on behalf of Michael Yeats and Simon & Schuster for the poem 'Memory' from *The Collected Poems of W.B. Yeats* (UK Title)/*The Collected Works of W.B. Yeats, Volume 1: The Poems*, (US Title) revised and edited by Richard J. Finneran (New York, Macmillan 1989).

Contributors

KHURSHID AHMAD
University of Surrey

GUY ASTON
University of Bologna

ANDREA DAVIES
Formerly University of Surrey

WILLIAM DODD
University of Birmingham

LAURA GAVIOLI
University of Bologna

GRAEME HUGHES
Lancaster University

GORDON INKSTER
Lancaster University

HOWARD JACKSON
*University of Central England
in Birmingham*

TIM JOHNS
University of Birmingham

RANDALL L. JONES
Brigham Young University

BERNHARD KETTEMANN
University of Graz

PHILIP KING
University of Birmingham

GEOFFREY LEECH
Lancaster University

WILLIAM LOUW
University of Zimbabwe

DIETER MINDT
Freie Universität Berlin

DAVID MINUGH
University of Stockholm

PAMELA PETERS
Macquarie University

ANTOINETTE RENOUF
University of Liverpool

JOHN M. SINCLAIR
University of Birmingham

EVE WILSON
University of Kent

General Introduction

Why this book?

Corpora have long been used in research. Since many researchers are also teachers, it is possible that corpora, or at least corpus-derived data, have also been used for some time in the teaching and learning process. So what has changed?

Firstly, computers have become smaller, cheaper and thus more widely available, both to teachers and to learners. The data stored on them has become more readily accessible to the user. Above all, the amount of data available from the outset in machine-readable form is far greater than even a few years ago. In this way the practical prerequisites for corpus-based teaching and learning have improved dramatically.

Secondly, the current approach to language description is strongly oriented towards usage. There is a general need to accommodate the apparent unpredictability of real data. This need stems in part from developments in speech and language technology. Systems, such as part-of-speech taggers, developed to work on written text, must be robust enough to deal with texts as they are, rather than texts as we might like them to be. In language teaching, too, the preference for 'authentic' texts requires both learners and teachers to cope with language which the textbooks do not predict. And of course the end product of language teaching, the ability to communicate, must ultimately take place in the real world, and not in a linguistically contrived one.

Finally, some of the impetus for this book may lie in changing views of the role of teachers and learners. Students are increasingly encouraged to take charge of their own learning. While this arises no doubt in part from economic pressures, it also reflects serious pedagogical concerns.

The contributors to this book are only a small number of those teachers around the world who exploit computerized language data, whether written or spoken, for teaching. Many, but not all, deal with the teaching of English; others have applied similar methods to the teaching of other languages. Some describe the use of corpora for helping learners to acquire a foreign language, with the main emphasis on increasing their proficiency. Others are more concerned with teaching *about* individual languages and language in general. Together they highlight just how many areas of language teaching and learning can profit from the use of corpora.

Anne Wichmann

1

Teaching and Language Corpora: a Convergence

GEOFFREY LEECH

There is every reason to believe that language corpora will have a role of growing importance in teaching. This book, and the workshop (TALC94) which gave birth to it, are testimonies to the richness of the interest and experience which are already being applied to the convergence of language teaching and language research, through the link of corpus-based methods.

1 Up to now

Until recently, teaching had little connection with the momentum behind the evolution of corpus-based methods in linguistics. There were other forces in play. But one of the functions of the TALC94 workshop, as the first-ever international (or even national) conference on corpora and teaching, was that it enabled us to learn, for the first time, about the whole range of largely unpublicized pedagogical activities making use of corpora.

The experience of ICAME (International Computer Archive of Modern English) has been especially indicative. For seventeen years, ICAME, with its annual conference and journal,[1] has spearheaded research developments in corpus linguistics, with particular reference to the English language. But it was not until 1992 that there was an item in the ICAME conference programme referring to the use of corpora in teaching. This was the paper by Steve Fligelstone, 'Some reflections on the question of teaching from a corpus linguistics perspective'. Fligelstone led a workshop at the 1992 conference in Nijmegen on the topic, and the paper was reworked for publication (Fligelstone 1993).

Future historians tracing the history of computer corpora in linguistics might easily assume that ICAME members had given no serious thought to the educational use of corpora up to that time. But this would be a false conclusion. Most of the members of ICAME were then, and still are, university teachers, and most of them will have increasingly been using their corpora and corpus-based techniques in teaching, as well as in research, for a number of years. In my own case, for example, I began using an incomplete prototype LOB (Lancaster–Oslo/Bergen) Corpus for postgraduate teaching as early as 1976, and this use of corpora in teaching has continued, and gradually been extended to new areas of the curriculum at Lancaster, ever since. The original 'trickle down' from research to teaching is now becoming a torrent!

The notion of 'trickle down' from research to teaching seems particularly appropriate to corpus linguistics. This is because the computer corpus, as a resource for finding out about language and texts, is totally neutral as to these two major interconnecting activities of universities. The corpus, purely as a resource, is rather like a shelf in a university library: it is there to be exploited, and the same resources are equally usable for research and teaching. The history of computer corpora, on the other hand, has been tied to the history of computer technology. Inevitably, while computers were limited to large mainframes available to the initiated few, computer corpora were largely restricted to research use. But as computers have grown smaller, cheaper, and massively more powerful, their use in teaching has grown immeasurably. It is natural that the movement from research to teaching has taken place in this way, as the information revolution in the use of computers has more and more extended itself from the laboratory to the classroom.

It is also evident that the corpus, as an information source, fits in very well with a dominant trend in university teaching philosophy over the past twenty years, which is the trend from *teaching as imparting knowledge* to *teaching as mediated learning* (cf. Laurillard 1993: 13–15). In this context, there is no longer a gulf between research and teaching (cf. Knowles 1990), since the student is placed in a position similar to that of a researcher, investigating and imaginatively making sense of the data available through observation of the corpus. As Tim Johns has said (quoted by Gavioli in this volume), [*Georges Clemenceau* (1841–1929): 'War is much too serious a thing to be left to the military.'] 'research is too serious to be left to the researchers': teaching is a natural extension of research. The student-centred paradigm of 'discovery learning' – or what Johns has called 'data-driven learning' – can scarcely be better exemplified than through the use of the computer corpus. Almost uniquely, among the information resources of which students make use in education, a text corpus is of primary interest because of what it is. Other resources, such as databases, are of interest indirectly, because of what they are 'about'. But a corpus is, of itself, a rich resource of authentic data containing structures, patterns and predictable features that are waiting to be 'unlocked' by the human intelligence. Perhaps the nearest equivalent, in other disciplines, is in the direct confrontation with data that occurs in the scientific laboratory, or in fieldwork. It is this experiential confrontation with the material of study that can make corpus work so rewarding for the student. And it often happens that a student working on a relatively small corpus assignment comes up with original observations and discoveries which have probably never been brought to notice before, even in the most detailed dictionaries and grammars of a language.

Having quoted Tim Johns, I should celebrate the nature of his contribution, as a prime example of a university teacher who has exploited the computer corpus mainly for teaching. Indeed, the above quotation 'research is too serious to be left to the researchers' reverses, by implication, the traditional donnish assumption that research or scholarship is the more important thing, and that teaching is just a spin-off from it, the vehicle whereby students are permitted to participate in the don's world of *recherché* knowledge. Tim Johns's earlier work in CALL (Computer-assisted Language Learning) – see Higgins and Johns (1984), Johns (1988) – naturally availed itself of the corpus-rich atmosphere of Birmingham, and he became among the first to advocate and to explore the use of corpora in teaching. Perhaps it is significant that Johns, being a teaching-oriented rather than research-oriented lecturer, never became a *habitué* of ICAME! And it is also significant that he was the first to insist that the use of computer corpora in teaching was itself a topic for research (Johns, this volume). (See also Johns 1991a, 1991b, 1993.)

Those, like Johns, who have been placing teaching with corpora at the forefront of our attention as a matter of primary interest, may well find my 'trickle down' metaphor unhelpful, or even offensive. 'Trickle down' implies that research is 'up there' as an élite activity, and teaching is 'down here' in a lower, subservient role. But, in the experience of many, there is not a one-way dependence of this kind. One finds that 'trickle up' from teaching to research can be just as important.

The *convergence* mentioned in my title is a natural coming together of teaching with research from various points of view. This is natural whether we consider it from the 'trickle down' point of view, where the resources and techniques used in research progressively become available for teaching, or from the Johns 'trickle up' point of view, where the development of language-teaching techniques naturally appropriates to itself the resources available for research, and becomes a topic for research in its own right. The convergence is aided by the increasing similarity, in higher education, of the paradigm for research and the paradigm for teaching (using and analysing resources in a self-access mode).

Research with corpora, over the past twenty years, has become an amazingly fertile development. Whereas as recently as ten years ago corpus-based methodology was the fringe activity of a tiny minority of eccentrics, it has now become the mainstream of computational linguistics, and has increasingly established itself in mainstream linguistics. This in itself means that corpus linguistics is appearing more and more as a part of the university curriculum in linguistics, both at undergraduate and postgraduate levels.

But the thing to avoid, if we can, is treating the use of corpora in teaching as a bandwagon. Teaching bandwagons, if driven too far and too fast, can do much harm to those on the receiving end. Some will remember that ten years ago, when the new educational possibilities of CALL were very much in the ascendancy, many warned heavily against too great an enthusiasm for this new toy – the computer in the language classroom. False expectations of the powers of technology, it was recalled, had been raised by an earlier innovation, the introduction of language laboratories. The warning was salutary: since the computer entered the classroom, students have learned a lot about how to handle computers. But has their knowledge of languages taken a great leap forward? The educational benefits of technologies are still far from fully understood and acknowledged.

At that time, Higgins and Johns (1984: 12) were among those who warned against a revolutionary zeal for computers. As a conception of the role of the computer in the classroom, Higgins (1988: 12–15) preferred the metaphor of the 'pedagogue' (in ancient

Greece, the slave who accompanied the pupil to school) to that of the 'magister' (the Roman 'master' to whom the pupil submitted in obedience). Unlike the magister, the pedagogue was merely a humble facilitator of the learning process. This view of the computer certainly comes to the fore when we think of corpora. The computer is simply the device that gives access, the intermediary between the learner and the corpus as a fountain of knowledge and understanding. But we may go even one step further, and say that the *corpus* itself has no more than the facilitative 'pedagogue' role. It enables the learner/student to explore, to investigate, to generalize, to test hypotheses; but it does not itself initiate or direct the path of learning.

It is timely, none the less, to welcome the emergence of the computer corpus as a linguistic learning resource. The convergence of research and teaching is already taking place – it is a *fait accompli*. Our task is to make the best use of it, and to exchange ideas on how the computer corpus can be exploited to the best advantage in the future. This means, first, exchanging experience on how we have used corpora in teaching in the past, and how we are developing these techniques at the present time. The time is right for taking stock. My plan is to do this by surveying the activities connecting corpora and teaching, and their motivations.

2   And now?

Like many fields of endeavour, the corpus-aided language teaching field can be thought of as containing a core – a central or focal area – and an expanding periphery. The core, which can be seen as the main concern of this book, is the direct use of corpora as resources for teaching. The periphery can be seen as a set of corpus applications which indirectly contribute to teaching. Both the core and the periphery are important for the way we think about the field, and for realizing its potential. Yet a further set of activities, more peripheral still, takes the form of teaching-oriented corpus developments. The follow list summarizes the activities I have in mind:

- Direct use of corpora in teaching:
  Teaching about
  Teaching to exploit
  Exploiting to teach

- Use of corpora indirectly applied to teaching:
  Reference publishing
  Materials development
  Language testing
- Further teaching-oriented corpus development:
  LSP corpora
  L1 and L2 developmental corpora
  Bilingual/multilingual corpora.

The three main headings above can be viewed as three concentric circles, starting with the innermost one, which will occupy our attention in the following section.

2.1   Direct use of corpora in teaching

What is the nature of the interaction between corpora and teaching? The three different ways in which corpora may be used in teaching, as listed above, are distinguished by Fligelstone (1993): *teaching about [corpora], teaching to exploit [corpora] and exploiting [corpora] to teach.*

Teaching about

The first of these is probably the least interesting or innovative. As I have already said, corpus linguistics, seen as a subdiscipline within linguistics, has now come of age (see Svartvik 1992), and is beginning to find its way into curricula, both postgraduate and undergraduate. One symptom of the 'arrival' of corpus linguistics is that introductory textbooks on the subject are already being written: I am aware of more than one such publication under preparation at present.

What does teaching corpus linguistics mean? Just as a student studying for a linguistics degree (or for that matter any language-related degree – say, in English or Italian) takes courses in such subjects as phonetics, syntax, sociolinguistics, or discourse analysis, there are now beginning to be courses on corpus linguistics, or courses containing corpus linguistics as a substantial component. I recently received a letter from an East European university asking me for a basic reading list on corpus linguistics, and some information about corpora and the software available. The letter enclosed an outline of a syllabus for a corpus linguistics course the author was planning to introduce. This was of interest to me, in showing that, for an academic who had not reached corpus linguistics directly through research involvement, the teaching of corpus linguistics was nevertheless becoming an important part of the curriculum.

As with other courses, the curriculum will tend to cover main areas of the subdiscipline: say, its history, its data and subject-matter, its methods of investigation, the models or theories it employs. In the case of corpus linguistics, inevitably important topics are: (a) what corpora exist?, (b) can they be accessed, analysed or exploited?, (c) what software can be used for this purpose?, (d) what are the applications of corpus linguistics? And arising out of these is a more philosophical or theoretical question: (e) what view of language and methods and goals of linguistic study is presented through corpus linguistics? How does this view compare with other views? (Here the Chomskian distinction between 'internalized' and 'externalized' language comes to the fore: corpus linguistics very much identifying its domain as the latter – see Chomsky 1988.)

In principle, of course, corpus linguistics could be taught as a purely academic subject, in which the students never get their hands on a computer, or gain access to a corpus. But, I would strongly suggest, almost more than any other branch of linguistics, corpus linguistics requires that students have 'hands on' experience of the subject: of the use and exploration of corpora. A course which did not provide access in this way would be like an astronomy course in which the students were never allowed access to a telescope: it would be a dull course indeed. Only through *using* corpora can one gain a first-hand sense of their potential. For example, in using a grammatically tagged corpus, one starts asking intelligent questions about how it is possible to build an automatic tagger. And one also considers questions of linguistic content such as: What sort of information does grammatical tagging give, or fail to give, about language? How can it help other aspects of language processing? Hence, 'Teaching about' naturally shades into Fligelstone's second teaching category, which is 'Teaching to exploit'.

Teaching to exploit

Since the main rationale of corpora in teaching is their immediate availability for students' use, it is important that the students should be able to acquire the necessary 'hands on' know-how, so that they can explore corpora for their own purposes. This activity of self-access exploitation can be to a greater or lesser degree manipulated by the teacher for the student's benefit; but however 'interventionist' behind the scenes, the teacher still remains cast in the role of adviser and facilitator, rather than the authoritative source of knowledge. (In fact, occasional bouts of ignorance on the part of the teacher can facilitate the process of learning enormously.) In the course of learning how to manipulate corpus searches, the student will need, at least initially, to be supplied with sample tasks or exercises, and with feedback on those exercises. To help there are published textbooks, such as Tribble and Jones (1990), exploring the use of the Longman Mini-Concordancer (LMC) package – authored by Brian Chandler.

Works such as Tribble and Jones (1990) are particularly tied to the use of pedagogical concordance programs. In spite of their accessibility to the learner, these imply certain limitations – such as the size of the corpus that can be accessed. However, more generally, it might be desirable to give students a broader sense of what corpora are capable of. At Lancaster, a postgraduate course in how to exploit corpora (designed mainly by Tony McEnery) enables students to progress from the simpler and more restricted packages, such as the LMC, to the more challenging ones, such as WordCruncher, which allow instant access to large 'standard' corpora of a million or so words, such as the LOB Corpus, the Brown Corpus, and the Helsinki Historical English Corpus. A still greater range of corpus searching is then provided for by the in-house 'CONCORD' facility (developed by Fligelstone), enabling students to search a wide range of tagged and syntactically annotated corpora, and enabling them to make use of annotations of grammatical categories (for example, in searches for adjective sequences, or passives, or phrasal verbs). A still vaster command of data will be possible in the near future, when we begin to make serious educational use of the custom-built SARA package for searching the 100-million-word BNC (British National Corpus). So, for our students, learning to exploit corpora in all their vastness and variety is a stage-by-stage process, graduating from simpler to more abstract or sophisticated tasks. This gradual progression is important, as the gentle 'nursery slopes' of the LMC are a means of wooing beginners to the use of the computer, while the more computer-literate will want to go further faster (see Renouf, this volume).

However, a course which teaches students to exploit corpora has a larger educational content than simply acquiring the know-how to use software – although this in itself can be important. By learning to interact with the corpora, students find themselves learning a great deal about language, and how to study language. They learn about the kinds of questions that can be usefully asked and answered by reference to a corpus of data. In using an annotated corpus – for example, the tagged LOB Corpus or the BNC – they also learn what the linguistic categories used in tagging mean, and the difficulties with defining linguistic categories in this or that way. So the process of getting to grips with the software invariably shades into getting to grips with the techniques of linguistic analysis.

Exploiting to teach

What this last activity means, for me, is making selective use of corpora in the teaching of language or linguistic courses which are not intrinsically computational and would traditionally be taught by non-corpus methods. All thorough-going corpus linguists believe that the study of corpora can illuminate virtually all areas of linguistic study. The merit of the corpus is simply to enable data to be delivered in a convenient form for the investigator, whatever area of linguistics he or she is concerned with. This certainly applies in the research sphere – where corpora are used for syntactic, lexical, semantic, sociolinguistic, stylistic, psycholinguistic and historical language studies – to mention just a few subdisciplines. But what applies to the research sphere also applies to the sphere of teaching: in virtually all branches of linguistics or language learning, confrontation with relevant data can be illuminating.

Again, if I can draw upon the experience of my own department in recent years: corpus-based work has been an integral component in a number of different courses, varying from first-year undergraduate to postgraduate levels. The areas chiefly involved are present-day English language, syntax, semantics, pedagogical grammar, and the historical study of English. Typically, students undertake assignments in which they select their own topic (let us say the progressive aspect in modern English), and are provided with contextualized corpus examples of sufficient variety and scope for the study of that topic. If it is felt that the corpus-based paradigm is being overworked through its recurrence in different courses,

I would emphasize the advantages of the great variety of corpora, datasets, and techniques that may be employed with this paradigm. I would also stress the need for balance between different educational tasks at university level. The critical and argumentative type of essay assignment, which is more or less standard in many areas of university study, should certainly not be abandoned, but should be balanced with the type of assignment (often, but not necessarily, using computer corpora) which invites the student to obtain, organize, and study real-language data according to individual choice. This latter type of task gives the student the realistic expectation of breaking new ground as a 'researcher', doing something which is a unique and individual contribution, rather than a reworking and evaluation of the research of others.

In a way, 'exploiting to teach' implies 'teaching to exploit'. How can a student gain access to the corpus for the purpose just described, without being taught the means of access? Well, there is a simple way, if so desired, of avoiding the student's confrontation with the computer, which is that the students be supplied with data in the form of print-outs from the corpus. This is the method we have used, to avoid the necessary 'nuts and bolts' type of instruction students have to go through if they are to obtain their own data from the corpus. Some colleagues will regard this as 'the easy way out', and very much a second best to the 'teaching to exploit' learning sessions which produce a better long-term result. But (again, in my experience) 'the easy way' ensures that the maximum number of students are able and willing to participate in this kind of learning experience. Neither technophobes nor those who wish to acquire the necessary corpus-searching skill are discouraged from going ahead in their own self-access mode.

2.1.1   The advantages of using the computer

It may be wondered, at this point, what are the advantages of the computer in setting up learning tasks? Here I will mention four particular benefits:

1   *Automatic searching, sorting, scoring.* The computer has immense speed and accuracy in carrying out certain low-level tasks, and can therefore deliver data in a form valuable to the human learner. Concordances and frequency lists are obvious examples.

2   *Promoting a learner-centred approach.* The computer brings flexibility of time and place, and adaptability to the student's need and motivation.

3   *Open-ended supply of language data.* The computer thus encourages an exploratory or discovery approach to learning.

4   *Enabling the learning process to be tailored.* The computer can customize the learning task to the individual's needs and wishes, rather than simply providing a standard set of examples or data.

2.1.2   Divergent and convergent paradigms of learning

The above advantages can be realized in two contrasting paradigms of computer-aided learning, which may be termed *divergent* and *convergent*. The concordance-based task exploited by Johns and others is already familiar enough, and may be characterized as 'divergent' in the sense that different learners, given the same data and the same set of task instructions, will end up with very different results and interpretations, all of which may be valid in their own way. The evaluation of how well a student has performed will be itself an open-ended task, in which the assessor has to exercise judgement about the student's powers of observation, analysis, inference, organization, presentation, and (last but not least) imagination.

Contrast this with another kind of learning task, which is 'convergent', in the sense that all students given the same task will, to the extent that they are successful, tend to converge on the same answer. On the face of it, this type of task does not have the merits of being 'open-ended and tailored to the learner's need' claimed for computer-aided learning above. One thinks of the well-tried formula of the multiple-choice test, in which learners simply have to select the correct answer from a closed range of possibilities. Many CALL packages have taken this form, and although they can to a degree exploit three of the four computer strengths, those of being 'automatic', 'learner-centred' (= self-access, etc.) and 'tailored' (= adaptive), they conspicuously lack the advantage of 'open-endedness' which is essential to the exploration-and-discovery learning approach.

The 'learner-centred' and 'tailored' qualities are fully realized only where the program is fully adaptable to the learner's individual needs and preferences. To go further, 'open-endedness' is achieved only where the learner has an ability to select from an unrestrictive range of responses, or even to come up with responses not envisaged by the teacher. These advantages of the computer corpus-based paradigm do not appear to apply, seemingly, where the goal of learning is precisely to attain the basic level of competence of distinguishing a correct from an incorrect analysis of some data. For such 'convergent' tasks, the well-tried formulae of multiple-choice, gap-filling, and other computer-delivered activities, though uncreative, would seem to be ideal.

Even here, though, a corpus-based approach can provide new advantages. Let us take, as an example, the need for students to acquire basic grammatical skills such as part-of-speech recognition and simple parsing. In a project sponsored by Lancaster University under the IHE (Innovation in Higher Education) scheme, we have developed and tested prototype programs for a self-access grammar tutor.[2] The software makes use of annotated (grammatically tagged and/or parsed) corpus data, and is in principle open-ended in the sense that the data can be selected from a very large data bank of text. The type of text, similarly, can be automatically varied – ringing the changes of spoken and written material, of different kinds of scientific materials, and so forth. From the student's point of view, the annotations are invisible on the screen, so that one very simple version of the task is to undertake part-of-speech identification by typing in labels which are then checked automatically by the computer against masked corpus annotations. Two experiments making use of this simple activity have so far indicated that the computer corpus-based technique of learning is more successful and also more congenial to students than more traditional techniques of learning grammar – such as being tutored by a grammar specialist, or using grammar textbooks. 'More successful' here means that (a) students on the whole achieve a higher accuracy rate, (b) they also achieve a greater quantity of analysis (more data being covered in the same time period), and (c) inter-student variation is smaller, perhaps indicating that the 'mental block' that afflicts many students in the study of grammar does not apply to the same degree in the computer-driven mode. One can only speculate about the reasons behind this promising result (preliminary as it is), but it appears likely that the following factors are in play. (1) The computer is not, as human teachers may be felt to be, judgemental about students' lack of grammatical knowledge. (2) The task gives students unlimited scope to try the same test repeatedly, to monitor their improvements in accuracy, to test their capabilities on realistic samples, selected (for example) randomly or according to text-type. This self-testing, trial-and-error learning has something in common with the experience of computer games, and appears to be more stimulating and challenging than one which relies on experts' explanations and rules (although in the computer-based mode, a 'Help' facility can also provide that kind of explicit guidance).

This grammar tutoring is just one example, illustrating how the strengths of corpus-assisted teaching can carry across from the divergent to the convergent paradigm of learning and evaluation. Further sophistications are clearly needful, such as the tailoring of corpus sentences to different levels of difficulty. For this purpose, it should be possible to develop a program which selects, from a corpus, sample sentences which fulfil certain criteria, such as brevity, complexity, the presence or absence of certain lexical or syntactic categories, combinations of categories, and so on (see Wilson, this volume). In this way, the program can provide a grading of examples for students to work on at different levels of attainment.

2.2   Use of corpora indirectly applied to teaching

In keeping with the movement from central to peripheral areas on my subject, I will deal with the remaining topics more briefly.

Reference publishing

Probably, most English language teachers who are familiar with the idea of a text corpus first acquired that familiarity through dictionaries. In 1987, something of a breakthrough in this field was achieved by the publication of the *Collins Cobuild English Language Dictionary*, with John Sinclair as its editor-in-chief. The Cobuild dictionary was the first English language dictionary to be based on a computer corpus, the Birmingham Collection of English texts. Other major British English language dictionary publishers followed suit – indeed, in the case of one publisher, a longer corpus involvement can be claimed, since Longman had supported the Survey of English Usage Corpus and the LOB Corpus projects since the 1960s and 1970s. Longman have used a 'corpus network' extensively in their dictionaries, in particular developing the Longman-Lancaster English Language Corpus. Oxford University

Press became corpus-oriented slightly later, and took the lead in developing the British National Corpus (Leech 1993), to which Longman and Chambers also contributed. Cambridge University Press has also joined the corpus club, with its Cambridge Language Survey. Dictionaries of other languages and publishers in other countries are also benefiting from the 'corpus revolution'.

This involvement of dictionary publishers with corpora is not entirely motivated by educational goals. But there is a close and obvious link between dictionary publishing and educational publishing, as is manifest in the particular contribution that corpora have made to educational dictionaries (particularly advanced EFL dictionaries, such as the *Oxford Advanced Learner's Dictionary of Current English* (4th edn, Hornby 1989) and the *Longman Dictionary of Contemporary English* (3rd edn, 1995). Among the advantages of corpus-based lexicography are that computer corpora can be searched quickly and exhaustively, can provide frequency data, can be easily processed to provide updated lists of words, can provide authentic examples for citation, and can readily be used by lexicographical teams (especially through the mediation of computer generated concordances) for updating and verifying other levels of description such as dictionary definitions. In fact, the arguments for corpus-based lexicography (automatic processing, authentic data, etc.) are very similar to the arguments for use of corpora in language teaching. But, through dictionary publishers, the resources are concentrated in one place, and are filtered through dictionary publication, and increasingly through other media, to the educational market. In this sense, then, educational users of improved dictionaries have benefited at one remove from the corpus revolution, without having to have access to computer resources.

Under the heading of 'Reference publishing', although we naturally think first about printed dictionaries, we should also be aware that conjunction of corpora and language reference resources is expanding in new directions. One direction is towards electronic modes of publication: interactive dictionary resources on CD-ROM, for example, are now becoming widespread.[3] Another direction is towards different kinds of reference work. As early as the 1970s (Quirk *et al.* 1972, 1985) reference grammars of English were drawing heavily on corpus materials, and a new degree of corpus-dependence was reached with the *Collins Cobuild English Grammar* (Sinclair 1990), for which it was claimed that all cited examples were drawn from the Birmingham corpus materials. Probably we still await the publication of the first thorough-going corpus-based grammar, in which all rules, generalizations, structures, etc., are derived from or tested against the evidence of 'real language' found in corpora. Another direction in which corpora are beginning to make an impact on reference publications is in the provision of frequency information, which in many respects is becoming available for the first time with the publication of corpus-based reference works. But there is a long way to go before the necessary manual and/or automatic processing provides us with 'push button' frequency information for word senses, grammatical structures, etc., in a form which the language teacher would find immediately useful. It is easy, however, to foresee that in the mid-term future, the corpus-based developments in reference publishing that I have mentioned will be readily available in combination: so that, for example, computer-delivered reference works of new kinds (frequency dictionaries, frequency thesauri, corpus grammars, and the like, interlinked with corpora) will be available in new and exciting forms, such as interactive access through multimedia and hypermedia.

Materials development

In the publishing world, there is a 'trickle down' process from large, scholarly works to smaller, non-specialist or educationally oriented works, as shown classically in the family of Oxford dictionaries deriving their pedigree from the *OED*. A similar 'trickle down' occurs with corpora. Large corpora provide the basis for large, scholarly dictionaries and grammars. But they also have a clear spin-off in the direction of teaching materials, as has been demonstrated by the *Cobuild* family of publications produced by Collins (now HarperCollins). From the *Cobuild* point of view, a philosophy which links corpora in reference publishing to corpora in ELT materials development is spelt out in Dave Willis's book entitled *The Lexical Syllabus: a new approach to language teaching* (Willis 1990). In this philosophy, stress is laid on the importance of frequency of occurrence, a form of information which is for the first time starting to become widely and informatively available to the language teacher through corpora. Yet we still await a comprehensive frequency dictionary of English, and West's ancient pre-electronic *A General Service List of English Words* (West 1953), first published in 1936, has still not been superseded.

The contributions of corpora to language-teaching materials can be thought of under three headings: (a) first, the provision in abundance of frequency information (see Mindt, this volume, for the relevance of frequency to ELT materials); (b) second, the availability of copious examples of authentic language in use; (c) third, the provision of computer-delivered learning packages, such as we have already discussed above. In the present context, I will concentrate only on the first of these, frequency information.

Whether we focus on lexical frequencies, as Willis does, or extend our interest to grammatical frequencies (e.g. frequency of grammatical structures), the revival of serious interest in the relevance of frequency to language teaching is well overdue. True, there are well-known objections, in applied linguistics, to the use of frequency criteria in deciding what to teach, when and to whom. Among them is the argument that frequency is only one of a number of criteria for deciding teaching priorities, and perhaps not the most important (van Els *et al.* 1984: 210–12). Another argument is that corpora, at least as they exist at present, are not the most reliable sources of frequency data: for example, a corpus of adult written English (which is the easiest kind of computer corpus to obtain) is not a good guide as to what is most frequent in the spoken language of children. Available lexical frequency lists, unfortunately, are still predominantly based on written language. Against these arguments, Kennedy (1992) argues cogently that language teachers, syllabus designers, and materials writers are wilfully ignoring compelling frequency evidence already available. Whatever the imperfections of the simple equation 'most frequent' = 'most important to learn', it is difficult to deny that the frequency information becoming available from corpora has an important empirical input to language learning materials.

Language testing

The arguments about corpora in direct language teaching (see 2.1 above) are of equal relevance to language testing. Testing, like teaching, benefits from the conjunction of computers and corpora in offering an *automatized, learner-centred, open-ended* and *tailored* confrontation with the wealth and variety of real-language data (see Alderson 1996 for some aspects of this). In fact, it seems that corpus-based CALL, of the 'convergent' type discussed in 2.1 above, can be characterized as self-testing. In convergent language/

linguistics teaching and in language testing, the same advantages of the corpus appear: in both cases, there is a strict control on the nature of the task, so that automatic scoring in terms of 'correct' and 'incorrect' responses is feasible. At the same time, the corpus provides the advantage of using genuine 'real-life' samples in sufficient quantity so that, if required, selection of test samples can be randomized. In principle, authentic samples of the language can be automatically graded by a range of criteria. And the general paradigm whereby the learner is confronted with a text sample, the grammatical characteristics of which are stored in the computer, but not visible on the screen, can be applied both to computer-based teaching and computer-based language testing.

2.3   Further teaching-oriented corpus development

One of the continuing difficulties for applications of corpora to language/linguistics teaching is the lack of suitable corpora. It is a sad fact that the types of corpora which are most easily available for the computer today consist largely of written texts, whereas the types of corpora which would most faithfully reflect the priorities of language learning would contain at least as much spoken material as written material.

To put it more generally: for human beings, experience of language is primarily spoken and secondarily written; for computers, conversely, language is primarily written and secondarily (via transcription) spoken. This difference in humans' and computers' experience of language is reflected in the history of corpus linguistics. The first computer corpora (e.g. the Brown Corpus, 1961–64) consisted of written English: only later, in the computerizing of the London–Lund Corpus in the mid-1970s (see Svartvik 1990) was it possible to produce corpora of spoken English – naturally, through the mediation of transcriptions (renderings of speech in written form). This prioritizing of the written language has persisted through the history of corpus development. For example, the BNC consists of *c.* 90 million words of written English, and only *c.* 10 million words of spoken language. Why this discrepancy? The reason, simply, is that spoken language is much more expensive to collect, at the present stage of technological progress, than written language. It costs roughly as much to collect 10 million words of spoken language (requiring, as this does, manual transcription) as to collect 90 million words of written English – and even then, the result is little more than a basic orthographic transcription.

On the other hand, the learning of spoken language is generally felt to be a *sine qua non* of language learning today: the idea of learning the written language, without being able to make use of the spoken language, makes good sense to a computer, but not to a human being.

This time-lag between the collection of written corpora and spoken corpora is no longer as important as it was. After all, there now exist corpora containing 10 million words or more of the spoken language. However, the general problem that the history of spoken and written language corpora reveals is that the corpora which are easiest to compile are not necessarily those which are most useful for language learning purposes. This leads to the question: what kinds of corpora do we need to develop, to make up the deficit between what corpora exist, and what corpora are needed for the best applications to language teaching? These resources are now being developed, albeit somewhat haphazardly.

LSP corpora

LSP, or 'Language for Specific Purposes', has an important place in the goals of language teaching. For example, many millions of people, throughout the world, need to know English particularly for a specialist subject which they are studying or professionally practising: science, technology, law, medicine – to mention a few. Although, again, the history of LSP thinking in applied linguistics has not favoured such an approach, it makes good sense to find out as much as we can about the linguistic characteristics of language varieties – including, for example, lexical frequencies, collocations, and characteristic grammatical structures. For this purpose, there is a clear need for LSP corpora. Such corpora are coming into existence gradually, by three different means. First, keen LSP linguists and teachers have developed their own corpora: early examples were the JDEST [science and technology] Corpus (Yang 1985) and the GPEC [petroleum industry] Corpus (Zhu 1989), both produced in China. Second, now that we have enormous general-purpose corpora, such as the BNC, it will be possible to select from such corpora a subcorpus dealing with a certain domain. (The informative written part of the BNC, for example, is divided into domains such as 'pure science', 'applied science', and 'social science': each of which might be regarded as an LSP subcorpus in its own right.) Third, research in language engineering is leading to the creation of corpora of what are termed 'sublanguages'. An example is a corpus of computer manuals. For language engineering purposes, it is found that ambitious tasks such as machine translation cannot be realistically attempted on languages in general, but become feasible when the task is restricted to a particular domain, or sublanguage. Once such corpora exist, there is nothing in principle to prevent their being used in educational applications.

L1 and L2 developmental corpora

Throughout the world, much language teaching is concentrated on children during the periods of primary and (particularly) secondary education. If we wish to use corpora in developing reference works or teaching and testing materials for these age groups, what kind of corpus should ideally be used? Surely the best kind of corpus would be one corresponding to the target language behaviour of the learners concerned. This will not be adult language, but children's language of the relevant age group. Hence the need to collect what may be called 'developmental corpora', representing the language as used by native speakers whose competence has not yet reached maturity. To some extent, this kind of material is being collected through CHILDES, the child language database centred in the USA (MacWhinney and Snow 1991). However, the function of CHILDES is focused more on the needs of researchers in language acquisition than on the needs of second language learners. The age groups from which material has been collected are naturally concentrated in the years of early childhood. Therefore a different approach to the acquisition of developmental corpora is needed, and one possibility is the collection of data from the mother-tongue reading materials used in the schooling of children at various ages and grades. Such a corpus was collected for *The American Heritage Word Frequency Book* (Carroll *et al.* 1971), although regrettably only the frequency lists from that corpus are available. The interest of this approach, however, was that the corpus was defined by *receptive* criteria (i.e. the range of language children were *exposed to*) rather than by *productive* criteria (i.e. the range of language the children used).

The availability of developmental corpora for English as L1 is patchy, but one recent development relevant to language learning in secondary education is the collection of a corpus of teenage British English (the COLT Corpus, see Haslerud and Stenström 1995), which has been incorporated into the BNC as part of its spoken language component.

Developmental corpora may be expected to provide a detailed picture of a type of language which corresponds most closely to target language behaviour of school-age non-native learners. Recently, however, a strong interest has developed in the collection and study of a different kind of developmental corpus: this time, an L2 development corpus, or a corpus of non-native learners' language behaviour. The most notable example of this kind of corpus initiative is the International Corpus of Learners' English (ICLE: see Granger 1993). The project aims at the collection of comparable corpora of learners' English from different native speaker populations: for example, the written English produced by French-speaking, Dutch-speaking and Chinese-speaking students. In effect, these are interlanguage corpora, which can be used to study, for example, the respects in which the language produced by the learners of one native language differs from that of those of other native languages, and ultimately from that of relevant groups of native speakers. At last it will be possible to give authoritative answers to such questions as: How far does native language interference influence the learner's English?; How far does classroom train- ing distort the pattern of a language learner's productions?; What are the most common types of learner errors?; or What avoidance strategies are adopted by learners in coping with features of the foreign language which have no counterpart, or an imperfect counterpart, in the native language?

The value of learners' language corpora is chiefly in Second Language Acquisition research, but they will also have a very practical application to the development of language-teaching and testing materials. At a relatively simple level, it may also be of direct importance to the language teacher to know (for example) which words and structures of the foreign language are typically overused, underused, or misused by non-native learners.

A momentum is gathering in the collection and compilation of L2 learners' corpora. In addition to the ICLE collection of corpora, it is worth mentioning two other examples: the Longman Learners' Corpus and a very large corpus (over 5 million words) of written English produced by Chinese-speaking students, and collected by John Milton in Hong Kong.

Bilingual/multilingual corpora

One final category of corpus should be mentioned: the bilingual or multilingual corpus, containing comparable text materials in different languages. In fact, there are different varieties of such corpora. Obviously one kind of variable is the number of languages involved: for instance, a bilingual corpus differs from a trilingual corpus on this score. Another variable is the extent to which the texts in the different languages match one another. Strictly, a *parallel* bilingual corpus is one where texts or text samples in the two languages are mutual translations. The term *comparable* corpus may be used for the looser concept of two corpora in different languages where the text categories, and perhaps individual samples, are chosen to correspond with one another as closely as possible.

In language technology, parallel corpora are now being developed vigorously as a key resource for the advancement of machine (or machine-aided) translation research. In the European Community, for example, two research projects, C.R.A.T.E.R. (McEnery *et al.* 1994) and Multext (Ide and Véronis 1994) are developing parallel corpus resources for a subset of European languages. One drawback, however, is that the kinds of parallel electronic texts which are available for this kind of research consist of highly specialized and often technical types of language. C.R.A.T.E.R., for example, is developing parallel corpora derived from the International Telecommunications Union documents, which happen to exist in parallel translations in a number of European languages. Another well-used corpus for this purpose is the bilingual Canadian Hansard Corpus, giving the proceedings of the Canadian Parliament in both French and English. Unless they can be 'captured' in this way from pre-existing translation materials, parallel corpora are at present difficult to obtain.[4] And it is particularly difficult to obtain or to compile a parallel corpus of texts of sufficient variety and interest to be useful for general-purpose language teaching. However, we may hope that such corpora will gradually establish themselves in the language-teaching arena as suitable materials become available, and as their pedagogical value becomes more widely recognized.

But what *is* the pedagogical value of a parallel corpus? At the simplest level, we may envisage a pedagogical tool, in effect, a bilingual concordance, perhaps with two windows on the screen (or perhaps two different-coloured lines of text) exhibiting the equivalent text units in the different languages. Software (already being worked on in various centres) will automatically identify such *translation units*, whether words, phrases, sentences, or other sections of text. A parallel concordance program will then be able to highlight the equivalent units. At one level, then, the parallel corpora can be used to exhibit translation equivalences which may then be compared and studied via concordance listings sorted in terms of either the source language or the target language. One can imagine, for example, examining all the instances of the English passive and their translations into Spanish, and then inducing from this a general account of the contrastive grammar of Spanish and English voice on the basis of these equivalences.

More ambitiously, parallel corpora will be able to provide frequency data of translation equivalence, and then feed these into more precise contrastive grammatical or lexical studies of two languages than has previously been possible.

Therefore, on the one hand, parallel corpora will contribute to pedagogical software (particularly in the teaching of translation), and on the other hand, they will contribute to research on translation equivalence which will then feed into language-teaching materials.

Conclusion: and the future?

I predict that one of the results of the 'corpus revolution', as it affects language learning, is that topics and techniques which have passed into relative oblivion through the influence of communicative teaching methodology will be brought back to life, and shown, much to everyone's surprise, to be not only highly informative for language teaching, but of fascinating interest. Among such topics and techniques, a number have been briefly discussed in this chapter: frequency and vocabulary studies, translation, and error analysis (in its broader conception as the study of learners' language).

But 'the corpus revolution' is a misnomer for a change which is taking place gradually, as suitable materials become available. This is a slow process, and, as exemplified with developmental corpora and parallel corpora, we may have to wait two or three decades before all the resources that we would like to have are readily available. The main cause of delay is that computers and corpora, even today, are comparatively expensive resources, whereas education is generally underfunded and cannot afford to develop resources of its own. Looking on the positive side, however, we should do our best to exploit for educational purposes the resources which are being built under the sponsorship of industry or commerce. (The British National Corpus is one example of such a resource.) Language engineering is likely to be a 'big earner' in the future, and language-learning activities can profit from software and corpus resources developed for those purposes. Just like the trickle-down from research to teaching, with which this chapter opened, the trickle-down from industry to teaching is something we should be ready to welcome and exploit.

Notes

1 Originally a newsletter entitled *ICAME News*, then from 1987 a journal under the new title *ICAME Journal.*
2 The results of the project are reported in McEnery, Baker and Wilson (1995).
3 For example, the *Longman Interactive English Dictionary CD-ROM* [Longman] and *Cobuild on CD-ROM* [HarperCollins].
4 However, as Steve Fligelstone has pointed out to me, parallel original and translated 'news digest' services on the Internet are now beginning to offer some hope in this regard.

Section A

Why Use Corpora?

Introduction

This section offers a justification, if such is needed, for the use of corpora in teaching languages and teaching about language. Each of the three papers considers a different aspect of the teaching and learning process.

First of all Sinclair raises the issue of *what* is taught. From long experience of corpus analysis, he challenges the 'common sense' view about how language, specifically English, is used. For example, corpora can reveal not only the frequency of individual lexical items but also, and crucially, 'the company they keep'. In his view, the priority traditionally given to the single word should give way to a much higher regard for multi-word units.

Mindt shares Sinclair's concern with authentic language usage, but concentrates in his contribution on the way the language is represented, or more often misrepresented, in commercial language-learning materials. He writes in the context of the German education system, but makes universally valid points about the processes, traditions and constraints which influence the design of language-learning materials. He argues strongly that insights gained from corpora should be reflected in the design of language materials, even at the most elementary stage.

Aston turns our attention from the language to the needs of the language learners. He discusses some of the theoretical issues which underly language learning and teaching. The use of corpora, he argues, can contribute both to learners' knowledge about language and to their proficiency in the language. Most importantly they offer the learner a new independence, allowing teachers to 'concentrate on their role as learning rather than language experts'.

2

Corpus Evidence in Language Description

JOHN M. SINCLAIR

In this chapter I wish to examine the impact of corpus-based research on language description, not least on those descriptions which underlie much of what is taught about English. It is a matter of speculation why some of the evidence I present here is not yet incorporated in the leading descriptions of English which emanate from formalist linguistic theories. One might reasonably suppose that after a generation of intense activity from the élite of linguistics intellectuals, most of the patterns relevant to the accurate description of English would by now have been recognized and built into the published grammars of the language.

Other chapters in this volume consider the direct applications of corpora in the teaching and learning process. Here I would like to discuss some of the more indirect ways in which computer-processed language data can, should and will have a powerful impact on language teaching.

1 From scarcity to superfluity

The linguistics of the twentieth century has been the linguistics of scarcity of evidence. Both in field work, concerning languages other than one's own, and in contemplating one's native language, the problem has been the lack of sufficient evidence.

Anyone who does not have full competence in a language of study has to get the crucial evidence from outside – through reading documents if the language is written, or listening to native speakers conversing. Beyond that, one can conduct various elicitation experiments, all artificial in one way or another. The gathering and processing of evidence has until recently been limited by the discrimination and attention-span of the researchers. Gradually, some instrumentation has aided the direct study of speech, and the invention of the wire recorder and tape recorder has been making a big contribution to the study of the spoken word since the 1950s.

But the quantity of data has been chronically inadequate for any reliable statements about grammar, vocabulary, usage, semantics or pragmatics. One of the most characteristic features of a natural language is its immense variability — across regional, social, cultural, institutional, etc., lines, and in individual freshness, wit and productivity. There is also a vocabulary of several thousand items in a natural language, giving a mathematically prodigious range of possible combinations.

In order to uncover the regularities of structure, to identify, if possible, exactly what the realizations are of meaningful choices, and to give precise shape to all the usual categories of linguistic description, it is necessary to assemble a large number of putative instances of each phenomenon. Given the well-known distribution of word tokens in a language (Zipf 1935), a large corpus or collection of texts is essential to provide a body of evidence.

An adequate corpus, of many millions of running words,[1] is beyond the organizing ability of an unaided researcher, or even a substantial group. It needs a computer with a larger memory store and sophisticated retrieval software. In very recent years this double resource of corpus and computer has been made available, for example, to the Cobuild lexicographers.

However, many linguists who have fluency in English do not feel that this evidence is necessary, valuable or even interesting. They put their faith in introspection and intuition, claiming to get closer to the abstract organization of the language by this method rather than by studying the output of spoken and written language as used in communication. For some, actual usage is distracting and probabilities are anathema.

The stance of the theoretical linguist must clearly change. Before large computer corpora became available, theoreticians were speculators in a subject where evidence was scarce. They trusted their judgement, backed hunches, tested hypotheses against what meagre data there was, and made bold assertions. Others followed them because they recognized high intellectual quality, and because the style of the theory suited them.

To move from scant evidence to introspection was, in a way, making a virtue of necessity. It has been, however, most disappointing that introspection grammars, after many years, do not produce output that comes near to actual usage. Hardline apologists will no doubt refuse to accept this as a criticism, pointing out all the non-linguistic factors that influence a verbal interaction in the real world.

However, the evidence from very large corpora offers another and more worrying reason for the mismatch between the output of introspective grammar and the way people talk and write. Patterns of usage, concord and coselection abound in the corpora and not many are familiar from published grammars. From the impromptu reactions of hundreds of fluent speakers, we can deduce that the intuitions about language which they can access are substantially at variance with their own language behaviour.

The difference is so marked and regular that it is likely to be systematic. Put starkly, it suggests that the main organizing procedures for composing utterances are subliminal, and not available to conscious introspection. Retrievable intuitions about language comprise a set of plausible decisions about the meaning and well-formedness of words and sentences treated as isolated events. The patterns of combination and interaction are not at present retrievable.

The next few years will no doubt see a considerable amount of adjustment, and a growing need for corpus evidence. New theoretical positions will be developed, and the relation between the linguist and the data will change.

Superfluity means that it will not be possible to examine all the evidence, and that it will become obviously unprofessional to select the evidence that suits a certain hypothesis. It means that procedures and conventions for accessing corpora and evaluating corpus evidence will have to be agreed and reference corpora established. It means that future speculations will have to be supported by convincing evidence to be taken seriously. On the technical side, superfluity means management and storage of language text pouring into the machines, and ingenious methods of acquisition, access and disposal.

2   Language teaching

Those who teach languages depend on those who describe them for their basic information and its stability and reliability. The syllabuses of language teaching reflect the theories and descriptions, as do the textbooks and examinations. At times the methodology of language teaching distances itself from developments in linguistics, and this is the case at present, and has been for some years.

Essentially, as I have pointed out before (Sinclair 1990), fashionable ELT methodology has paid little attention to the state of language description, behaving as if the facts of English structure were no longer in dispute. In practical terms this has led to the growth and maintenance of a mythology about English (Willis 1990) which language teachers take for granted, but much of which is challenged by corpus evidence (Mindt 1986 and this volume). A few leading figures in applied linguistics (e.g. Widdowson 1992) effectively endorse this complacency by casting doubt on the relevance of corpus findings to the process of teaching and learning languages.

Very large collections of language text will shortly become available cheaply on CD-ROM. Quite young learners will gain access to this and will become self-taught DDL (data-driven learning) students. Problems will arise when the textual evidence does not fit the precepts of classroom and textbook, and the mythology will prove no match for the facts. Although still perhaps marginal for Widdowson, corpus data will become central to the daily concerns of language teachers.

A preliminary response to those who believe that corpus evidence need not affect language teaching is to be found in Sinclair (1992) and this is not the place to argue the case further.

3   Some precepts

In this chapter I do not wish to be understood as a methodologist. I am not advocating any particular way of teaching languages. My points are couched as a set of precepts for language teachers regardless of which method they prefer to use. Some of them are clearly more in tune with one approach to language than another, and therefore the precepts below may seem more or less in tune with what is already going on in a variety of classrooms.

The precepts centre on data, and arise from observations about the nature of language. They are not concerned with psychological or pedagogical approaches to language teaching.

3.1   Present real examples only

This is perhaps the first lesson to be learned from corpus study. Language cannot be invented; it can only be captured.

At the simplest level of practicality, it is probably easier to search through a file of relevant examples for what is required than to think up something that sounds natural. When 'sounds natural' is examined closely, it usually transpires that it is almost impossible to invent an adequate example; attempts by language teachers, lexicographers and others to represent usage are often embarrassing and never reliable.

This is not to say that we should frown on every decent attempt made in urgent circumstances, e.g. during a lesson. The point only arises when teacher or textbook is drawing attention to the example as a whole as a model of English usage, or if a learner is likely to expect such a model, for example in a dictionary. In such a case it would be most unwise to offer examples which are unattested, or to make major changes to actual instances.

It is a hangover from the period of scarce evidence, that people should believe, as some do, that their ideas about what language is like are superior (for language-teaching purposes) to what language is really like. Sometimes it is said that even with huge corpora, it is difficult to find examples of some phenomena. That is true, because many words are not common at all. But ultimately the searcher who cannot find evidence will be forced to reconsider the importance of a very rare phenomenon as compared to the rich variety of frequent patterns.

Another potential snag is that a real example may be mixed up with other material which is unsuitable for the job in hand. This, again, is true though it is not so much of a problem with large corpora. Also it is important to be sure that other patterns which co-occur with a cited word or phrase are actually independent of it.

The experience of Cobuild has been increasingly to accept the textual evidence, in all its detail. Since we are just at the beginning of corpus-based study, we do not know which details are essential, which important, which optional, which indicative, which transitory, which random and which distracting. Until we know, the editing of examples remains very conservative.

Some years ago it was argued that if a good example took the form of a relative clause, there would be no obstacle to replacing the relative pronoun by an ordinary one, and making any other adjustments to turn it into a possible main clause. However, some of the results of this editing sounded slightly odd.

Take the word *borrow*. It is strongly associated with modal verbs, in particular *can*. In an unbiased selection of 20 instances from a spoken corpus, *can* was used 11 times. Other modals were *shall, must, had to*, and *'ll*, once each. Other instances of modal-like meaning were *perhaps* (1), *allowed to* (1), *if* (1), giving a total of 18 out of the 20. The other two were

(a)   . . . every book which people borrow; . . .
(b)   . . . those who borrow from fifteen to thirty . . .

The relative clauses are the only ones that do not attract an expression of tentativeness. Hence it would be misleading to present these made up into freestanding clauses.

If such details turn out to make the difference between the attested example (c) and the invented one (d)

(c)   People can borrow books according to . . .
(d)   People borrow books

then the rashness of total invention is obvious, no matter how experienced the presenter.

3.2   Know your intuition

Your intuition about language, whether as a language teacher, a learner or just a user, is a most important asset. As was pointed out earlier in this chapter, it gives you instant information, mainly about two things

(a)   the meanings of words in isolation
(b)   the well-formedness of sentences in isolation.

It also gives a variety of information about styles and registers, and of words, phrases and sentences considered in isolation.

It is not, however, reliable about the way words and sentences are combined in actual communication. The organization of language in use does seem to be largely subliminal, and although it is instantly recognizable, it is not easy to retrieve. Other factors cut across, so that we may retrieve more readily a few exceptions rather than the rule.

For example, in Sinclair (1992) I showed how our intuitive position about the adjective *glad* is at variance with the principal ways
in which it is used. Native speakers are almost bound to disagree
with the observation that *glad* usually occurs in a predicative position. This is the effect of a few biblical phrases like *glad tidings*,
which are the exceptions, and a very small number of compounds
like *glad rags*. Otherwise *glad* is predicative.

A fairly cursory inspection of predicative *glad* reveals another
generalization that is not usually retrievable. *Glad* is almost always
followed by the reason for the gladness – usually with prepositions
about, of, infinitive *to* or a *that*-clause. This is so reliable that, if the
reason is not articulated, it is inferred.

Such a pattern is not noted with the ordinary run of adjectives.

However even the commonest adjective shows patterns that one
can hardly imagine will be retrieved. The adjective *nice* selects the
indefinite article *a* and most emphatically rejects the definite article
the. When in predicative position, it attracts strongly a modifier
such as *very, pretty, extremely*. When attributive, it is commonly found
with another adjective with which it combines in meaning, so that
a nice relaxing time is nice because it is relaxing. Where *nice* immediately precedes a noun, and has no modifier itself, the nouns
it goes with seem to be frequently selected from a few short lists
– *day, evening*, etc., *boys, girls*, etc., and *surprise*. Often there are set
phrases.

The most neutral adjective, then, has strong patterns associated
with it.

Collocations present a similar picture. It is easy to retrieve *open*
with *door* but what about *answer*? Work on the cumulative effects
of collocation, leading to 'semantic prosodies' is forging ahead
with Louw (1991) laying the groundwork.

Matters of wit, curiosity and love of the unusual, the absurd, etc.,
have a further impact on the intuition. These things are memor-
able, and ordinary things are not. The computer does not discrim-
inate. It is therefore important to know when one's intuition is
reasonably trustworthy and when it is not. Teachers may be tempted
into all sorts of contortions of argument to explain, for example,
how the meaning of *take* is preserved in *take a photograph, a bath,
notes, care* and a hundred other regularly occurring objects. Intuition should on occasion give way to common sense.

The subliminal patterns of language are those which the learner
must command in order to become fluent. It is a pedagogical

decision how to present them; my only concern is to provide them, and to argue for their central importance in language learning. It really is now time to conduct a full review of the facts of English, as presented in language teaching, and compare them with the facts as presented in corpus research.

3.3   Inspect contexts

Strictly speaking, I should write 'inspect co-texts', because 'context' often has a wider meaning than the surrounding text. Following on the evidence given so far, I would advocate a much closer inspection of the verbal environment of a word or phrase than is usual in language teaching. A great deal is to be learned from this exercise.

The nature and extent of multi-word choices is one area where thousands of examples can be found. A corpus will provide neutral evidence. For example, the English word *eye* is mainly used in phrases concerning inspection, appraisal, attention, where it combines with other words, e.g. *naked*. It is easy enough to retrieve the fact that *naked* always precedes *eye* (whereas *caught*, for example, does not). A little more introspection may suggest that *the* is obligatory in front of *naked*. A preposition in front of *the* is a safe bet, but it is quite likely that a person will retrieve one of them (e.g. *with*) and forget the other one (*to*). In virtually every case there is, in front of the preposition, an expression to do with seeing. Here we must move from exact phrasing to something more semantic. It may be *see* itself, or *spot, observe, recognized*; or it may be *visible, perceptible*.

There is still another component of this complex unit of meaning. In a large number of cases the 'see' expression is preceded by another expression, suggesting difficulty. A typical realization is *just*, but there are many, and not all are entirely convincing. At times the difficulty is just hinted at.

The existence of many such intricate patterns leads us to the hypothesis of co-selection – that the choice of the phrase *the naked eye* is a result of the same decision that led to 'difficulty' and 'visibility' being realized in the same clause. Co-selection tends to undermine the notion of word-meaning, and examples accumulate. In Sinclair (1991) I point out that frequently an adjective such as *physical* modifies nouns such as *appearance* and *action*, which

already contain the notion 'physical' quite prominently. It is difficult, in the face of the evidence, to continue to rely on the idea
of each word delivering its little nugget of meaning. Rather we
should see the words of a language as acting more like the letters
of an alphabet – each one contributing to the recognizable shape
of the higher unit, but not necessarily adding a clearly defined
meaning.

In language teaching, the multi-word items have traditionally
been treated as of lower priority than the single words, with notable
exceptions such as phrasal verbs in English, which are unavoidable.
Co-selection is not in my experience an object of attention and this
is quite understandable since the evidence is only now becoming
available.

Room must be found for these common and typical features of
a language – perhaps at the expense of teaching large numbers of
isolated words and meanings.

3.4   Teach by meaning

This is a precept that might appear superfluous, but it certainly is
not, especially in the teaching of grammar. The principle behind
it is that meaning has a profound effect on structure; hence if a
word has two meanings one can predict with some confidence two
structures at least.

Dictionaries rarely recognize this and list meanings without
reporting on structures; grammars seem to take most words as
having just one meaning despite what the dictionaries say. As an
example I can do no better than quote from the Introduction to
Collins Cobuild English Grammar (Sinclair 1990).

'. . . in one meaning a verb may be transitive, and in another meaning intransitive'.

An instance of this is 'manage' which in its meaning of 'be responsible for controlling an organisation, business or system' is transitive
and in its meaning of be able to continue with a reasonable way of
life, even though you do not have much money, is intransitive, usually followed by an adverbial phrase

Drouet returned to Ecuador to *manage* a travel agency
I don't know if I can *manage* much longer

. . . Another example is a verb referring to physical senses such as
'see', 'feel', 'hear' and 'smell'. When such a verb is used to refer to

the present time, it is typically preceded by the modal 'can' or 'can't' rather than being in the simple present tense:

I can *see* George's face as clearly as if he were here with me

However some of the verbs can be used with other, non-physical meanings, and in the other meanings the simple present tense is much used.

I *see* you had a good trip

This grammar is a halfway house between grammars which ignore the meaning of words, and dictionaries which give some grammatical information. We have left out reference to uncommon meanings, and we only occasionally draw attention to distinctions of meanings that entail a different grammar.

If you think about it, it is obvious that different meanings of a word are likely to occur in different structures. The meaning of a word includes the relations it makes with other words; so a verb such as 'see' in its physical meaning is likely to go along with a noun that means what was seen or perhaps by an adverb such as 'well' which gives an evaluation of the power of seeing. When 'see' is used to mean something like 'understand', it will naturally be followed by a 'that' clause. On the rare occasions when it has a noun group as object, the noun will be something like 'problem', 'paint', or 'position' – nouns describing messages.

On other occasions I have pointed out that, for example, some words exist as noun and verb, and have two meanings. The more concrete, narrow meaning goes with the noun, and the more figurative, vaguer meaning goes with the verb. The word *combat* shows this. As a noun it means actual physical fighting; as a verb it means something like 'struggle against', usually with abstractions like inflation, recession, etc. Although such distinctions are easy to appreciate when pointed out, they are not always distinguishable grammatically.

The learner is faced with a large and confusing learning load. Any regular linking of form and meaning is likely to cut down the load, while providing a rationale for the link.

Most grammars lack the evidence for pursuing form–meaning distinctions through the broad generalizations and down into the detail. Yet if grammatical classes can be listed, as they can with a corpus, then the grammar will become much tighter. As the classes become smaller, so their relation to meaning becomes clearer.

Collins Cobuild English Grammar, Chapter 10, gives a number of examples of such detailed, or delicate classes.

3.5   Highlight productivity

Perhaps the most profound impact that a corpus will have on language teaching is in the demonstration of permissible variety. Novelty and innovation are not always highly regarded as features of communication, but they are major features of current English. Both in recognition and production they are of great concern to the teacher and learner. Absence of them from textbooks is caused by authors' reliance on inauthentic materials, and leads to a duller curriculum.

A corpus allows variation to be observed and described – like the example of *the naked eye* above. It indicates what changes can be made without distorting or obscuring the meaning; what combinations are likely to be acceptable. By understanding the meaning of an expression the learner can develop unique and personal utterances which are almost guaranteed to be acceptable, and which have the added charm of the new.

Let me give but one example. It is very likely that, when the grammar of a corpus is fully articulated, there will be a huge mass of productive opportunities identified. Many or possibly most classes will be open-ended. *Collins Cobuild English Grammar* (pp. 110–12) shows an analysis of the structure

   a(n) X of Y

The first noun, X, is realized by such things as measures *pint, yard, ounce*, etc.; informal portions *blob, dash, lump, shred*, etc.; shapes *shaft, stick, tuft*, etc.; flows of liquid *dribble, jet, spurt*, etc.; containers *bag, bucket, tank, tub*, etc.; formal collectives *herd, flock, team*, etc.; and informal collectives *bunch, clump, group*, etc. Each of these sets is potentially open-ended; anything, for example, that is recognized as a container will do. Some things that are not recognized as a container will do. Some things that are not recognized may be pressed into service by another productive device: adding *-ful* onto the end of a container. *Bag* becomes *bagful*, etc. Now almost anything can become a container – a skirtful, a houseful, a shipful, etc.

I am not advocating as a methodologist that we should teach languages in a way which emphasizes individual creativity (though I would certainly subscribe to the notion). I am pointing out that ordinary everyday language is the product of individual creativity and the variation associated with it is one of the principal features of text and discourse. Hence, if that is what language is like, that is what should be taught. There is no way that authentic language use can be presented without this feature being prominent.

4   Conclusion

I have tried to devise some precepts for language teachers from the first fruits of corpus study. Language corpora are becoming available cheaply, sometimes free. The likely impact on language teaching will be profound – indeed the whole shape of linguistics may alter at speed.

Corpora provide many challenges for the linguist, whether theoretical or applied, and for the language teacher. Why, we may ask, are strong structural patterns not recorded in grammars? Why is the evidence of what does occur given low priority beside speculative statements of what might occur, even though its chances are close to zero? Why is the distinction between intuition and actuality not explicated throughout?

For the language teacher, the precepts given below carry implications of similar questions.

Present real examples only
Know your intuition
Inspect contexts
Teach by meaning
Highlight productivity.

For the learner, there are no extra challenges beyond the perennial problems of language idiosyncrasy and complexity. Corpora will clarify, give priorities, reduce exceptions and liberate the creative spirit.

Note

1   The Bank of English is an online selection of 200 million words of current English from a total holding at present of over 500 million words. A balance is maintained in the proportion of spoken material and the main types of written language – newspapers, magazines and printed books – so that each category accounts for around 50 million words; and there is a small collection of ephemera.

The Spoken section includes 15 million words of unscripted conversations, recorded using a variety of techniques, including samples organized by the British Market Research Bureau. About 50 million words come from America, and smaller amounts from other native-speaking sources. The Bank of English is twice the size of the nearest comparable corpus, and contains by far the largest collection of transcribed speech.

The original corpus was established in 1980 as a standard reference point for current English, and has been frequently updated to maintain this position. For some time now, every word in the corpus has had a part-of-speech tag, so that the grammatical searches could be substantially speeded up. It has also been fully parsed by a team at the University of Helsinki, and the current task is to integrate the parse information within the retrieval system.

The retrieval system, called *Lookup*, is an exceptionally efficient and user-friendly means of access for language researchers to the riches of the corpus. The dozen or so main components of the corpus (e.g. British Books, The National Public Radio of Washington, DC) can be grouped to form corpora for individual lines of enquiry, and the queries can specify words, phrases, inflected variants, grammar codes and framework patterns in very flexible combinations. The system will also compute collocational profiles and find representative examples of patterns. *Lookup* is updated several times a year. The corpus and the retrieval system are used by Cobuild mainly for lexicography, and by corpus linguists as the starting point for a wide variety of research projects. They have always been available to researchers, and with the advance of networking technology, the Bank of English is now available all over the world through the Cobuild Direct Internet and e-mail service (information from direct@cobuild.collins.co.uk).

3

Corpora and the Teaching of English in Germany

DIETER MINDT

This chapter is divided into three parts: the first deals with some general points on teaching materials and their relation to grammars, with special reference to Germany; the second part outlines some of the essential points of a corpus-based approach for the development of a grammar for the foreign language learner; the third part presents three examples of new findings which affect the way in which grammatical items are selected, graded and presented in teaching materials. The first example is the teaching of *any*, the second example the description of *will* and *would*, the third example concerns irregular verbs of English.

1 Teaching materials and their relation to grammars

English is the first and most important foreign language in German schools. Every student in German secondary schools (age 10/11 to 16/17) has to learn at least one foreign language. For about 95 per cent of all students, English is either the first or only foreign language.

There is a vast range of textbooks for teaching English as a foreign language. These textbooks are generally based on a grammatical syllabus. Both the grammatical syllabus and its content (the functions of different grammatical structures) rely on two main sources. The first source is a long-standing tradition of English language teaching, the second is the accepted grammatical knowledge as we find it in current handbooks of English grammar.

The observation that textbooks are based on these two sources is not only true of Germany. A closer look at textbooks used in other countries reveals that we are also dealing with a more general problem.

Both these sources are of questionable value. Tradition, even if it is most venerable, cannot serve as a substitute for research. The current grammatical handbooks of English grammar are not always based on specific research (e.g. Alexander 1988). Grammars which are based on research generally rely on foundations which are theoretical rather than applied. For this reason such grammars do not take into account the requirements of foreign language teaching.

It is important to note at this point that there can be nothing like the best grammar of English from which every other grammatical description could be derived. Let us for a moment compare the reality of language with the reality of the world. The physical reality of the world is represented by maps. There are different types of maps and their differences are due to the purposes they are designed for. The map for a railway user is totally different from maps designed for motorists, and again those who might want to use public footpaths will not find any information relevant to them in either railway maps or maps for motorists.

The same is true of grammar. Grammar is an abstract representation of the physical reality of language, i.e. each grammar is a map of the language. Languages are so complex that no grammar can account for the totality of the language. Each grammar focuses on certain aspects of the language while necessarily neglecting others. The content and form of a grammar are determined by its specific objectives. The rationale of each grammar affects the selection of data, the choice and scope of its categories, the use of specific tools of analysis and the presentation of the results of the preceding research.

My claim is that there is at present no comprehensive grammar for the aim of teaching English as a foreign language. At the Freie Universität in Berlin, we are in the process of developing such a grammar for the verb system of English.

2 The development of a grammar for the foreign language learner

In the approach we are using there are three fundamental steps (see Figure 3.1):

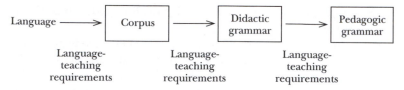

Figure 3.1   The way to grammars for the foreign language learner

- the compilation of a corpus of language data
- the construction of a didactic grammar from this corpus
- the derivation of pedagogical grammars from the didactic grammar.

Each of the three steps is fundamentally determined by the purposes of foreign language teaching: the corpus has to be compiled according to the learning objectives of a specific language course or group of courses (e.g. spoken English for courses which aim at communication in everyday life situations, business letters for courses in business correspondence, etc.).

The didactic grammar is based on the analysis of the corpus according to questions which have their origin in the needs of foreign language teaching. The didactic grammar is designed to give a descriptive account of the morphological, syntactic, semantic and, where necessary, pragmatic features of the corpus along with distributional statements about these features.

The pedagogic grammar is prescriptive. It is based on the didactic grammar and selects those features from the didactic grammar which are central, recurring and invariant. In addition, the selection is determined by the objectives of specific courses, the age of the learners, their development, their cognitive capabilities and their affective dispositions as well as their sociocultural backgrounds.

Our present work is concerned with the development of a didactic grammar, since the construction of a didactic grammar is the initial step for all follow-up work. It goes without saying that our work is based on machine-readable language corpora and that the analysis of the corpus basically relies on computational procedures (see Mindt and Tesch 1991). They have been described in Mindt (1988) together with some preliminary findings. Further results have been published in Mindt (1987, 1992) and Tesch (1990).

For all areas of grammar which we have studied so far it has become clear that the English which is taught in German textbooks is at variance with the language used by native speakers (see

Mindt 1989). The same is true of statements in a number of widely used handbooks of English grammar on which these textbooks are based.

3 Examples of new findings

3.1 The teaching of any

The teaching of *any* is characteristically based on sentences such as

> *There **were some** nice restaurants in Malaga,*
> *but there **weren't any** English restaurants.*
> ***Were** there **any** English boys at the hotel?*
> (*English in Action* 1980: 17)

Any is normally contrasted with *some* and the following rules are given:

> *Some* is generally used in affirmative sentences, *any* in questions and negations ('*Some* wird meist in bejahten Sätzen gebraucht, *any* in Fragen und verneinten Sätzen.')
> (*English in Action* 1980: 111)

The use of *some* and *any* and their compounds has been studied by Tesch (1990) within the framework of a didactic grammar. As a result she has developed a set of linguistic rules (Tesch 1990: 343f). In addition she has taken the first step into a pedagogic grammar and has suggested a new approach for the teaching of *any*.

Tesch (1990: 338) distinguishes three types of *any* and gives the following examples:

> *Any 1: I thought **any** fool would know*
> *Any 2: I shan't get **any** scripts from the assistants before then*
> *Any 3: But is there **any** truth in it?*

Any 1 generally occurs in affirmative and declarative sentences and applies to a referent whose existence is presupposed. Type 1 makes up more than 50 per cent of all cases of *any*.

Any 2 occurs in negative and declarative sentences and applies to a referent whose existence is not presupposed. This type covers between 30 and 40 per cent of all instances in authentic texts.

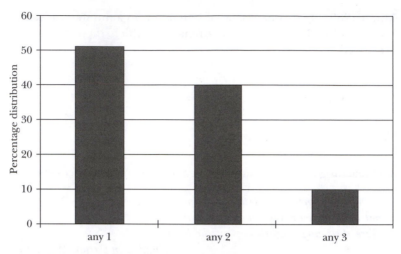

Figure 3.2   Distribution of *any 1, any 2* and *any 3*

Any 3 occurs in affirmative and interrogative sentences and applies to a referent whose existence is not presupposed. This type makes up about 10 per cent of all cases of *any.*

The relative distribution of the three types of *any* is illustrated in Figure 3.2.

Any 1 is the most frequent type, but is rarely mentioned in teaching materials and often only marginally covered in grammars of contemporary English. It is interesting to note that, although *any 1* is not explicitly taught, it occurs in textbooks of English with the same frequency that can be found in authentic texts. There is, however, one notable exception. *Any 1* does not occur at all in lessons where *any* is consciously taught. In these cases the use of *any* is restricted to *any 2* and *any 3.*

Tesch (1990: 345f) proposes a new approach in the teaching of *some* and *any.* The grading she suggests is not assumed to take place within one lesson but would normally spread over several teaching units.

Step 1: Introduction of *some* as a plural form of the indefinite article *a*:

a *house*   **some** *houses*
an *apple*   **some** *apples*

Step 2: Expansion of *some* to uncountable singular nouns:

some *milk*
some *butter*

Step 3: Introduction of *any 1*, contrasted with *every*. (Situation: a basket full of apples, all of them polished.)

*You can take **any** apple.   **Every** apple has been polished.*

Step 4: Introduction of *any 2:*

*I haven't got **anything** for you*
*There isn't **anybody** here*

Step 5: Introduction of *any 3*, contrasted with *some*:

*Are there **any** problems?   Would you like **some** tea?*

The traditional opposition of *some* and *any*, which is normally introduced as the first distinction and at the very beginning, only occurs in step 5 (for fast learners it would be possible to combine steps 4 and 5). The new grading emphasizes the main uses of *some* and *any* contrasting them step by step with their appropriate counterparts in a new and unconventional way which is consistent with the use of *some* and *any* by native speakers.

3.2   *The description of* will *and* would

In a large number of grammars *will* and *would* are treated within the same framework of reference. *Would* is generally considered as the past tense form of *will.* This sort of description is also found in grammars used for teaching purposes (e.g. Ungerer *et al.* 1984).

The joint description of *will* and *would* is historically and etymologically correct. In the course of the history of English, however, the two modal verbs have taken different developments.

In our study of the meaning of modal verbs (see Mindt 1995) we have made a distinction between temporal meaning and modal meaning. The following remarks will be restricted to the modal meanings of *will* and *would*.

There are five principal meanings for *will* and *would*. Three of them make up *c.* 97 per cent of all cases of *will* and four of them make up *c.* 95 per cent of all cases of *would*:

certainty/prediction, volition/intention, possibility/high probability, hypothetical event or result, and habit.

Certainty/prediction:

> *one speaker predicts that unemployment **will** considerably increase*
> *soon Jonathan **would** be two years old*

Volition/intention:

> *spectacles could do something for his eyesight, but he **won't** wear them*
> *because of a pardonable vanity*

Possibility/high probability:

> *it's remotely possible that they **won't** be swept off their feet as I have been*
> *don't you think it **would** be wonderful to live like that?*

Hypothetical event or result:

> *if you were a very forward kid, maybe it **wouldn't** bother you*

Habit:

> *usually, when he came home from school, he **would** free the bird from*
> *its cage, and it **would** fly around the room*

In fictional texts we have found that *will* and *would* have different semantic profiles as follows (see Mindt 1995):

	will	*would*
certainty / prediction	*c.* 71%	*c.* 31%
volition / intention	*c.* 16%	
possibility / high probability	*c.* 10%	*c.* 33%
hypothetical event or result		*c.* 18%
habit		*c.* 13%

This distribution of the meanings of *will* and *would* is represented graphically in Figure 3.3, which makes it clear that because of their different semantic profiles, *will* and *would* should be treated separately not only in a grammar for teaching purposes but also in teaching materials.

The result of our studies also emphasizes the importance of distributional data in grammars for teaching purposes. Without distributional data there can be no informed grading of the functions of a grammatical form in a language course. The absence of distributional data in almost all preceding grammars results in a grading that is based on intuition rather than on empirical evidence and very often does not reflect the actual use of English.

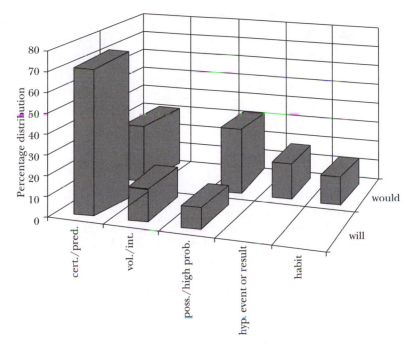

Figure 3.3   Semantic profiles of *will* and *would*

3.3   The treatment of irregular verbs

Irregular verbs belong to the most important parts of the English verbal system. They are especially important for the foreign language learner.

A study of the verbs in LOB and Brown has shown that irregular verb forms are more frequent than verb forms of regular verbs. The absolute frequencies of regular and irregular verbs in these two corpora are as follows:

	number of different verbs (types)	number of different occurrences (tokens)
Regular verbs	4,240	141,403
Irregular verbs	160	192,868

Figure 3.4 gives a graphic representation of the distribution of regular and irregular verbs (types) and their occurrences (tokens).

Only 160 irregular verbs with 192,868 verb forms make up more than 57 per cent of all verb forms in LOB and Brown. The number

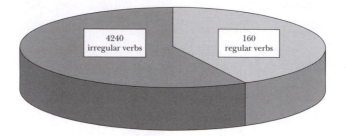

Figure 3.4   Distribution of regular and irregular verbs

of regular verbs is 4240 which is *c.* 42 per cent of all occurrences of verb forms in the two corpora.

These findings were the basis for the development of a learning list of irregular verbs in English. In this list the verbs are ranked in the order of the frequency they have in the two corpora (Grabowski and Mindt 1994, 1995). The list does not include the three most frequent irregular verbs (*be, have* and *do*) since these verbs have to be learned independently at a very early stage. The forms of *be* are required in order to use the progressive and the passive, the forms of *have* for the perfect and past perfect, *do* is required for questions, negations and emphasis.

The new corpus-based learning list presents the irregular verbs of English in an order that gives the learner the maximum yield at each individual step. Even if the learning process is broken off, the learner can be sure of having learned the most important verbs irrespective of when the learning process is broken off.

In addition, the new list is an important tool for the course planner. The list presents an empirical basis for the selection and gradation of irregular verbs in courses for English language teaching.

The traditional lists of irregular verbs are in alphabetical order and do not take the actual occurrence of the verbs into account. For the learner, the teacher and the course planner the traditional lists give no help for the selection and gradation of verbs.

In order to compare the expense of time and the return, which the learner gets, we have set our learning list alongside a traditional alphabetical list from a widely used textbook in Germany (*Learning English: Green Line 6* 1989: 145).

Figure 3.5 shows that if the learner has mastered the first five verbs of our learning list (*say, make, go, take, come*) he or she is familiar with more than 27 per cent of all irregular verb forms

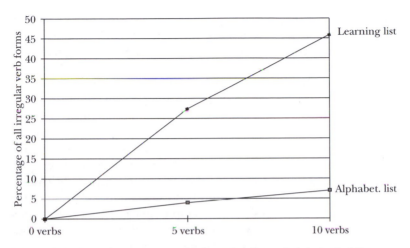

Figure 3.5   Learning progress with learning list and alphabetical list

of English. The corresponding figure for the alphabetical list is 3.6 per cent (*beat, become, begin, bet, bite*). After ten verbs of our learning list (*say, make, go, take, come, see, know, get, give, find*) the learner has mastered 45.6 per cent of the verb patterns of irregular verbs. With the same expense of time the learner of the traditional list has learned 6.4 per cent of the verb forms.

4   Summary

I began with some general remarks on the relationship of teaching materials and grammars and the observation that teaching materials are very often at variance with authentic language use. I then gave an outline of the foundations which underlie the construction of a grammar for the foreign language learner, which is presently under development.

In addition, I have presented some new findings which could influence the construction of language-teaching materials. For *any*, our studies have shown that its most frequent use is generally not taught in German schools, which is also likely to be true for courses outside Germany. The new findings suggest a different gradation and presentation of the functions of *some* and *any*.

The traditional description of *will* and *would* does not take distributional data of their different modal meanings into account, because such data are not supplied by current grammars of English. *Will* and *would* have in fact different semantic profiles which should be adequately reflected in grammars and teaching materials of English.

A new learning list of irregular verbs which we have developed on the basis of machine-readable corpora presents the verbs in an order that reflects their importance in actual language use. For the learner it offers the maximum yield at each point of the learning process. For the course planner it supplies a new basis for the selection and gradation of these verbs in language courses.

The examples point out that the traditional approach leads to language courses which very often do not adequately reflect the use of present-day English. The examples make it clear that corpus-based studies of grammar which are geared to foreign language teaching can do much to bring the teaching of English into better accordance with actual language use.

4

Enriching the Learning Environment: Corpora in ELT

GUY ASTON

1 Introduction

The proliferation of text in electronic form on disk, CD-ROM and over computer networks, and of software to access it rapidly, offers teachers and learners an enormous range of material which might be used for language-learning purposes. Faced with this abundance, one task for applied linguistics is to ask how the purposes of language pedagogy may best be served by access to corpora of foreign language texts, be these electronic publications of books, periodicals or encyclopaedias, corpora specially constructed for lexicography or grammatical description, such as Cobuild and the British National Corpus, or simply *ad hoc* collections put together by the user.

Widdowson (1991, 1993) stresses that as the objective of pedagogy is to enable the learner to use the foreign language, proposals for corpus use must be justified in relation to theories of what that ability consists of and how it is acquired. In this paper I note how different theoretical premises point to different uses of corpora as resources for language learning, first outlining some simple uses which make relatively weak assumptions, and then moving on to discuss the role of corpus use from the perspective of communicative language teaching in its 'weak' and 'strong' versions (Howatt 1984), arguing that corpora can play a useful role in the acquisition and restructuring of the schematic knowledge underlying communicative competence (Widdowson 1983; Skehan 1993).

In so doing I shall focus on corpora consisting of collections of newspaper texts. All the British quality press is now readily available in machine-readable form (see Minugh, this volume): the examples here are taken from the CD-ROM of *The Independent* for 1992, along with a smaller collection of articles from *The Independent* for 1989 published for use with the concordancing program MicroConcord (Corpus A: Scott and Johns 1993). There are, I shall argue, pedagogic advantages in using relatively homogeneous, domain-specific corpora, and newspapers have a well-established role in contemporary language teaching, being one of the most widely read forms of English, and of interest to many categories of learners:

> Learners find newspapers motivating because they offer interesting, relevant, topical, and varied information. Equally importantly, for many, they provide one of the more obvious keys for opening up the foreign society, its preoccupations, its habitual ways of thought, and its prejudices. For these very reasons, newspaper material is among the most challenging the learner is called upon to face.
>
> (Grundy 1993: 3)

2   Corpora as sources of texts and contexts

Perhaps the most obvious pedagogic use of corpora is to treat them as sources of classroom materials which the teacher can select from and adapt according to requirements. Two kinds of operation which can typically be carried out with a newspaper collection are to obtain (a) texts with particular characteristics (text retrieval), (b) smaller contexts which exemplify particular linguistic phenomena (concordancing).

(a) Teachers often go outside textbooks to find appropriate texts, and newspapers are a frequently used resource. Provided that selection criteria can be suitably formulated in terms of lexis (a relatively simple task if a text on a particular topic is needed), newspaper CD-ROMs can generally provide a more rapidly accessible and wider range of candidate texts than piles of cuttings. The associated software enables all the articles in which specified words or combinations occur to be found, scanned to establish that they effectively match requirements, and then printed or saved to disk. Thus for a class in which an interest in astronomy had emerged, we might look in *The Independent* for a text dealing with the planet Venus, obtaining a headline list of all those articles published in October 1992 to contain the word *Venus*. (See Figure 4.1.)

In this apparently motley assortment, two articles (26 and 11 OCT 92) clearly refer to the planet. By generating a list for the whole year, and perusing the actual texts in uncertain cases, we obtain

IND 31 OCT 92 / Expensive souvenirs from the big house: Country house sales can be great fun. But private buyers rarely pick up bargains, says John Windsor
IND 26 OCT 92 / There comes a time in every star's life . . . : The variable brightness of stars helps us to work out how far away and how old they are. Heather Couper and Nigel Henbest explain
IND 25 OCT 92 / The Year-By-Year Quiz
IND 25 OCT 92 / 5 TOP TENS
IND 25 OCT 92 / BOOKS / Low Hum & Little Lo: Humbert Humbert, narrator of 'Lolita', is a sadist, narcissist and sexual deviant: so why should we think Nabokov's novel morally acceptable?
IND 21 OCT 92 / Tennis: Graf has date with nostalgia: The defending champion finds the time to take a sentimental journey
IND 20 OCT 92 / MUSIC / Perfect mix: Edward Seckerson reviews Glyndebourne Touring Opera's The Rake's Progress
IND 13 OCT 92 / Obituary: Bill Rowe
IND 11 OCT 92 / Opinions: Is there life on other planets?
IND 10 OCT 92 / Art Market: Delhi in-crowd bids with one eye on taxman
IND 07 OCT 92 / MUSIC / Notices: New Queen's Hall Orchestra – Barbican Hall, EC1
IND 07 OCT 92 / Obituary: Denholm Elliott
IND 05 OCT 92 / Hippie days are here again
IND 03 OCT 92 / Auctions: Lightly draped ladies for the garden

Figure 4.1   Headline list of articles containing 'Venus'

a subcorpus of 20 articles dealing with Venus from which to choose an appropriate one for this class.

(b) Teachers also regularly need to come up with examples of a particular expression or construction. Concordancing software such as the Longman Mini-Concordancer (Chandler 1989) or MicroConcord (Scott and Johns 1993) allows retrieval from a given collection of texts (including subcorpora downloaded by the previous procedure) of all the contexts in which specified expressions occur. These contexts can be viewed, selected and sorted in a variety of ways before being printed or saved, giving the teacher a range of examples with which to illustrate a particular usage. For instance, when wanting to explain the use of the word *dire*, the concordance in Figure 4.2 – sorted by the word following *dire* – exemplified its collocation with the general nouns *consequences, need, peril, situation* and *time.*

A characteristic feature of these operations of text and context retrieval is that they rarely provide simply what the user was expecting. The retrieval of texts containing the word *Venus* revealed references not just to the planet and the goddess, but also to the Venus fly-trap. Along with my original ideas of *consequences, peril, situation, straits*, the concordance in Figure 4.2 reminded me of the use of *dire* with *need* – as well as introducing me to the existence of *Dire*

East Berlin </bl> <st> <p> AROUND the dire brick pile which is Gethsemane Church
ks have suggested that there could be dire consequences for the City should the
with bombs and rockets, take off from Dire Dawa and head west. <p> The estimated
light from Addis Ababa had stopped at Dire Dawa but had picked up no passengers.
n civil servant said he would stay in Dire Dawa, for a week if necessary, rather
legal. The arrival of the flight from Dire Dawa, where the khat is grown, is met
6–9, 9–6, 9–5, 9–5 on Saturday, is in dire need of a rest. <p> Had Beeson lost t
test time, when they were in the most dire need of calm, clear orders, when ever
have done nothing. Irish racing is in dire peril,' Jonathan Irwin, the showman o
s. <p> 'It is an accepted practice in dire situations such as this that the boar
bels, including Fine Young Cannibals, Dire straits and Bon Jovi as well as perfo
r in what one fanzine has dubbed the 'Dire Straits and lager guide'. In it, the
ing areas like Wallis and Horne and a dire time in housebuilding to limit the de
ure on continued reaction to August's dire trade figures, fell to a low against

Figure 4.2   Concordance showing allocation of 'dire'

Dawa in Ethiopia. Such unexpected (or at any rate unthought of)
cases may have positive pedagogic spin-offs: they complement the
teacher's intuition, thereby assisting in the selection of appropriate examples, and they suggest curiosities – such as the Dire Straits
and Dire Dawa allusions – which may be motivating for learners.
In both these respects the use of a corpus can enrich the material
available for learning.

3   Corpus use within the communicative paradigm

The above proposals, bland as they may seem, may be restricted
according to the assumptions that we make about the nature of
the learning process. As formulated, they suggest that the teacher
may filter and adjust corpus output prior to pedagogic use. The
appropriacy of such mediation is, however, debatable. Many would
maintain that texts and contexts used with learners should reproduce authentic target behaviour, and that the unmediated use of
corpora of naturally occurring text provides an excellent means
of meeting this requirement (e.g. Sinclair 1991). Others would
argue that it is important for texts and contexts to allow learners
to engage as participants in the discourse process, seeing authenticity as a feature of this process rather than of the textual product
(Widdowson 1979): this perspective would suggest that learners
themselves should be allowed to select texts and contexts in the
light of their communicative requirements, which may imply using
corpora of simplified as well as of naturally occurring text. In this

section I want to investigate more closely the implications of different theoretical assumptions, stressing the way in which one particular feature of corpus use – its potential for retrieving multiple texts or contexts of a given type – appears particularly relevant in the light of current theory.

The communicative approach to pedagogy assumes that learners need to acquire an ability to communicate through the language. What Howatt (1984: 279) terms the 'weak version' of the approach assumes that this objective can be achieved by teaching a syllabus of propositional and illocutionary acts in particular genres, and by designing situations which allow for their use in communication. From this perspective, it has been suggested that corpus-based descriptions of the foreign language and its registers can help create general and specific-purpose syllabuses (Sinclair 1991, 1992; Willis 1990; Biber *et al.* 1994), with concordancing being employed to identify and exemplify typical acts and their realizations, and those situation-types in which their use may be appropriate (Willis 1990; Flowerdew 1993; Ma 1993). Concordances of particular phenomena can also be used as data to engage the learner in hypothesis-testing as to particular rules of language use (Johns 1986, 1991a; Jordan 1992; Murison-Bowie 1993). This approach implies the use of corpora which are representative of the genre or genres to be taught, so that typical target uses can be identified.

Such a 'needs-based' approach to pedagogy has however been criticized as confusing learning ends with means (Widdowson 1983, 1991). Partly in response to these criticisms, what Howatt terms the 'strong version' of the communicative approach proposes that the syllabus should be viewed as a series of problem-solving tasks, specifying contexts rather than contents for learning (Prabhu 1987). Stressing a distinction between procedural and declarative knowledge (knowing how to vs knowing that – Faerch and Kasper 1984), it considers the former to underlie effective use, which it sees as developing primarily through participation in discourse with non-linguistic goals. Opportunity for use and motivation are judged the principal conditions for learning (Corder 1986). The role of declarative knowledge, which is instead held to develop through attentive observation of discourse (Schmidt 1990; Aston 1988: ch. 4; McCarthy and Carter 1993: ch. 5), has been widely debated (cf. Krashen 1982), but there appears a degree of consensus that it may facilitate proceduralization insofar as it can be related by the learner to participatory experience (Brumfit 1984; Prabhu 1987).

This perspective suggests different roles for corpora, seeing them on the one hand as a source of problem-solving tasks where the learner participates in the discourse (most obviously involving reading and discussion of retrieved texts), and on the other as a source of opportunities to observe and analyse, but in such a manner as to make the resulting information relevant to activities of discourse participation (be these corpus-based or otherwise).

From this perspective, the retrieval of texts and contexts from a specific domain of use, such as a newspaper collection, would appear to have considerable potential for enabling acquisition of procedural and declarative knowledge and facilitating their interaction. Both types of knowledge, it has been argued, take a schematic form (Widdowson 1989). For instance, rather than generating and interpreting utterances by combining/analysing morphemes on the basis of generalized grammatical and pragmatic rules, users appear to make use of larger memorized chunks associated with particular types of problem in particular types of context, instantiating these as necessary with relatively simple modifications (Bolinger 1976; Pawley and Syder 1983): work in corpus linguistics has provided evidence in favour of this view, showing the extent of recurrent co-selection of lexicogrammatical forms with relatively simple variation (Sinclair 1991). The acquisition of memorized schemata, which may be of varying sizes and of varying generality (Winograd 1977), can be seen as involving two complementary and progressive processes of knowledge restructuring (Skehan 1993). On the one hand, a degree of variation across contexts may prompt the analysis of larger, more context-specific schemata to form smaller, more generalized ones. Thus a learner may acquire a repeated utterance as a single chunk associated with a specific situation-type, only successively analysing this into components as a result of encountered variations. On the other hand, the repeated combination of smaller and more general schemata in recurrent situations may lead to the synthesis of larger, more context-specific ones, which can then be retrieved and instantiated as wholes, in a process analogous to that of script-formation (Schank and Abelson 1975). In both these processes, a key role appears to be played by multiple occurrences across a limited variety of contexts, suggesting that it may be appropriate for pedagogy to use relatively homogeneous collections of data, so as to provide the repetition and minor variation necessary for restructuring to take place. In what follows I shall outline some activities where newspaper corpora serve as sources of multiple texts and contexts, permitting discourse participation and observation, and allowing inference from the latter of declarative information that can be related to occasions of procedural use.

4 Multiple texts, multiple contexts

Seen as resources for discourse participation, newspaper CD-ROMs offer a convenient way of locating material for the vast array of reading activities for which newspapers are used in communicative pedagogy. Being specifically designed to allow the user to find articles of specified types or dealing with specified topics, they can be used with a variety of communicative goals: to find out about a country and its problems; to investigate arguments and attitudes concerning pollution, nuclear proliferation, other nations, etc.; or even as a source of entertainment (e.g. by retrieving articles containing the word *joke*). With respect to the printed newspaper, however, they make it easier to retrieve a range of similar texts as a basis for information exchange and discussion, and thereby provide learners with a range of similar discourse experiences which may facilitate the restructuring of procedural knowledge. It is also easier to involve learners in the selection process, deciding search criteria and scanning the output to identify articles relevant to their purposes and interests. Such involvement can increase the range of opportunities and motivation for participating in discourse (as well as providing practice in a type of reading – scanning for relevance – which is absent in classrooms where texts are pre-selected by teachers). Even irrelevant texts can often excite curiosity, tempting a closer reading and a search for further similar items which is learner-motivated and learner-directed – rather like browsing in a bookshop or library (Aston 1996).

Moving to a declarative perspective, the retrieval of multiple texts can highlight recurrent patternings for observation and analysis. If the texts have similar topics, semantic fields may recur with similar lexicogrammatical content; if they are of similar types, they may also show regularities in information and rhetorical structuring. For instance, for a classroom exercise eight articles were retrieved from *The Independent*, all of which reported on the same murder trial. After jigsaw reading of these to pool information about the crime in question, learners looked for similarities in the way this information was presented. The features they noted included:

- many initial sentences took a routine form 'A [profession-descriptor] [witnessed some event potentially related to the murder of a woman], a jury/court heard/was told yesterday';
- these sentences were followed by an expanded description of the event witnessed, the witness this time being identified by name, age, and geographical origin in that order;
- the location of the trial was specified, in a subsequent sentence, as 'Shrewsbury Crown Court' (rather than, say, 'the Crown Court in Shrewsbury');
- if this fact had not been previously mentioned, the final sentence stated that the accused had denied the murder;
- the accused was consistently referred to as the killer – murder is the charge, killing the event giving rise to it.

It might seem that if learners have already managed to understand and convey the content, this kind of analysis is detached from communicative concerns. Its relevance can, however, easily be increased by asking learners to produce similar texts to those retrieved, where the regularities noted can be related directly to their experience as discourse producers. In the case just described, each group was subsequently asked to invent a murder scenario, and to write newspaper reports on a trial relating to it. In another one, students were first asked to produce texts of their own reporting a given piece of news, and then to see how far these corresponded to texts retrieved from the corpus.

In this manner, the texts retrieved from the corpus serve as a source of declarative knowledge to aid discourse participation. A similar role may be played by the retrieval of multiple contexts through concordancing. During writing, for instance, concordancing can provide evidence for the use of an expression in a particular collocation or situation-type, complementing the dictionary as a reference tool. Thus a concordance of *decline* in the MicroConcord *Independent* Corpus shows that a *decline* is *slow, long, sharp, steep, n per cent* or *relative*, and that it is mainly used to refer to business matters and the fortunes of sports teams – again underlining how a domain-specific corpus is more likely to provide the learner with appropriate information for the topic and text-type concerned. Similarly in reading work, concordancing may offer evidence in favour of a particular hypothesis as to meaning (Minugh, this volume), and in cases where specialized terminology is involved, may even provide a definition. Thus in the following text, problems were posed by the meaning of *Nupe*:

Clarke 'to blame for ambulance dispute'

By Andy Gliniecki

An Ambulance workers' union leader yesterday accused Kenneth Clarke, the Secretary of State for Health, of intransigence, as union officials prepared for today's meeting at Acas.

Roger Poole, the staff's chief negotiator, and a senior *Nupe* official, said: 'Kenneth Clarke's refusal to talk proves conclusively who is responsible for the continuation of the dispute. Mr Clarke knows how serious this dispute is but he is prepared to risk people's lives rather than talk.' . . .

but the following concordanced examples from *The Independent* effectively explained the term:

white-collar union Nalgo together with **Nupe** and the Transport and
cretary of the public employees' union **Nupe**, said that local manage
mon suffered by nurses,' **Nupe**, the union supporting the case, said
deputy general secretary of **Nupe**, the public sector workers' union,

On occasion, instead of providing examples which match the learner's current problem, retrieval from a corpus may highlight different patterns, suggesting that the current use is in some way marked. Louw (1991, 1993, this volume) has proposed that concordancing provides learners with a means to understand ironic or poetic deviation by an understanding of the recurrent connotations or 'semantic prosody' of particular forms. Here, too, the use of a corpus of texts of the same genre can provide clues as to the features at issue. A concordance of *too far* from *The Independent* facilitates appreciation of the pun in the following headline to a theatre review

A fridge too far: Dinner Dance – Lyric Hammersmith

by evidencing the recurrent expression *a bridge too far*, in the figurative sense of exaggeration and overreaching (as well as, nicely, its 'literal' use in the title of Attenborough's film). By highlighting regularities with respect to which a particular case may be heard as conforming or deviant, the corpus provides ' "bottom up" *textual evidence* for what has until now been regarded as "top down" *prior knowledge* in the act of reading' (Louw 1993: 161), allowing the formation of declarative schemata that relate to a particular procedural problem.

5   Some practical problems

5.1   Learning to look for regularities

While use of a corpus to confirm a hypothesis as to meaning or the existence of a particular usage may simply involve a search for one example that matches the problem, most of the uses examined imply a search for recurrences over multiple texts or contexts. While the search for a single instance parallels learners' experience of other tools such as grammars, dictionaries and encyclopaedias, searching for recurrences may be conceptually less familiar. If the observation of repetition and variation in multiple texts and contexts is to help them to infer declarative schemata, learners may need to be made aware of how corpus data can suggest regularities of use, and to understand the potential relevance of the latter for learning. It seems important to stress that such regularities need not correspond to the generalized statements familiar from grammars and dictionaries. A concordance for *since* from *The Independent*, as well as confirming the general rule that *since* occurs with expressions referring to points of past time (Jordan 1992), highlights a number of particular patterns – clause-initial *since then*; clause-medial *long since* – which may be learned as larger and more context-specific schemata. Being derived from a limited range of data, they may be neither fully generalizable nor fully accurate, but they none the less arguably offer the learner intermediate reference points in a process of progressive restructuring.

Given the traditional emphasis in pedagogy on maximally generalized rules, learners may need training in attending to partial regularities of this kind. Learners may need practice in identifying patterns of collocation, colligation, connotation and discourse structuring; and at the same time to appreciate the relevance of noting such regularities to their own learning. The structure in Figure 4.3 was developed to discuss the notion of schematic knowledge with learners, and to make them aware of the many kinds of regularities present in discourse and the extent to which users operate with fixed or semi-fixed associations. It is based on a distinction between syntagmatic associations (on the horizontal axis) at the levels of meanings (informational/rhetorical structure) and of forms (collocation/colligation/semantic prosodies), and paradigmatic associations (on the vertical axis) between situation and meaning (genre and register conventions), between meaning and form (conventional speech act and referring procedures), and between situation and form (routine formulae, technical terminology):

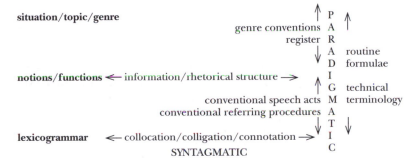

Figure 4.3

By making learners aware of such regularities and of their importance in language use and learning, and by showing them how they can be highlighted in corpora through the use of retrieval, selection and sorting procedures, we also move in the direction of independent use of corpora as resources for autonomous learning (Aston, 1996; Gavioli, this volume).

5.2   Grading

Awareness of rationale, along with practice, may help learners develop strategies for interrogating corpora and interpreting data. Corpus-based activities need to be designed bearing in mind the need for learners to acquire the ability to exploit these resources. The initial reactions of most teachers and of many learners to using corpora, particularly where multiple texts and contexts are retrieved, often stress their linguistic difficulty. While ease of access to corpora clearly depends on linguistic competence, there are a number of other variables which can be manipulated to control difficulty and hence grade activities.

5.2.1   Simplify the data

Most of the examples from newspaper corpora cited in this paper are clearly more suitable for use with relatively advanced learners. At more elementary levels, either a simpler corpus can be found or constructed by the teacher, selecting and/or modifying texts to be included on the basis of their presumed accessibility, or access may be mediated, with the teacher filtering the texts and contexts retrieved to ensure their appropriacy and comprehensibility.

5.2.2   Select familiar/predictable data

Working with corpora on familiar topics and consisting of familiar text-types may reduce task difficulty, since in discourse 'the word works indexically to key in with and complement a context of shared knowledge' (Widdowson 1993: 309). Short news items, for instance, are familiar as a genre to most learners, having wide-ranging cross-cultural similarities (Bell 1991), and can be selected to deal with familiar topics. Willis (1993) makes the more radical proposal of creating corpora consisting solely of texts that learners have previously studied. But even where the particular texts included are unfamiliar, accessibility would seem likely to be enhanced if the variety of text-types is restricted and the learner is both familiar with those types and aware of the composition of the corpus.

5.2.3   Reduce the quantity of data

If the corpus is small, it is easier for learners (individually, or as a group) to become familiar with its component texts. While a larger corpus may provide more choice of texts or contexts, the fact of having to deal with more data (even simply to discard it) may increase difficulty of use. Though a small corpus is inherently less likely to display recurrences than a larger one, the use of highly homogeneous collections, such as the murder trial group described in section 4 above, may counteract this tendency, presenting multiple instances of features specific to that particular text-type. Working with a corpus of a few thousand words can also help learners understand how the nature of the corpus influences retrieved output, and what sorts of questions may require larger or different corpora to provide answers.

5.2.4 Simplify the task

Tasks vary in the amount of data that needs to be read, and the depth of reading involved. Some tasks may allow learners to discard data that is not immediately accessible, as when choosing texts for personal reading, in contrast with others which require analysis of all the data retrieved. Difficulty also depends on the type of analysis required: some tasks may only require recognition of superficial regularities – for instance, a search for collocational patterns – whereas others may require a contextualized interpretation of the various texts or contexts, as in searches for connotational regularities or semantic prosodies. Analysis in terms of familiar, predetermined categories may be easier than where the learner has to devise an appropriate categorization. And many tasks can be easier for learners to carry out in pairs or groups, where linguistic and encyclopaedic knowledge can be pooled.

6 Conclusions

Overall, corpora seem able to significantly enrich the learning environment, by providing opportunities for using English and observing regularities in this use. At the same time they can reduce the learner's dependency on the teacher, and the teacher's on the textbook, allowing teachers to concentrate on their role as learning rather than language experts.

From a pedagogic perspective, any collection of homogeneously encoded texts can constitute a corpus provided that the texts and contexts that are retrievable from it form a suitable basis for language learning. The inherent interest of newspaper collections, the fact that they belong to essentially familiar text-types, and their relative homogeneity, makes them seem a particularly appropriate source. On the one hand, these features facilitate access for users who, lacking the interpretative skills of the native-speaker and the descriptive skills of the trained linguist, may have difficulty in making sense of and categorizing instances retrieved from unfamiliar and widely differing contexts; on the other, they facilitate the design of tasks which evidence repetition and minor variation across multiple texts and contexts, aiding the acquisition of procedural and declarative schemata and their interaction. If acquisition is a matter of progressive approximation to native-speaker competence, restructuring on the basis of limited, non-representative but understandable and motivating data seems a natural part of that process.

Apart from the issue of difficulty discussed in the last section, the obvious criticism that can be levelled at the use of such a restricted corpus as a single newspaper is that learners may seem implicitly invited to conform to a single model – *The Independent*'s house style – and to treat this as typical English. It is clearly important that learners should be made aware of the limits of this or any other corpus: analysis of its composition, reflection on its conditions of production, and comparison with other corpora may help learners understand how different collections of texts can provide different kinds of information. It may be useful for different groups within a class to work with different corpora and compare their findings. If a bank of such corpora is progressively built up within the teaching institution, learners may acquire the ability to select appropriate corpora for particular tasks, progressively increasing the size of the overall text-base upon which they can draw.

Section B

Teaching Languages

Introduction

In the first section of this book we were given an insight into three crucial aspects of language study: first the nature of the language itself, then the role of the teacher in providing learning materials, and finally the theoretical and practical aspects of the learning process. In this section, Minugh comments on some issues involved in the first of these. He recounts the strains and hazards of being a native 'informant' in his adopted Sweden; newspaper CD-ROMs, he argues, have at last provided him, and his students too, with an up-to-date ally in the quest for what is English. Many teachers will identify with the problems he describes. Whether native speaker or not, teachers find themselves more or less willingly in the role of language authority. As Aston pointed out in the previous section, corpora can to some extent relieve the teachers of this burden, allowing them to concentrate on facilitating the language-learning process. However, it is not enough to leave students alone with the data. As Gavioli stresses in her chapter, students need to be trained to interpret and classify corpus-derived data.

The chapters by Johns and Wilson both emphasize the need to guide the learner while still providing authentic and representative language. Their chapters both belong to the area of CALL and both aim to give learners independence. Johns, in particular, regards the ideal learning situation as being 'driven' by the data. Teachers of course frequently make assumptions, both implicit and explicit, about what learners need. Johns' chapter is remarkable in that he has built into his system the means of testing those assumptions. By monitoring the route students take through his

CALL program he is able to observe the extent to which their needs as language learners are met.

Corpus compilation favours written data. So, in the main, does language teaching. It is a strange thing that while the procedural part of language learning, the 'doing' part, gives considerable importance to oral competence and concentrates in so doing on the situational and functional dimensions of language use, much of the declarative knowledge, 'knowing about', is based on a study of the written word. The existence of spoken corpora, such as the corpus of spoken German, collected and described by Jones in his chapter, has at last allowed learners to capture the spoken word and investigate it. The enormous resources necessary to transcribe conversational data make his corpus a unique and invaluable source of information about the spoken language. This particular corpus has been so designed to allow the study of language variation, in particular the regional differences in the German-speaking world.

The issue of language variation is also raised by Gavioli. In her chapter she points out that it is possible to subdivide existing bodies of data, such as newspaper CD-ROM texts, in order to create other more specialized sets of texts, grouped for example according to topic or genre. In this way comparisons can be made between language patterning in different text types. Anyone with access to a corpus of conversation can, of course, extend this grouping to discourse types.

It is important that this book does not concentrate solely on the English language. Both Jones and Dodds show the value of corpora in the teaching of German, and Gavioli describes comparative study of English and Italian. Finally, the chapter by Ahmad and Davies presents a further case for the value of corpora. The Welsh corpus data they describe supports teaching the language not least in order to preserve it.

Finally, lest corpus-based learning be seen as entirely a matter of learning *about* language, let it be said that the procedures involved can and do provide an excellent reason to communicate in the language. The concept of 'authenticity' is thus not only relevant to the source texts themselves; the very authentic process of discovery, which is an integral part of working with corpora, provides an equally authentic reason for using the language.

5

All the Language that's Fit to Print: Using British and American Newspaper CD-ROMs as Corpora

DAVID MINUGH

Two interconnected technological advances – the increasing availability of English-language newspapers and magazines on CD-ROM, and the advent of CD-ROM readers as standard PC equipment – now provide us with a relatively sophisticated tool for the exploration of a number of areas in contemporary vocabulary and syntax studies. The simplicity and accessibility of this procedure open up corpus studies for the first time to language students at relatively elementary levels, without major investments in hardware or long apprenticeships in computer software management, while simultaneously providing opportunities for language investigation that will reward even the most advanced student. For the EFL teacher and student, it provides a wealth of information on collocations and usage far beyond what handbooks can provide.

The genesis of this paper lies in my years of experience as an *utländsk lektor*, or 'foreign lecturer' at the University of Stockholm. For nearly two decades now, I have been repeatedly called upon to make intuitively based pronouncements upon the acceptability of the English produced by students and – rather more gingerly – that of my Swedish colleagues. Over the years, my brash American certainty about what is 'correct' has been somewhat dampened by the repeated ability of said colleagues to produce counter-evidence about many aspects of my own language, not to mention the curious variant called British English.

It is thus imperative for me to spend time back in the States, where I can 'refresh' my intuition, and correct my expatriate folly of assuming that nothing has changed in my absence. While doing so one summer, I was bemused to see on a highway overpass a spray-paint message proclaiming: 'Harry is a dweeb.' Not being personally acquainted with Harry, I couldn't vouch for his personal character, but it was his categorization as a *dweeb* that nonplussed me, even if linguistic and social intuition indicated that the epithet was probably less than approving.

Predictably enough, a sweep through recent learner and reference dictionaries will draw a blank: nothing in the *Longman Dictionary of Contemporary English* (*LDOCE*) (1987), *Webster's Ninth* (1988), the second edition of the *Oxford English Dictionary* (*OED*) (1989), John Wells' *Longman Pronunciation Dictionary* (1990), *Collins English Dictionary* (1991), or the *Longman Dictionary of English Language and Culture* (1993). Modern slang dictionaries, however, confirm its existence from the early 1980s on; moreover, it was familiar enough to the students in my graduate seminar at Wesleyan University that summer.[1]

1   CD-ROMs and new words

Up to this point, my story is one familiar enough to language teachers abroad. Keeping up with a living language means visits back home, extensive reading, a sharp ear for novelties and a considerable dose of optimism. Early corpora such as Brown and LOB were a revolution in their time, but their 1961 English is not exactly the place to look for new arrivals! In 1992, other, more extensive modern corpora, such as the Birmingham Cobuild Corpus, were the sort of mainframe pipe-dream that visiting firemen spoke of, well out of the reach of the average university lecturer. It was at that point that I discovered that Wesleyan's library had a CD-ROM version of *The New York Times* (*NYT*) on trial loan. Within seconds I found that *dweeb* had gained a firm footing even in written American, with eight instances in the 1991 *NYT*.

This brings me to my first point: *contemporary newspaper CD-ROMs are a rich mine for instances of new words or phrases.* Even if one is extraordinarily assiduous, conscientiously noting down everything that catches one's eye, it can often take months or even years to amass more than a few examples of a given item, unless it is highly predictable in specific contexts. CD-ROM newspaper corpora will, however, usually provide a wealth of examples, even for items that at first do not seem very frequent.

What is perhaps not as immediately obvious to scholars working in what approximates a monolingual, monocultural environment such as the US or the UK is my second point: *newspaper CD-ROMs provide us with the ability to track the extent to which a new item leapfrogs from one dialect area into another.* (As newspapers from Australia and elsewhere are released in CD-ROM form, the possibilities for comparison of course become even wider.) Particularly in today's world, many EFL students are interested in this latter aspect as a matter of self-defence, faced as they are with UK-oriented teachers and US-produced videos! In the case of *dweeb*, incidentally, *The Times* and *The Independent* used it in one and two articles, respectively, in 1992, the latter admittedly while quoting from an American novel.

When looking at vocabulary changes, one may also wish to follow semantic shifts, conversion to metaphor, and the like – again, something difficult to do without corpora to draw on. To begin with an older example, the *OED* suggests that the phrase *[to undergo] a sea change* had begun breaking away from its Shakespearean origins at least as early as 1948, when, in the literary history of England he co-edited, none other than Albert C. Baugh used it in a footnote on medieval romances. The *OED* provides three subsequent examples of this extended use, only one of which is completely non-literary in nature. An inkling of how widespread this metaphorical use has now become may be gleaned from the *The Times* of 1992 which provides us with 45 articles mentioning a *sea change*, of which only two contain what may be an oblique reference to Shakespeare. Current learner dictionaries are thus quite right in teaching this as an idiom rather than a quote.

A much more recent example may be found in the phrase *the glass ceiling*, which seems to have started out as an Americanism.[2] First, two examples of it in its 'normal' use, the latter of which already contains the seeds of a potential *glass X* pattern:[3]

> The daughters of NOW's founders . . . are . . . disheartened to have hit the glass ceiling at work. (*NYT*, 1 March 1992)

> Catalyst Inc. contends that not only is there a 'glass ceiling' that prevents many women from reaching top levels but there is also a 'glass wall' that blocks them from gaining the broader line experience they need in addition to the staff jobs many hold as middle managers. (*NYT*, 29 March 1992)

An obvious extension (to another minority group) has already taken place by the time we look at our next example:

> Hispanic legislators . . . opposed the plan because they believe [New York] state's Hispanic population is large enough to merit two new seats . . . 'It doesn't make any sense that we should agree to a glass ceiling of two when it has already been proven that you can do three,' said Assemblyman Roberto Ramirez.   (*NYT*, 10 June 1992)

The shift to a political arena completely stripped of minority implications is complete in the following, slightly earlier, example from presidential candidate Paul Tsongas:

> Today is the day we become the breakthrough kid. I'll no longer have that glass ceiling called regional appeal.
>
> (*NYT*, 8 March 1992)

The key point here is, of course, not the history of this idiom, but how easy it is to observe the development of a new collocation, and by extension, *how easy it is for our students to explore these areas.* Given access to even one such CD-ROM, they can get a feel for how new phrases are actually being used – and with several such CD-ROMs from different papers and years, they can begin to follow developments at a level of detail that previously only dictionary staff could hope to achieve.

2   CD-ROMs and current usage

A related form of activity is where students can use these CD-ROM corpora to check their intuitions about current usage against the statements of the dictionaries. While this particular type of exercise can be done with most modern corpora, the relatively central position that newspapers such as *The Times* and *The Independent*, or *The New York Times* and *The Washington Post* hold in our culture makes them arguably among the most interesting corpora for student work, which is why this particular example will be given at length.[4]

Consider the following dictionary definitions of the word *fondle*:

- If you *fondle* someone or something, you touch them gently with a stroking movement, usually to show your love or affection for them (*Cobuild*)
- to touch gently and lovingly; stroke softly (*LDOCE*)
- to touch or stroke lovingly (*Oxford American Dictionary*)
- to handle tenderly, lovingly or lingeringly: caress (*Webster's Ninth*)

A student reading an article about the case where boxer Mike Tyson was convicted of rape will find that he is repeatedly referred to as 'violent' and a 'serial buttocks-fondler', which seems rather at odds with the above definitions. Rather than argue about whether this is a nonce use of the word, we can turn to, say, *The Independent* CD-ROM for 1992, which records a total of 33 uses of *fondle*. We find, for example,

> ... [men] tentatively or lasciviously buy underwear for the women in their lives. Here is the chance to fondle expensive basques and bras, stockings and slips in the softest silks.   (9 December)

> ... celebrating the early raunchy days of jazz it positively blushes with its own daring. Tarts strut their stuff, punters fondle and gloat and everyone does a lot of pumping, grinding, shimmying jazz dance to a score featuring ...   (24 July)

> [Sinead O'Connor] wore a nipple-revealing string vest on stage in Gothenberg and fondled herself on stage, saying afterwards: 'I believe I can do whatever I like with my own body.'   (29 November)

> She alleged she watched from a wall as the couple kissed, embraced and fondled for half an hour in the back of Miss Allan's car.
> (22 July)

> ... London, was ordered to pay a further £200 out of his own pocket after an industrial tribunal heard that he fondled the secretary's breasts.   (19 May)

> Investigations are still under way into events at the Tailhook Convention, where at least 26 women were allegedly fondled and even undressed after being forced to run the gauntlet through aviators on the third floor ...   (14 August)

In the interests of cross-Atlantic harmony, I will not reveal the name of the politician referred to in the next example:

> He will never be a shamelessly theatrical orator in the Thatcher or Heseltine class, but he knows where the Tory party likes to be tickled and fondled. And he tickles. He fondles.   (10 October)

Of its 33 instances, 6 deal with the Tyson case; of the remainder, only at most 3 appear to match the dictionary definitions, with another 11 involving overt sexual arousal, and the remaining 13 containing a clear element of sexual harassment, an element totally absent in the dictionary definitions.[5]

As before, the point of this exercise is not to criticize this specific shortcoming of our current dictionaries, but rather to point out that the CD-ROM search can put students in the driver's seat, as it were, *enabling them to explore their own intuitions about how words are actually used.* In the overwhelming majority of cases they will find that the dictionary makers do indeed know what they are doing, but by wrestling with questions of style, register, tone, allusion and so on in these concrete examples, our students will become considerably more sophisticated users of dictionaries. In addition, they will gain a greater sense of the ways in which native speakers create variations on a theme, as with Catalyst Incorporated's *glass wall*, explicitly derived from *the glass ceiling.*[6]

Another point worth reiterating is the fact that a newspaper CD-ROM forms an (admittedly limited) corpus, rather than merely being examples, thus providing us with a greater sense of how common such uses are – a point to which we now shall turn.

A classic problem of language learning, that of homonyms or polysemous words, can be made into a challenge for students: take, for instance, the word *wake.* No university-level EFL student would fail to recognize its meaning in, say, the Everly Brothers' 'Wake up, Little Susie, wake up!', but how common are the other meanings suggested by the dictionary? Cobuild suggests in its Introduction (1988: xix) that it will provide its definitions in a pedagogically meaningful order, here offering (1) wake up, (2) a boat's wake, (3) leave in one's wake, (4) something follows as a consequence, (5) a wake for the dead. An examination of *The Independent*, January–March 1992, yields the data in Figure 5.1 (where senses 3 and 4 have been combined).

Here, the key point is not to confirm Cobuild's choices, but rather that the newspaper corpora allow students to draw their

Sense	Examples (n = 256)	Percentage
Wake up	69	27
Ship's wake	7	3
Consequence	170	66
Mourning	9	3
(Place name)	1	

Figure 5.1 Occurrences of the word *wake* according to meaning (*The Independent* January–March 1992)

own conclusions and compare them to the dictionary, rather than merely accepting the authority of the latter.[7] Cases where student findings disagree with Cobuild might then lead to fruitful discussion of possible causes.

Without wishing to dwell on this point, I might add that it also has obvious repercussions for selecting meaning in vocabulary testing. For example, for student groups beyond the beginner level, the most important meaning of *wake* to test is clearly the metaphorical use of the ship's wake.[8] At least for some EFL environments, this choice is doubly important, since the equivalent concrete term in, e.g. German (*Kielwasser*) apparently does not have this abstract sense, and the Swedish term (*kölvatten*) seems to be much less common in the abstract sense than in English – and we know that it is precisely these abstract areas where schools are least likely to prepare their students.[9]

3   Beyond the dictionaries

It has long been known that corpora can provide information on collocations, and newspaper CD-ROMs fulfil this task with aplomb. The fact that they are such large corpora here operates powerfully in their favour: I still remember the shock I got when I found that the Brown and LOB corpora, at a million words apiece, could together produce only one instance each of *Merry Christmas!* and *Happy Christmas!* By contrast, in 1992 alone *The Times* used these expressions 33 times and *The Independent* 43 times.[10]

When searching for already-established collocations, the up-to-dateness of the corpus is, of course, nearly irrelevant, but size is vital, and it is clear that the newspaper CD-ROMs are a considerable improvement on this score. There is, however, another factor of major importance for collocations: such searches are often fruitless in current dictionaries of English, owing simply to the fact that English normally writes N+N compounds as separate words; one need only consult a German or Scandinavian dictionary to note the difference! Although recent years have seen considerable improvement in dictionaries in this area, the EFL learner is never quite sure whether a given collocation is not in the dictionary because it is a transparent formation, like *glass slipper*, or because it is not yet recorded, like *glass ceiling* (known only to Longman's latest dictionary), or because it does not exist in English, like the

Swedish term *glasberget* (the proverbial glass mountain upon which a 29-year-old maiden in want of a suitor is said to sit), or because it is/was used by only a specific ethnic or social group, such as the *Gold Mountain*, a Chinese-American name for America.

At a minimum, one might argue that a failure to find a collocation in several current newspaper CD-ROMs would argue for a relatively restricted provenance of the item in question. And again, the simplicity of working with such corpora means that the students themselves can check on such items directly. One is even tempted to speculate whether this might not prove most salutary for those students who have difficulty believing that English could possibly lack an idiom they know and use frequently in their own native language!

Another area of interest may be found in the area of lexical choice between competing items that appear identical to non-native speakers, yet are clearly distinguished by native speakers. The following example, which derives from student questions in a translation class, will serve to illustrate this point.

The underlying Swedish text concerned medical treatment, and the key term was *hjärttransplantation* (heart transplant/transplantation), Swedish offering only the one form in *-transplantation*. Norstedts' *SSEO* (1993), the best bilingual Swedish – English dictionary, suggested *transplantation*, with the reservation that the individual operation should be called a *transplant*. This text was originally used as a test, and the native speakers marking it all agreed that *heart transplant(s)* was the only suitable choice, even though it was used in a relatively abstract sense: 'Most Englishmen regard heart transplants as an expensive, but routine operation.' Nearly all our students (some 300 this past year alone), however, opted for *transplantations*. Were we wrong? How could we explain our choice?

I turned to *The New York Times* CD-ROM (January–October 1992) to examine this problem. The striking results are shown in Figure 5.2.

Among the examples found, one might mention the *Cardiac Transplant Clinic*, *The Journal of Heart and Lung Transplantation* and *The Journal of Cell Transplantation*. These latter examples appear to point to a need for a greater degree of abstraction before the form in *-ation* is triggered. Regardless of the reasons, it clearly demonstrated to our students that our resistance to the use of *heart transplantation* was not merely a whim of their teachers, but one which,

[Type]	transplant	transplantation
[simplex]	317	23
Heart	22	0
Liver	28	0
Kidney	15	1
Fetal tissue	13	1

Figure 5.2   Occurrences of the words *transplant* and *transplantation* in *The New York Times* (January–October 1992)

at a minimum, we shared with *The New York Times*.[11] Moreover, since the corpus is in the university library, freely available to students, they can double-check our claims – and we have made it known that challenges to marking on our translation tests will carry much greater weight if backed up by such evidence!

4   CD-ROMs and grammar

As with any relatively large corpus, one lexis-related starting point for grammar questions in newspaper CD-ROM corpora might be matters such as irregular verbs.[12] Take, for example, the American alternative past forms *sneaked* and *snuck*: *The New York Times* used them 60 and 18 times, respectively, during January–October 1992, while *The Independent* had 42 and 0, *The Times* 38 and 2. There are details involved that would need to be checked, such as which form of the past we are dealing with, and whether the form occurs more than once in an article, but the trend is clear: the alternative form *snuck* still seems to be less likely (in written journalism, at least), but already far too common to be stigmatized as incorrect in American.[13] The two instances of *snuck* in *The Times* seem to be purely British in nature, and suggest that we should watch for further developments there – but the lack of examples in *The Independent* suggests that we should not hold our breath on this one. Similar explorations easily suggest themselves, perhaps the easiest being a systematic sweep through the footnotes in the relevant sections of one's favourite EFL grammar.

Newspaper CD-ROMs can, of course, be mined for information about the grammatical constructions involved in, for example, collocations. One instance that came up in our discussions when marking student translations concerned the types of clause permitted after the phrase *It is [high/about/Ø] time* . . . Swedish grammars have long offered students the choice between *for* + infinitive (*for us to leave*) or *that* + subjunctive (*that you did something about that nasty cough of yours*).[14] But even a minimal search of *The New York Times* for *high time* in the period January to March 1992 revealed that the situation is far more complex. Ignoring the single example of *high time* with no modifier, a total of 13 examples were found, as follows:

- high time + to-infinitive: 5 instances
  Ex.: Whatever the fate of this year's nominee, it is in the party's best interest to change the system. It's high time for the Democratic Party to rediscover democracy.   (3 March)

- high time + subjunctive infinitive: 1 instance
  Ex.: Consequently it is high time that ethnic Russians, those who suffered most under Communism, be given preferential treatment and that a strictly Russian ethnic quota be restored to remedy seven decades of injustice.   (20 February)

- high time + present (indicative or subjunctive): 3 instances
  Ex.: That is why it is high time that Hispanics begin to see that the party on the other side may be able to help them become successful. The Democratic Party has taken both Hispanics and blacks for granted.   (9 February)

- high time + past (indicative or subjunctive): 4 instances
  Ex.: . . . last September Hurley rewrote its zoning to create a historic district that encompasses all 25 houses, now privately owned and occupied. Previously, only about half the houses were within a historic district created in 1967.
  'Probably because some homeowner objected to being part of the district, they left out one side of the street,' said Town Councilman Fred C. Doty. 'It was high time we treated these houses as a whole.'   (26 January)
  In response, many Chinese intellectuals argue that the regime ultimately will crumble because it brutalizes demonstrators and refuses to listen to criticism, and in this sense human rights issues are central. It is high time, they say, that the West gave the same support for freedom in China that was long standard in Eastern Europe and the Soviet Union.   (26 January)

Preliminary investigations of this construction in *The New York Times* for 1990–92 indicate that the picture is approximately the same, with a clearer dominance of the infinitive form, and with some 100 examples.[15] By way of comparison, it might be mentioned that the Brown and LOB corpora together contained only a handful of instances.

Another area worth considering is the numerous rules given in school and university grammars. In cases where such rules are hedged by means of phrases such as 'usually, often' or the like, students can go to the corpora and examine a series of examples. I regard this as relatively important, and of interest above all for future teachers, it being vital that they gain insight into the fact that the rules in the school grammars they will be using are necessarily overly simplistic and categorical.

If we consider for example the rules for applying the definite article in English, a distinction can be made between *play* + <sport> and *play* + *the* + <musical instrument>; this used to be regularly tested, at least in Swedish schools.[16] Yet even relatively casual listeners will know that this is a rule jazz and rock musicians often honour in the breach. Due to the limitations of the search functions in newspaper CD-ROMs, searching for phrases involving *the* requires a little ingenuity, in this case searching for *play* <within 2> *piano/trumpet/sax/kazoo/sitar/organ/washboard* and so on.[17] Extracting a minicorpus of, say, 100 examples and putting it into handout form takes only two or three hours, yet its size will provide students with adequate input to discuss in detail, rather than merely learn, the complex patterns governing the choice of the article in this context.

5   Styles and registers

By selecting and comparing distributions of items from the various text types (as defined by the producers of CD-ROMs), such as sports, editorials or economic news, one can compare grammatical and lexical features from these various subgenres. One might test, for example, whether *dark horse* is more common as a political metaphor ('an outsider, unexpected candidate') or a racing term;[18] or one might examine whether contractions are more common in editorials than in book reviews. In short, newspaper CD-ROMs can in this respect fill the same function as many other corpora, although admittedly within a narrower range of registers.

6   Advantages

By this time, the major advantages of using newspaper CD-ROMs should be clear, and need little additional comment. They include:

- their large size (30–50 million words)[19]
- their user-friendliness, including easy installation
- their well-defined corpora (one newspaper/year per CD-ROM)
- their various genres correspond to people's daily reading experience
- their low minimum hardware specifications
- purchase costs can be shared with other departments or the library
- their number and geographical range are steadily increasing.

Several additional advantages deserve a brief additional comment. One fringe benefit of using a newspaper corpus is that there may very well be information available about the item itself. An example of this is to be found in our earlier search for the missing *dweeb*: two of the instances from *The New York Times* 1992 turned out to be articles discussing modern American slang, including notes on usage, etymology, and references to newly published works in the area!

Another major advantage for the foreign learner is the sheer fascination of all the various news items that catch their eye as they read them for a specific phrase. While this tends to slow down their specific task, it can lead them into all sorts of interesting byways lined with new vocabulary.

Finally, of particular interest is their enormous potential for advanced learners – a group hitherto badly neglected in the CALL world. Many of the areas I have touched upon contain elements that can involve considerable linguistic sophistication and engage even those at near-native levels of fluency.

7   Disadvantages

A few of the disadvantages of these CD-ROMs have already been mentioned, such as the lack of information about the corpora as such, not least the exact size of each CD-ROM corpus. Several other disadvantages stem from essentially the same source, i.e. the fact that they were developed for information retrieval rather than language investigations:

- the search system is a given part of the packet and cannot be changed in any significant way
- the most frequent words are classified as 'noise' and cannot be searched for[20]
- many CD-ROMs, such as those produced by UMI, currently can dump only the entire article, including the CD-ROM's information about it (date, type, author and so on)[21]
- the 'pop-up' word frequency lists in, e.g. UMI and Chadwyck-Healey CD-ROMs are incomplete ('noise words' are omitted) and cannot be saved to disk.[22]

8 Conclusion

As more and more newspaper CD-ROMs become available, it is to be hoped that it will become possible to persuade the companies involved to consider our interests when developing their software and storage systems.

But it is not only the indifference of commercial interests that is involved: one of the saddest ironies in this chronicle is that I was utterly unable to convince the Wesleyan University librarians that it was worth investing in these CD-ROMs for the study of their own language – they chose to return the trial package. It is my fervent hope that this chapter will have provided you with the arguments needed to introduce newspaper CD-ROMs to your own students. As for Wesleyan, if worst comes to worst, I shall leave them a donation for that purpose in my will.

Notes

1 It is found in for example *Bloomsbury Dictionary of Contemporary Slang* (1990) and the earlier *New Dictionary of American Slang* (1986). It makes its first general appearance in *Webster's Tenth* (1993).
2 *The Independent* 1992 contains 6 instances of it in clearly British discourses; by 1993, the number had risen to 11, with a further two instances dealing with America and Japan, respectively; and in 1994

it contained 26 instances, including one of an economy approaching its glass ceiling!

3   A further semantic echo of the metaphor may be seen in the subsequent development of the 'sticky floor' said to keep most women firmly in the lower echelons of organizations. See Anne H. Soukhanov's 'Word watch' in the December 1993 issue of *The Atlantic* (p. 148).

4   For a more general discussion of corpora and their relation to language, see, e.g. the Nobel Symposium 82 publication *Directions in Corpus Linguistics* (Svartvik 1992), particularly Christian Mair's 'Comments', pp. 98–9.

5   Newspaper CD-ROMs can of course also be used to investigate gender and language in many different ways – for example, the choice of lexical items such as *chair/chairman/chairwoman/chairperson*.

6   This is particularly striking in headlines, which often exhibit complex word play, such as playing off an article's actual subject against the normal (metaphorical) meaning of an idiom in the headline. Consider, for example, the title 'Major's gift horse looks down in the mouth' (*The Independent*, 10 April 1994), about the illnesses and uses of the stallion presented to the PM by the President of Turkmenistan in March 1993.

7   Cf. Graeme Kennedy's comment: 'Increasingly, the most professional teachers expect evidence to justify positions taken, and teacher trainees should receive statistical information as part of the description of English or whatever language they are learning to teach' (1992: 367).

8   This particular idiom is of interest as an expression of causation. See the discussion in Kennedy (1992: 355–6).

9   See Ljung (1990) on the patterns of Swedish high school vocabulary in English. As such teaching comes at the tail end of nearly ten years of studies in English, matters are presumably no better in most other EFL teaching situations.

10 In this connection, one of the disadvantages of newspaper CD-ROMs should be mentioned: because they are commercial products primarily designed to aid people interested in information retrieval, they contain no information about the actual nature of the individual corpus, beyond the obvious fact that they contain the newspaper texts and captions. Thus the actual size of newspaper corpora must at present be estimated from occurrences of a series of lexical items, or by other approximations. One might note that the main files seem to be on the order of 300–600 megabytes, which suggests a corpus size in the neighbourhood of 30–50 million words. A comparison of 262 items (essentially the first searchable word from each letter of the alphabet in frequency bands 5–15 [i.e. items 5000 to 14,999] of

the 18 million word Cobuild Corpus of 1987, as utilized by Ljung (1990)) with the average annual figures for *The New York Times* 1990–92 yielded a ratio of 2.51 to 1, suggesting a *NYT* CD-ROM size of 45 million words, but other approximations yield results as low as 15–20 million. It should not be impossible for UMI and Chadwyck-Healey to determine a more exact measure.

11 As a footnote, I might add that a search of *The Independent*, 1992, yielded 241 instances of *transplant*, none of *transplantation*.

12 For a discussion on verb forms in general and teaching, see the discussion in Kennedy (1992: 341–3).

13 An instance may be found in Wallace Chafe's contribution to the Nobel Symposium (Svartvik 1992: 91).

14 The point does not seem to be covered in Quirk *et al.* (1985), although it is indirectly dealt with in part in section 14.24n, and hinted at in 17.30.

15 See Lavelle and Minugh (forthcoming).

16 Swedish omits the definite article in the equivalent constructions. Svartvik and Sager (1975: 29) stated the *sport/instrument* distinction as a flat rule; their third edition (1985: 29) more cautiously states that this is normally [*oftast*] the case. More recent grammars take the same line: e.g. Johansson and Stevens (1988: 16) [*i regel* 'as a rule']; Ljung and Ohlander (1992: 46) [*vanligen* 'usually', with a special note on rock and jazz music].

17 While the exact procedure will vary from corpus to corpus, the basic pattern is identical across the board, and shifting among corpora should cause students no real trouble.

18 In BrE the latter seems to dominate, in AmE the former.

19 See note 10, above. A drawback of the *NYT* CD-ROM is that the same article can appear in several parallel suburban sections on a given Sunday.

20 Indirectly, of course, they can sometimes be made accessible by dumping out a batch of collocations and using a word-processing or concordance program to narrow the search. This can, however, be rather clumsy, or even impossible: if we were to look for *[It is] about time* in, say, *The New York Times* for 1990, we would have to first extract 50,952 articles containing *time* (something the search program refuses to do). Chadwyck-Healey's more sophisticated software would allow us to narrow the search to a week or two, after which one could run, e.g. Oxford's MicroConcord on the resultant file and actually obtain useful data.

21 The Chadwyck-Healey CD-ROMs can dump a three-line context, which greatly facilitates large searches. Unfortunately, the program cannot suppress the citation information, and in addition places a page break (ASCII character 12) between entries; if this latter point causes trouble

(as when, e.g. Word 5 tries to format a 2000 page document), strip the character away before loading the file into the word-processing program.

22   A department with an interest in comparing lexical frequencies and access to a decent programmer can probably solve the practical problems involved, although our tentative contacts with UMI indicate that they are not particularly interested in helping; the legal implications would also need to be worked out.

6

Exploring Texts through the Concordancer: Guiding the Learner

LAURA GAVIOLI

1 Active learning with corpora: getting students to act as researchers

The approach taken in this paper is based on a very similar point of view to that expressed by Johns (1991a: 2).

> The perception that 'reseach is too serious to be left to the researchers': that the language learner is also, essentially, a research worker whose learning needs to be driven by access to linguistic data.

Johns redefines the role of the computer in the classroom from that of a 'surrogate teacher or tutor' to that of an informant. It follows that, rather than making the machine more intelligent in answering learner-generated questions, a pedagogy of the foreign language should be concerned with making the learner 'more intelligent' in posing questions and interpreting responses. While, on the one hand, this entails training teachers in corpus and concordance analysis (see Renouf, this volume), on the other it stresses the need of providing students with the means of interpreting the data produced by the machine. Simply giving students direct access to the data produced by the computer is not enough to make them research workers. As Barnett (1993) notes, the use of computer applications in the classroom can easily fall into the trap of leaving learners too much alone, overwhelmed by information and resources. Besides being familiar with the software, processing a corpus of authentic texts involves a range of levels of linguistic and metalinguistic knowledge which can enable students to categorize occurrences, identify regularities and generalize from them. The process of leading the students to interpret the data is, in my view, as good a language-learning activity as that which it aims to make possible, i.e. teaching the students to use the concordancer as a resource to obtain information about the language.

This chapter focuses on the processes involved in analysing text corpora and in interpreting computer-derived data, and the need to elaborate activities which introduce students gradually to data analysis. Examples of such activities are proposed in sections 2.3 and 4.2. My study is based on a joint research project, which has been carried out at the School for Interpreters and Translators of the University of Bologna over the last two years, aimed at investigating the use of multilingual corpora in the training of students of interpretation/translation (Aston 1996). The corpora used are collections of newspaper articles in three languages: English, Italian and French. Newspaper corpora seemed useful to us not only because newspaper texts form the bulk of the main resource materials used by foreign language teachers at any level (Grundy 1993), but also because they provide a variety of different texts and show a certain degree of comparability in the languages we are considering, both in the text types that can be found and in the topics dealt with. Besides this, newspaper texts in electronic format (CD-ROM) are easy to obtain and are reasonably priced. The data presented in this chapter is derived from corpora of about 1 million words of English (MicroConcord corpus A) and 1 million words of Italian (mainly *Il Sole 24 Ore*, plus a sample from *La Repubblica, Il Mattino* and *La Stampa*).

2   Some characteristics of corpus data

There are two main aspects to be taken into account when introducing analysis of corpus-derived data in the classroom: first, the data does not generally provide an immediate answer to the original question of the research, as it must be edited and interpreted; second, the data is corpus-derived, and therefore does not illustrate characteristics of 'the language' in general, but rather of the particular language of the corpus examined. This section clarifies these two aspects of corpus analysis and their implications for using data for language-learning activities.

2.1 Interpreting the data

Although it permits us to deal with actual occurrences of language, a corpus is not 'the real language'. Large as it may be, and even when selected in order to be as representative of the language as possible, a corpus does not include all the possible occurrences of language and inevitably includes patterns which might not be recurrent at all, and which might sound odd to a native speaker (Edwards 1993). When we look for information about a pattern of language through the concordancer we get only the collocations in which the search word appears in the corpus.

It is a common experience that those who use a concordancer for the first time to check the meaning of a word or a pattern of words, find that many of the examples occurring in the list of concordances are not very illuminating. Concordance-derived data may not provide immediate evidence for the question posed by the researcher and may instead provide an answer to some other question. As Sinclair notes: 'the most actual examples are unrepresentative of the pattern of the word or phrase for which they are chosen' (1991: 99). Let's take an example. A search for the word *rift*, initiated by the question 'What does *rift* mean?' provided the data in Figure 6.1 (overleaf) (the search was carried out with MicroConcord, Scott and Johns 1993).

Although the meaning of *rift* can more or less be guessed, it is not an immediate answer and a non-native speaker would presumably check the guess in the dictionary before attempting to use or translate the word. What is immediately visible, in these examples, is that *between* is a very common first right collocate of *rift* (five occurrences out of nine examples). This suggests that a *rift* generally implies two (not more) parties. Looking at the list more carefully, we can find other evidence for this assessment in example 1 – in which *between* does not occur but the number of parties involved in the rift is in fact two (Brady and Charlton) – and in example 8 (the 'makers' of architecture and its 'users'). This can be easily seen simply by moving the cursor to the right of the screen or by pressing 'enter' on the example to get more context (most concordancers allow such operations):

'the Prince of Wales Rules OK?', will highlight, yet again, the deep **rift** that separates the makers of architecture in this country from its users.

```
1 ent emollient correspondence has has healed the  rift  and Brady remains within Charlton's embrace, hi
2 fore word came of Mr Afanasyev's departure, the   rift  between Mr Yeltsin and the Soviet establishment
3 on described weekend press reports of a serious   rift  between Eurotunnel and Transmanche Link, the co
4 ver-reacted even more than usual. Evidence of a   rift  between the Prime Minister and the Chancellor,
5 lting discontinuity that has caused the current   rift  between architect and layman. The thread must b
6 armony was lost: As debate again highlights the  rift  between professional and layman, Dan Cruickshan
7 s in city elections on 29 October. <p> A public  rift  in Catholic politics surfaced last week when th
8 Rules OK?', will highlight, yet again, the deep  rift  that separates the makers of architecture in th
9 </dt> <h1> Runcie attack on 'Pharisees' revives  rift  with Tories </h1> <b1> By JAMES DALRYMPLE </b1>
```

Figure 6.1 Concordance of 'rift'

Whatever the meaning of *rift*, then, what these examples clearly suggest is that 'a rift' occurs between two parties (7 out of 9 occurrences).

The examples derived from computer concordancing are samples of actual language occurrences, but they may not provide immediate answers to the questions posed. Answers are obtained only through interpretation and categorization carried out by the researcher. If students are to act as research workers when faced with such data, we have to introduce them to the process of interpretation and categorization and to show them what this process entails.

2.2 Limitations of the data

The problems involved in interpreting the data above are clearly a consequence of the corpus used. The fact that the corpus is a collection of newspaper articles instead of, say, geology texts, might explain why *rift* is never used in its literal meaning (a fissure in the earth/rock), for which examples are provided in the *Cobuild Dictionary*. Corpora are created to fit particular research projects (Leech and Fligelstone 1992) and as Sinclair observes: 'the beginning of any corpus study is the creation of the corpus itself [. . .] The results are only as good as the corpus' (1991: 13). By processing a corpus of texts different from newspaper articles, it is very likely that we would obtain different examples of *rift* which might suggest different uses or regularities. Flowerdew (1993: 236) notes that the extent to which the corpus is processed affects the data resulting from the concordance. Contrasting the Cobuild Corpus and a specific corpus containing only texts dealing with biology, he shows that there is a great difference in the data provided. While in the Cobuild Corpus the twenty most frequent nouns are:

time, people, way, man, years, work, world, thing, day, children, life, men, fact, house, kind, year, place, home, sort, end

in the biology corpus they are:

cell, cells, water, membrane, food, plant, root, molecules, plants, wall, energy, concentration, organisms, cytoplasm, animal, stem, structure, body, part, animals.

In the English newspaper corpus we are considering, a concordance of the word *criminal* showed that its three most frequent collocates are respectively *war, act* and *law,* suggesting that *war criminal, criminal act* and *criminal law* are recurrent patterns for the word *criminal* in this corpus. An analysis of a corpus of academic texts of social sciences (about 200,000 words of the MicroConcord corpus B) showed that the three most frequent collocations were *criminal law, criminal liability* and *English criminal,* and there were no occurrences of *war criminal.*

It is evident that the data obtained through concordancing is strictly connected to the corpus examined. Further generalization of data-derived results may be obtained, in the classroom, through corroboration by means of other reference materials, such as dictionaries, grammars and possibly other corpora.

2.3   A simple task: reconstructing a text

The strict connection between the concordance data and the corpus has to be explained clearly in order to enable the student-researcher to interpret the data and the resulting 'findings' (see also Stubbs and Gerbig 1993). As shown above, concordances and frequency tables provide a certain amount of information about the corpus examined, particularly when the corpus is specific, like Flowerdew's biology corpus, and not too big. Concordance analysis based on a very restricted corpus provides quite detailed information about its texts' content and organization, both in terms of syntagmatic and paradigmatic associations (see Aston, this volume). The activity I shall describe here is an analysis of a single short text (281 words) taken from *The Independent* (26/1/93) and is set out in a worksheet at the end of this chapter. Frequency counts and concordances are exploited to guide the students in 'reconstructing' the text; this helps them consider the interrelations between the data and the text(s) they are derived from. The software used is the Longman Mini-Concordancer (Chandler 1989) and a word processor.

Students were first presented with lists of frequency and were asked to make hypotheses about the topic dealt with in the article (see Figure 6.2). The list shows that out of the 12 words, 10 are 'grammatical' (articles, pronouns, prepositions or auxiliaries). The only two lexical words in the list are *drivers* and *young. Drivers* is also a highly frequent word (third in the list). This might suggest that the text is about drivers (possibly young drivers) and students

the	14	in	6	are	4
of	10	they	6	on	4
drivers	8	a	5	their	4
to	7	for	5	young	4

Figure 6.2 Twelve most frequent words in article from *The Independent*

can be invited to make hypotheses about topics regarding drivers (rules for drivers, good/bad drivers, car accidents, etc.) which might be dealt with in the text.

A list of the next most frequent words in the text was then shown to the students to provide them with more clues to guess the text topic (see worksheet). Here words like *accident, cars* and *deaths* may lead the students to determine that the article deals with young drivers' deaths in car accidents.

Students were then asked to look at a concordance of the most frequent lexical words to get further clues about the text's topic. The worksheet shows the concordance of the pattern 'driv*', to find both *drivers* and *driving.*

Recurrent combinations like *young drivers, prohibited from driving, barring them from driving* and *banning them from driving* provided further clues as to the topic of the text. At this point both the concordance and the frequency lists were removed and the students were asked to write a text as close as possible to the one analysed.

Besides being a reading/writing exercise, this activity shows that data derived from text processing provides clues about the text(s) examined and can guide students to read and interpret this data as samples of the corpus, rather than as general occurrences of the language. Further research can then be stimulated on larger corpora to see, e.g. how often 'young drivers' are mentioned in the context of 'car accidents' in newspapers, different uses of *bar, ban* and *prohibit,* used as synonyms here, or further information about British government restrictions on drivers in general.

3 The concordancer as an instrument to 'read' a corpus

It will be clear, by now, that using a concordancer as a language informant is not the same thing as using a dictionary or a grammar.

A dictionary and a grammar provide information on the basis of data that has already been interpreted and generalized, a concordancer simply provides the data. In the activity proposed in 2.3, I mentioned the possibility of considering data derived from concordancing as clues to a text that is being processed. The next problem is how this data might be used in the classroom to explore a larger corpus of texts and analyse its recurrent features.

Interpreting corpus-derived data, such as lists of concordances, involves reading at various levels to confirm or contrast hypotheses. A simple 'look' at the data might suggest certain recurrent lexical patterns; the concordance may subsequently be read focusing on single examples which attract attention for some reason; or the analyst might want to read more, or even all, of the text where some 'curious' example comes from. For example, in the concordance considered in Figure 6.1, with *rift* as a keyword, we saw that 'a rift' generally involved two parties. While in 5 out of 9 occurrences this was immediately clear from the KWIC concordance, thanks to the collocation with *between*, students have to read longer extracts in order to identify the two parties in lines 1 and 8. Reading even longer extracts is required to identify the two parties in lines 7 and 9. Figure 6.3 shows the wider context for line 7 of the concordance.

Therefore, exploring the hypothesis that 'a rift' occurs between two and not more parties involves a three-stage reading process: (a) the concordance as a list; (b) a closer reading of particular lines from the list; and (c) a reading of some texts containing the examples. As shown in the experiment reported in the next section of this chapter, such activity increases the students' curiosity about items encountered during reading and consequently their involvement in the research process. For example, in line 1 in Figure 6.1, we can see that a rift can be 'healed', which might imply a search for other things that might be 'healed'. If the search implies some 'sociocultural' aspects instead of the meaning or function of a word, still more intensive reading will often be involved. For example, the analysis of a concordance of *top nation* over a corpus of about 3 million words from *The Independent,* carried out by one of our students at the University of Bologna (Di Concilio 1993), to find out which nation the expression actually referred to, involved reading several articles to be able to establish that it referred to England in 90 per cent of cases and, incidentally, that it always referred to England in the past.

For church and state it's divorce: Italian style
From MICHAEL SHERIDAN in Rome

EVEN THOSE students of Italian Catholic politics enchanted by Byzantine matters are nostalgic this autumn for the days when schism was a simple affair.

Important changes are afoot within the network of personal relationships which have cemented state and church power in Italy since the war. The church hierarchy, which daily seems to see less that is Christian in the Christian Democrat party, is divorcing itself from its traditional allies.

Ironically, it is the proconsuls of that great exemplar of Vatican influence, Giulio Andreotti, Prime Minister for the sixth time, who are exciting church disapproval. His faction has triumphed over the reformist elements of Christian Democracy, headed by the ousted leader and premier, Ciriaco De Mita. In the sweetness of victory, Mr Andreotti's Roman cohorts have forgotten that they are mortal and, in the eyes of many churchmen, their greed and arrogance now risk bringing Catholic politics into disrepute.

The Pope's Vicar of Rome, Cardinal Ugo Poletti, has taken to scolding the Christian Democrats for their divisions which may bring victory for the secular parties and the Communists in city elections on 29 October.

A public rift in Catholic politics surfaced last week when the Communion and Liberation movement severed its ties with a powerful weekly magazine, Il Sabato, run by Andreotti supporters. The magazine exploited popular Catholic themes, such as anti-abortion campaigning and family values to channel middle-class resentment into a political movement. The movement promoted single-issue politics but invariably delivered its machine vote to the Christian Democrats. [. . .]

Figure 6.3   Text containing a single occurrence of 'rift'

This process of reading, moving from the concordance to the text(s) and vice-versa on the basis of a hypothesis, is very similar to the process entailed in the idea of hypertext 'navigation'. According to studies in hypermedia and hypertext (Nielsen 1990; Maioli *et al.* 1991), the hypertext structure represents the natural process of reading which is not linear but based on free associations of mind. McKenna and Seeve-McKenna (1992) point out that while traditional media present information in a linear, sequential manner, the way we think is naturally associative and knowledge itself is based on a series of intrinsic interconnections. They argue that 'hypertext allows the learner to construct knowledge via "web learning" moving from maps of interrelated concepts to construct an increasingly detailed model' (1992: 71). On this basis hypertext has been used in language learning to guide students to read long texts like novels or stories (Evans 1993; Hult *et al.* 1990) through 'nodes' where interrelations can be picked up and the 'web' can be entered leaving the student free to move inside it. Treating corpora and concordances as a hypertext leaves readers free to

follow their own associations, formulating, falsifying or supporting hypotheses they have in mind or that are suggested to them
during the research process. Because corpus-derived data do not
offer immediate answers to students' questions, they are often the
starting point rather than the result of the research process, i.e.
they offer the material which initiates investigation into a research
problem. The reading of data and texts is guided by the mental
process of the student-researcher.

Concordance-based research can thus lead the students to read
quickly large amounts of material to find out information about
topics, words, or expressions they might find interesting. The concordancer can give the students the chance to go through corpora
in order to collect the pieces of information they are interested in,
exploiting a process which is in many ways similar to that involved
in reading articles from a printed newspaper. Such extensive
reading activities, besides being in themselves learning activities
(cf. Klapper 1992; Grenfell 1992), help students to achieve familiarity with the corpus they are processing. This familiarity permits
them to see more clearly the kind of interrelations existing between the corpus examined and the data derived, and can help
the students to contextualize the degree of generalization of their
'discoveries'.

4   Reading a multilingual corpus: sample activities

Although text corpora are usually exploited for linguistic research,
they may also be regarded as sources of comparative information
about different social, political and cultural aspects of the country
speaking the language in question. As shown in section 2.2 above,
a comparison of frequency lists of words derived from the Cobuild
Corpus and a specific biology corpus suggested quite clearly what
was in the latter. Frequency lists of words derived from two comparable corpora of British and American English, the Brown Corpus
and the LOB Corpus, have been analysed to exemplify differences
between the two varieties of English in domains such as sport,
travel and transport, administration and politics, etc. (Leech and
Fallon 1992: 38ff). Parallel corpora of newspapers in different languages may also be processed to contrast aspects connected with the
culture of the country in question, raising interesting hypotheses
about culture-specific linguistic aspects of the different countries
and providing stimuli for reading and research.

Interesting work might, for example, be done in the classroom with loan words. A search of the word *top*, for instance, that has been borrowed into Italian, showed that the three most frequent collocations with *top* in the Italian corpus are *desk top*, *top secret* and *top management*. While *top management* is a very frequent collocation in English too, we have one single occurrence of both *desk top* and *top secret*, the latter occurring in inverted commas. Very frequent collocations in English are *top* + <number> (*top 10*, *top 20*, etc.) and *top class*. Both expressions exist in Italian, but they do not occur at all in the corpus, possibly raising the hypothesis that they are more frequently found in different contexts. A further search was then carried out to see if *top* occurred in contexts where Italy or England were mentioned. With both the Longman Mini-Concordancer and MicroConcord it is possible to specify a 'context word' in a specified horizon (a certain number of words to the right or to the left of the search word). Our search was done with *top* as a search word and the patterns 'engl*' or 'brit*' in a horizon of 9 words to the right and 9 words to the left. This provided 20 occurrences, of which 18 were from sports articles. A similar search in the Italian corpus with 'ita*' as a context word provided no occurrences. The search word was then changed to a possible Italian equivalent of *top*, viz. *migliore*. A search with 'ita*' as a context word and the pattern 'miglior*' as the search word provided 20 occurrences, of which only 4 were in fact with the adjective *migliore/i*. Three of these concerned sport, the fourth concerned wines. The remaining 16 examples were not occurrences of the adjective *migliore*, but of the verb *migliorare* ('improve').

This data is of course not conclusive for linguistic or sociolinguistic generalizations of cross-cultural features, needing corroboration with further research on corpora of different texts or collected with different criteria. It shows, however, how parallel corpora of newspaper articles in two languages can be exploited in the classroom to raise hypotheses for further reading and research.

The differences found in the use of the words *top* and *migliore* might lead students to find out if they are really equivalent, or in which contexts they are equivalent and in which they are not; if *migliorare* and *improve* act as equivalents; or if there are any broader differences in the newspaper language of sports in the two corpora. In the next activity reported, a group of eight students, using computers in pairs, were guided to look for differences in the use of patterns and expressions moving from the English to the Italian

---

What is crucial in English and Italian?

Look at the two concordances with the words *crucial* and *cruciale* and:

a. Write down as many expressions as you can which are similar in the two languages or might be considered appropriate translations of each other. You can use the concordancer to generate other data

b. On a separate piece of paper, write down other patterns/expressions you have noticed during your analysis.

English

```
 1 pt by the President to reinstate a crucial, and so far unadopted, paragraph in
 2 m stall 15. <p> Fitness should be crucial at Chepstow, the jumping season's
 3 nounced its intentions will have a crucial bearing on whether it can put toget
 4 the pilots' claim, seeing it as a crucial challenge to the cornerstone of his
 5 common access protocol Tramp is a crucial component, will set the standard for
 6 s themselves had to pronounce on a crucial compromise resolution whose text
 7 cted council members. By sharp and crucial contrast, the metals trade, which ac
 8 marked, on the eve of yesterday's crucial debate: 'This party is interested in
 9 tria on 22 May, before some of the crucial decisions about the repatriations wer
10 o modern ones. This is not so: the crucial difference between old and new is ho
11 ls group was forced to withdraw a crucial dollars 400m junk-bond offering bec
12 other exchange, will give Liffe a crucial edge in the increasingly competitive
13 for Harriet's affections. <p> The crucial element of the package is undoubt
14 in pay (and recruitment) wil be crucial factors in escaping from what Mr
15 on, Snook's countryman may prove a crucial figure in Bedford's cause. A sniping
```

Italian

```
 1 a ridosso della penisola arabica e cruciale per il controllo dell'Oceano Indiano?
 2 la carta di credito sono i fattori cruciali su cui insistere. In merito al primo
 3 ttori che rivestono un' importanza cruciale per l' efficacia generale dell' econo
 4 Per quanto riguarda l' importanza cruciale della credibilita' e delle anticipazio
 5 paccature su un tema di importanza cruciale come l' Uem – l' ipotesi di una soluz
 6 estro' insistendo sull' importanza cruciale del regolamento Cee antitrust ne
 7 u uno dei temi centrali e insieme cruciali dell' attuale congiuntura europea. E
 8 rra che spirano dal Golfo, il mese cruciale di Piazza Affari, gia' alle prese con
 9 Nazioni Unite. <In questo momento cruciale della storia, e' molto importante
10 rapporto Stato-Regioni e' un nodo cruciale. Maccanico, dal canto suo, ha ricord
11 o sotto questo aspetto. Parimenti cruciale infine e' il riferimento all' andamen
12 lermo ha preso in esame il periodo cruciale che va dall'aprile del 1981, dopo la
13 cardiopatici sottolineano i punti cruciali: <P Discorso> 'E' utile affrontare il
14 a' d' intervento europee. Il punto cruciale non consiste nella quantita', ma ne
15 . E' dunque la second fase quella cruciale per la costruzione dell' Unione mon
```

Figure 6.4 Concordance-based activity

corpus and vice versa. Students were shown two concordances with the words *crucial* and *cruciale* and a set of instructions (see Figure 6.4).

It could be seen from the students' reports that while there were lists of parallel expressions with the words *crucial/cruciale* (*crucial point/punto cruciale; crucial factors/fattori cruciali; crucial role/ ruolo cruciale*, etc.) there were also many findings not directly connected with them. It seems that the comparison between the two initial concordances gave the students access to an exploratory 'web', which led them to move from one corpus to the other in search of further equivalent words/patterns. From their reports it seems that they not only got more and more involved in the research, but also gradually learned to categorize and generalize the data. While the reports generally start with lists including all the expressions they noticed, at the end more general observations occur, such as the fact that while in English *crucial* is used in superlative forms (*the most crucial*), in Italian *cruciale* seems to have an inherently superlative meaning and no such forms as *il più cruciale* (literally 'the most crucial') are found. Reports also contain lists of collocations the students may also want to learn (e.g. all the adjectives collocating with *point*), and other observations, such as the fact that while there are only two adjectives colligating, with *moment* with a meaning similar to that of *crucial* (*drastic* and *decisive*) there are at least four collocating with *momento* (critico, culminante, fatidico, importante). Findings related to the word *match* show that in English this word typically collocates with expressions specifying the match or championship concerned (*European Championship match, Toshiba County Championship match*, etc.); in Italian there are more generic expressions such as *partita di campionato* ('championship match') without any specification of which 'campionato' is being referred to. Regarding the word *match*, students also noticed that expressions such as *football match* or its Italian equivalent *partita di pallone* never occur in articles dealing with football.

This activity is an example of how exploration through the concordancer can be exploited with bilingual corpora. Students can navigate through the corpora to discover differences in the use of the same word or of apparently similar ones, or even in the way that more 'sociocultural' topics such as the World Cup (which appears in the English concordance with the word *crucial* and which probably gave rise to the search for *match* discussed above) are treated in the two (or possibly more) corpora. It is made evident to the students that the concordancer is a means to analyse actual occurrences of language and that although these occurrences can provide 'illuminating' guesses about the use of the language, these guesses and findings need corroboration by means of other reference materials. The 'navigation' process entailed in interpreting data from multilingual corpora is based on hypotheses of a cross-cultural nature. Regularities derived from one language are contrasted with different regularities derived from the other language, which may in turn suggest new patterns and key words to search for. The concordancer is thus exploited here as a means of learning about the foreign language and the students' own.

5   Conclusion

Using the computer as a source of information about the foreign language in the classroom requires more than simply giving students direct access to data. Learners need also to be introduced to the process by which the data can be analysed. If students are to learn to edit and classify data, they must be shown how to read frequency tables, and concordances. This can lead students to formulate hypotheses, which can then be confirmed or falsified by consulting more text. This process of 'navigating' through the corpora leads to extensive reading of texts. Students thus learn to use the concordancer as an instrument for research and learning.

The concordancer provides data which has to be interpreted, and in this way the role of the corpus as an informant in the classroom is different from that of traditional reference material such as dictionaries or grammars. Instead of offering a description it provides a source of material on which students can base their own description. One may regard the role of dictionaries and grammars as complementary to corpora, in that they may serve to support or, indeed, contradict data-driven hypotheses.

Research on one corpus can be complemented with research on others. A parallel corpus in another language permits students to carry out contrastive analyses of language patterns. An additional corpus in the same language, but containing a different selection of texts compiled according to different criteria, allows one to check, for example, if a highly recurrent pattern in a specialized corpus is equally frequent in a more general one. A 'general' newspaper corpus may be subdivided to create more restricted ones, for instance of business articles, or, even more specifically, of business articles on a particular topic. These subcorpora can also be compiled in two languages, providing students with parallel words and expressions in a specific domain (see also Zanettin 1994).

Analysis of subcorpora highlights associations between words and their context. Students might be led to look at text–context associations of recurrent expressions in particular fields, such as the recurrence of *membrane* in Flowerdew's biology corpus, or of *criminal liability* in the corpus of academic texts about social sciences, or recurrent sequential positions of expressions in particular text-types, such as *until* [*very*] *recently*, which is recurrently sentence-initial in social science academic papers.

The above shows clearly the potential offered to learners by the concordancer to explore text and context in corpora, and in so doing to build their own mental constructs about how language works.

Appendix: Worksheet

a. This activity relates to one article taken from the *Independent*. The Longman Mini-Concordancer (Chandler 1989) has been used to calculate all the words occurring at least four times in the article. Look at the list below and make hypotheses about the topic dealt with in the article. The numbers on the right represent the occurrences of the words in the text.

the	14	in	6	are	4
of	10	they	6	on	4
drivers	8	a	5	their	4
to	7	for	5	young	4

b. Now look at the words occurring 3 times and 2 times. Do they provide some more clues to identify the text-topic?

accidents	3	cent	2	or	2
been	3	certain	2	other	2
driving	3	considered	2	per	2
from	3	deaths	2	plates	2
is	3	has	2	said	2
move	3	have	2	such	2
after	2	involving	2	them	2
an	2	Ireland	2	there	2
be	2	more	2	two	2
being	2	new	2	were	2
by	2	Northern	2	with	2
Carlisle	2	number	2	would	2
cars	2	options	2	years	2

c. You may have noticed that the most frequently recurrent lexical word in these lists is *drivers* and there are also 3 instances of *driving.* Use the Mini-Concordancer to search for the pattern '**driv***' to find all the forms relating to this stem. Then look at the concordance and try to guess:

(i) what drivers does the text deal with?
(ii) what is the problem with these drivers?

> Restrictions on young **drivers** considered Two schemes to restri
> red Two schemes to restrict young **drivers** soon after they pass their tests
> rn over the number of deaths such **drivers** cause. The Government is conside
> Government is considering making **drivers** put 'P-plates' on their cars for
> option being looked at is for new **drivers** to display 'R-plates' barring th
> sing a total alcohol ban on young **drivers** or, as suggested by the Automobi
> nalty points, compared with other **drivers** who are only banned when they ha
> ister for roads, said that of all **drivers,** 10 per cent were aged 21 or you
> st. They would be prohibited from **driving** above a certain speed. In Northe
> play 'R-plated' barring them from **driving** certain types of vehicles until
> le Association, banning them from **driving** if they collect four penalty poi

d. Now remove the concordance and the frequency lists. On the basis of the information you have collected, write a text which you think might resemble the one used for the analyses above (the original text is 281 words long).

e. Type your text with a word processor and then save it in DOS format. Ask your teacher for instructions.

f. Calculate the frequency of the words used in your text (use the frequency function in the Mini-Concordancer). Are the most frequent words in your text different from the most frequent words in the original?

original text				**your text**
the	14	on	4	
of	10	their	4	
drivers	8	young	4	
to	7	accidents	3	
in	6	been	3	
they	6	driving	3	
a	5	from	3	
for	5	is	3	
are	4	move	3	

g. What words appear in both lists? Do a concordance on these, first on the original text, then on yours. Are there differences in the contexts in which they are used?

h. Now read the original text. Is this text similar to yours? Complete the table following the text.

Restrictions on young drivers considered

Two schemes to restrict young drivers soon after they pass their tests are being considered because of concern over the number of deaths such drivers cause. The Government is considering making drivers put 'P-plates' on their cars for up to two years after passing their test. They would be prohibited from driving above a certain speed. In Northern Ireland, where such a scheme has been in operation since 1968, the limit, even on motorways, is 45mph. A more stringent option being looked at is for new drivers to display 'R-plates' barring them from driving certain types of vehicles until they have gained more experience. Other options include imposing a total alcohol ban on young drivers or, as suggested by the Automobile Association, banning them from driving if they collect four penalty points, compared with other drivers who are only banned when they have 12. Kenneth Carlisle, the minister for roads, said that of all drivers, 10 per cent were aged 21 or younger, yet they were involved in 20 per cent of accidents involving casualties. The Royal Society for the Prevention of Accidents welcomed the move: 'We would like to see an experiment, for say three years, with this. Although there are similar measures in New Zealand, Northern Ireland and France, there hasn't been much analysis of the results.' Most motoring organizations support the move except the AA which said it was an 'administrative nightmare'. The move has been prompted by a number of well-publicized accidents involving several deaths of young people killed in high performance cars, usually belonging to their parents. The options are expected to be presented to Mr. Carlisle in the next couple of months.

	original	**yours**
text-type	news report	....
topic	young drivers	....
function	informing about a problem	....

i. Take the frequency list of the words in your text and choose 15 words that occur only once. Use a word processor and create a cloze exercise substituting each of these words with a series of 6 dashes (_____). Make a list of the words you have deleted and put it in alphabetical order at the end of the text. Print the page out and pass it to the student next to you. Ask her/him to fill in the blanks using the words at the bottom of the text.

j. Discuss together the texts you have filled in. Are there words you have doubts about? Think together of better choices to fill in the blanks. You might like to use:

(i) a dictionary;   (ii) the Mini-Concordancer on a larger corpus

7

Contexts: the Background, Development and Trialling of a Concordance-based CALL Program

TIM JOHNS

1 Background

Contexts is a Computer-assisted Language Learning (CALL) program which has its origin in work undertaken at Birmingham University since 1987/8 involving the rewriting of materials for the Remedial Grammar course offered by the English for Overseas Students Unit. These materials are based on examples of authentic usage recovered from a corpus by means of a concordancer (Johns 1991b, 1993). The aim has been to exclude invented examples of English as far as possible, whether for presentation or for practice. The only exceptions allowed are those created not by the teacher but by the students to express their own ideas.

Development of the materials has proceeded largely by trial and error to ascertain which tasks are within the grasp of the student and which not, and which activities seem to be effective and which not. The materials have also been influenced by examples provided by our colleagues in the Cobuild project, though we aim to give our students more direct access to and engagement with the source data than has been usual in the Cobuild materials. We have also benefited from our experience in the Unit in using the concordancer to respond to students' problems and queries in the course of one-to-one consultations (Johns 1988, 1991a).

From work so far, we have established a number of basic principles:

1. The materials are used not only in teaching specific features of the language, but also in developing the student's ability to puzzle

out how the language works. The central metaphors embodying the approach are those of the learner as 'linguistic researcher', testing and revising hypotheses, or as 'language detective', learning to recognize and interpret clues from context ('Every student a Sherlock Holmes').

2. The most frequently used sequence of activities in the materials consists of a research (R) task or tasks followed by a practice (P) task or tasks and improvization (I) activities. However, the RPI sequence is not invariable and other sequences also occur, such as RI (where the research activity leads directly into an improvization activity) or PRI (where the research activity is based on material used for a practice activity).

3. Students can be given fairly simple research tasks involving mark-up of the contexts to identify collocations, etc.:

- How many different verbs are shown with this structure?
- What are the expressions with the pattern '*at* ____ *time*'?
- A word is present in the right context of citations 1–8 that is not present in the right context of citations 9–16. What is it?

Such tasks are, of course, 'closed' in the sense that the result is known to the teacher in advance (cf. the lab experiment in science teaching). The materials also include more complex tasks – e.g. those involving classification of contexts, or possible explanations of the presence or absence of a feature:

- Identify the contexts in which this structure has a clearly positive meaning, and those in which it has a clearly negative meaning. What do you conclude from your results?
- Using clues from the context, what can you discover about the places and institutions named in these citations?
- A word is present in the right context of citations 1–16 that is not present in the right context of citations 9–16. What is it? Can you explain why it is missing in 9–16?
- Judging from these citations, is this structure used more often in formal or informal varieties of English?

These tasks are more open, in that there may well be more than one possible classification or explanation of a phenomenon in the data. In addition, students define their own tasks as they start noticing features of the data for themselves – at times features that had not previously been noticed by the teacher.

4. A number of exercise types for practice have been developed based on gapping and reordering of citations. Of these, the most characteristic is the 'One Item, Many Contexts' (OIMC) exercise which approaches a research task in that it demonstrates 'hypothesis-testing in action'. The number of citations presented for each item in OIMC exercises is constrained by the overall length of the hand-out: at most seven citations are used, and for many exercises three or five citations.

5. Improvization tasks are based on questions and skeleton statements to prompt students to create their own statements, serious or frivolous. These tasks are often framed to exploit to the maximum the wide range of national and cultural backgrounds among our students, and their shared experience as overseas students at a British university, e.g.:

- 'In your country, what does a boy do if he wants to meet a girl he likes?'
- 'When I arrived in Birmingham, I was shocked by _____.

6. Working from data leads to a radical revision of preconceived ideas about what one should be teaching as well as how one might teach it.

(a)   The simple principle 'It is probably not worth teaching anything that does not occur at least x times in a corpus of y million words' (x and y being redefinable taking into consideration the level of the learners) makes it possible to exclude immediately much that is traditionally enshrined in classroom tradition.

(b)   *Pari passu* the work suggests ways of dealing with areas of language which have traditionally been poorly taught or regarded as unteachable (e.g. article usage) and reveals areas of language structure (e.g. the contextual patterning of nouns) that have been neglected both descriptively and pedagogically.

(c)   The data controls not only which features of the language are taught, but which exponents are presented and which meanings are taken as primary (e.g. in Academic English, *may*, showing an estimate of probability based on 'theory', versus *can*, showing an estimate of probability based on 'experience').

(d)   More fundamentally, the traditional division between independent 'levels' of language (e.g. lexis–syntax–discourse) appears increasingly untenable once one starts to place at the centre of one's concern the ways in which words behave in context. As a result, although the materials have for the most part a syntactic/functional starting point, they could (as the students themselves have observed) as well be labelled 'Remedial Vocabulary' as 'Remedial Grammar'.

7. Students adapt rapidly to the idea of working from data. It soon becomes normal – neither particularly threatening nor particularly 'exciting'.

2 Development

In 1992 I started to consider how some of the basic approaches developed for the Remedial Grammar materials might be incorporated in a computer-assisted language learning program that could be used by students as a supplement to the classroom sessions. Such a program could have a lexical rather than syntactic starting-point, giving students an opportunity to investigate and work with a 'core' vocabulary of, say, 1000 words of English. The Contexts program developed from that idea: the form it took was influenced by the various students and teachers who saw and worked with early versions. It incorporates many of their suggestions, and has benefited also from a published 'preview' of the program (Waitzbauer 1994). If I had had the programming skill I would probably have written it from the start as a mouse-driven Windows program: as I did not, I wrote it mouse-free for the Zbasic-PC compiler version 4.71 (32 Bit Software Inc.) which produces fast and compact code.

The data used as a source for the citations used in the program is a 3-million word corpus chosen to give a rough reflection of an overseas student's life in Birmingham, both on and off the campus:

- The popular scientific journal *New Scientist*
- The scientific research journal *Nature*
- Transcripts of lectures given in the University of Birmingham
- Newspapers – *The Times, The Guardian* and *The Independent*
- 'Domestic' texts such as Spock on Child Rearing and Conran on Household Management.

In addition one or or two 'interloper' texts were allowed, for example Frederick Forsyth's *The Day of the Jackal* to give an occasional glimpse of sex-and-violence.

KWIC (Key Words in Context) citations for the selected items for the program are recovered using MicroConcord (Oxford University Press) and saved to disc. Items selected may include not only words, but also prefixes and suffixes. From the total, ten are selected for the program using the following criteria:

(a)   The citations should give as accurate a representation as possible of the range of syntactic/collocational environments of the item in the corpus as revealed by the full concordance.

(b)   Where possible, the selected citations should represent the range of genres/topics shown by the full concordance for that item.

(c)   The citations should be reasonably comprehensible when torn in fixed-width KWIC format from the context in which they occur (a challenge when the DOS screen accommodates only 80 characters across).

Using simple authoring conventions (for example, the start of the key item must be in column 37 from the left hand margin), the selected citations are edited and assembled in files up to, and usually equal to, 50 items in length. Currently, citations have been prepared for 975 items in 24 files which are defined in terms of word class (e.g. Nouns 1, Adjectives 3 – the numbering giving an approximate indication of the difficulty of the items and their contexts), topic (e.g. body parts) or genre (e.g. Scientific papers). The main screens of Contexts[1] are given below.

Title screen

From the Title screen the user may choose, at this point only, to modify the screen colours used before starting the program.

Top screen

From the Top screen the following options are available:

(a)   An on-screen Guide to the program, giving information on how to operate the program and pedagogical advice on how to obtain the maximum learning benefit from it.

(b) An Index to all the items (words, prefixes, suffixes) available
to the program.
(c) Choice of file to work on.

Choose screen

This screen gives basic information about the file selected (number of items, range of citations available for each item). From this screen the user decides whether to work with the file in Show mode (research) or Quiz mode (practice), and if the latter, how many questions to attempt (steps of 10).

Show screen

The bottom half of the screen shows a list of the items in the files: by running a cursor around the list the user may inspect in the top half of the screen all the citations, presented in random order, for any item in the list. The options available on the Show screen are:

(a) The user may Mark (highlight) any item in the list, the effect of marking being to ensure that marked items will be included in a subsequent Quiz on that file – or, if more are marked than are to be selected, that the selection is made only from marked items. This facility gives the user a way of overriding the random selection of Quiz.
(b) If there is a live printer attached to the computer, the user may print out the citations for any item in the list, either as shown on the screen, or with a standard-length gap in place of the key item – a quick way for teachers to prepare teaching materials!
(c) The user may request research tasks, if these are available, for any item. A 'bank' of up to 10 tasks may be specified for each item, with a maximum of three being presented on request. Where more than three research tasks are available, they are selected by the program in such a way that the first is general and quite easy, requiring special attention to all the contexts of the key item; the second (often a follow-up to the first) also general, and possibly a little more difficult; and the third more detailed, requiring attention to one or two citations from the total.

Quiz screen

The Quiz uses the OIMC format in a presentation based on one developed by Paul Doyle as a classroom activity using the over-head projector (Doyle 1992). A single gapped citation, randomly selected from those available, is shown at the top of the screen, users being able to ask for as many more as they need up to the total available in order to find the missing item. Quiz offers the following facilities:

(a)   When the user types in an answer, the program is able to distinguish between those which are Correct, those which are Wrong, and those which are Almost Correct (mis-spellings and mis-typings identified by a Fuzzy Matching routine based on one first presented in Higgins and Johns (1984)). If an answer is identified as Almost Correct a clue or clues are provided to help the user to find the right answer – e.g.:

```
Don't switch letters around
You left out (a letter/n letters)
You inserted (a letter/n letters)
Be careful over doubled letters
Be careful over a, e, i, o and u
Your answer is (much) too long
Your answer is (rather/much) too short
Look at the nth letter
```

In order to accommodate data for languages such as French and German that use diacritics within the standard IBM character set, the program is also able to offer the following clues:

```
Don't add unnecessary accents
You chose the wrong accent(s)
You left out (an accent/n accents)
```

(b)   Having found the right answer, the user is encouraged to study the citations carefully before moving on to the next item.

(c)   If all the citations have been presented and the user is still unable to find the correct answer, (s)he may ask to See it.

(d)   The user may exit the Quiz before completing the number of questions requested.

(e)   A Help facility is provided, the user being able to See a list of the items selected for the Quiz.

(f)   When users complete a Quiz (or exit early from it) they are offered alternative analyses of their performance:

(i)   An objective report on what they have done:

> Number of questions attempted
> Number of correct answers
> Number of correct answers found on the basis of three or fewer citations
> Number of wrong guesses
> Number of mis-spellings
> Number of times user asked to See the correct answer
> Average time spent answering questions
> Average time spent studying citations
> Number of times Help requested, and total time spent studying Help.

(ii) An evaluation generated on the basis of the user's overall performance, and any features of that performance outside the normal range. For example:

> O.K. But try to complete the quiz next time!
>
> I'm sure you can do better next time!
>
> Well done. Perhaps you should continue work with this file for a while.
>
> Not bad, but try not to do so much random guessing next time!
>
> Magnificent work! Time to try a new file!

3   Trialling

The program is now available, with the assistance of the University's Centre for Computer-based Learning, on the campus high-speed network so that students can access and work with it in a cluster in or near to their own department or faculty.

The version of the program made available on the network has been rewritten so that it 'logs' students' sessions with the program, storing information on which choices were made by the user, which items were dealt with in Quiz, the length of time taken over each activity, and so on. The log files are stored on the CCBL file-server, and are regularly amalgamated into larger files. It is hoped that in time the logged information will provide a useful source of evidence for research into student learning behaviour

1 T[body parts]	LQNNNNNNNNDFKNKKNNNNNKNKNKHFNKEATX
2 T[body parts]	LSMYLQWNWWWWWWHNHWWNNHWWNNFWHKHWNWHWNWHWNWHNKETGX
3 T[business]	LSLQKWWHWWHHWHKKKKWWHWHKWWWKKKWWHKA
T[body parts]	LQWWNFFHKKWKKWKWKWHWHWNNNNKKNKWWHWNFKALTX
4 TG[business]	LQNHHWHHNNNNNNNNDHWWHWWNNNNNNKEALTX
5 T[adjectives – 1*]	LQHWHWWHKKHKHKHKKWHKHKKALQNHKHWHKHWNNHKKHKHKKKKKATX
6 T[body parts]	LQKNWWWNKNNNNKWNNWNNNNNNDEATX
7 T[prepositions]	LQHWKHWHWNHKHWNHWHWHWHKHWHNHKHNHNHWHKHKHWHNHFHKHNHNHHKALSTIGGGX
8 CTGI[body parts]	LSMMMMMLQKHKKFKWKNNKKNKNNNNNNNNDKA
T[business]	LS
T[house & garden]	LS
T[prefixes]	LS
T[prepositions]	LS
T[verbs – 5*]	LSTX

* This indicates which of a number of similar files the student is working on

C	Colour menu	R	Research task(s) requested in Show
T	Move to Top screen	P	Print gapped citations in Show
L	Move to Choose screen	U	Print ungapped citations in Show
I	Inspect Index	T[ ]	Title of file selected
G	Inspect Guide	Q	Select Quiz
S	Select Show	N	Another citation requested
M	Item marked in Show	K	Correct answer in Quiz
Y	Item unmarked in Show		

F	Mis-spelling in Quiz
W	Wrong answer in Quiz
D	See correct answer in Quiz
H	Help requested in Quiz
E	Early exit from Quiz
V	Improvizations at end of Quiz
A	Analysis at end of Quiz
X	Quit program

Figure 7.1 'Session histories' showing sequence of choices made by students working with contexts

in a CALL environment, and how that behaviour may change over time. Meanwhile, the logs of the first 50 student sessions logged after the program had been available for just over a month reveal certain features of student behaviour that were clearly enough defined – and in some respects unexpected – to warrant a revision of the program. The most revealing component of the data from that point of view is the 'Session Histories' in which each action taken by the user is recorded as an upper-case character in a string. A few examples from the early log files are shown in Figure 7.1, together with a key.

Some features of the early Session Histories are unsurprising. For example, files defined in terms of topic (e.g. 'body parts', 'business' and 'house and garden') seem to be preferred to those defined in terms of parts of speech (e.g. 'Nouns 1', 'Adjectives 2' or 'Verbs 3'). Other features of the data were more unexpected, and, for the author of the program, initially disappointing:

(a) In only 15 per cent of the histories did the users investigate the data in a file by using the Show option before they attempted to do a Quiz.

(b) Only occasionally did the users ask for the full number of citations in Quiz before attempting a guess at the answer. It is striking that in nearly 50 per cent of cases they attempted to guess the answer on the basis of one citation only, thus depriving themselves of the assistance given by multiple contexts.

(c) Features (a) and (b) are together almost certainly the main factors underlying the most striking feature of the data: that 58 per cent (255/437) of all guesses were wrong, and only 38 per cent (116/437) correct, 4 per cent (16/437) being mis-spellings. A user could probably tolerate having about 20 per cent of his or her answers rejected, and would certainly prefer less: the figure of 58 per cent is likely to be the main reason why in 77 per cent of cases users exited from a Quiz without completing it, no doubt disappointed with the program, and with themselves, that the tasks it set were 'too difficult'.

The pattern of behaviour described above was no doubt due in part to users' unfamiliarity with the program. Although the students were probably using the program for the first time in most sessions, the user referred to the Guide at the start in only four cases. It may also have something in common with items we noticed in the early 1980s with the first text manipulation programs such as Storyboard (Higgins) and Jumbler (Johns). Given the wide range of student choices offered in those programs (a range that we saw as one of the main justifications for CALL over language-learning materials presented through other media), a number of students appeared to want to make the program as difficult for themselves as possible. They would, for example, refuse to look at the text in advance or to ask for 'free' words in Storyboard, or they would always choose the 'Difficult' options in Jumbler. The source of this phenomenon appears to lie in human pride and competitiveness: the user is engaged in his or her own private battle with the computer, and any help offered would detract from the value of the anticipated victory.

The evidence offered by the early log files was supplemented by feedback from a group of Malaysian teachers who worked with the program for three two-hour sessions towards the end of 1993, keeping a diary of the work they did with the program. My colleague Philip King organized and conducted the sessions to avoid as far as possible any Pygmalion effect from the presence of the author of the program. Some teachers later used their diaries to write an evaluation of the program. The evaluations give some support to the decisions made when the program was being developed – for example:

> Overall, I find the Quiz challenging . . . By going through the Show mode and the Quiz mode, I become aware of the use of common words, . . . learn new words . . . and how these words are used in different contexts. Indirectly, I feel that my general knowledge had increased as the program covers a range of topics. I am also exposed to special words used in different fields: for example, 'a true fish', 'Pat Eddery was beaten a short neck by Kitwood' and 'Robson will perform a holding role in midfield'.

One teacher found from experience the value of using the Mark facility in Show:

> After doing the third Quiz, I decided not to Mark any of the words that appear in the Show mode. When I was doing the Quiz I found that I was making random guesses . . . The same thing happened when I used the Help mode.

The same teacher also had some interesting observations on how she used the Analysis option at the end of the Quiz:

... the Analysis gives very encouraging comments. But, after going through a few quizzes, I found myself focusing on the statement which tells me the time I took to deal with each question and to study the contexts. I try to improve on the time with each Quiz. However, later on, as I went through more quizzes, I wasn't interested in reading the comments except for the last comment. It gives me a general idea of my experience in the Quiz.

At the same time, their observations throw light on the difficulties learners may encounter in adjusting to fundamental features of the 'data-driven learning' (DDL) method – for example the 'One Item, Many Contexts' format:

> (At first) I felt cheated. The program only accepts the exact words that have been programmed, although the words that I have chosen fit the sentences. As I progress through the other files, this feeling wears off and I found that it's more challenging to find a word that fits several contexts. It made me look 'deeper' into the word, how it's used in different contexts.

One student made the valuable observation that the fact that a word is frequent and (apparently) well known does not necessarily mean that it will be easy to guess from its collocations:

> The word quite seems to be a familiar word, but I do not know why I find difficulty in guessing the word (twice!). I've studied the ten contexts using the Show mode and did not find any difficulty in understanding the sentences. I've also looked up the word in the dictionary and did not find anything that is unfamiliar. This word puzzles me.

The problem of 'unexplained' features of the contexts seemed to remain the major problem of the DDL method for some students. The program's on-screen guide offers advice that the user should not be over-perfectionist in trying to understand everything:

> Don't worry that there may be some contexts that you do not understand completely. The important thing is that there should be some contexts that you DO understand: as you work with the program you will find you understand more and more.

Nevertheless, some students were clearly worried by anything in the citations that was not immediately clear, and critical of the program on that account:

A closer study of the contexts revealed certain phrases or metaphors that are beyond my comprehension, especially when the shown parts of the sentences concerned do not offer sufficient contextual clues.

This student suggested that an on-screen dictionary could solve the problem. The considerable scope that such a dictionary would require is illustrated by the following comment, prompted by a reference to the (bowdlerized) version of Lyndon Johnson's famous comment on Gerald Ford:

The second sentence 'because they have insufficient brain to walk and chew gum at the same time' does not make sense to me. I consulted a few coursemates and the result is still negative.

Two months after the workshops, the teachers were asked to come together for a further feedback session with the author of the progam. One of the most interesting aspects of the session was the fact that some of them could, without referring to their notes, still remember many of the observations they had made concerning the collocations and connotations of particular words. The evidence of the effect of DDL methods in terms of memory is, at present, limited (see Stevens 1991), or, as in the present case, anecdotal: this is an area which deserves further investigation. At the same time, although the teachers were clearly better prepared than the 'casual' users of the program logged over the network, and made more intelligent use of it, the same 'beat the machine' effect was detectable. Half of them confessed to not wanting to use Show before Quiz, and another group (overlapping the first, but not coterminous with it) had tried always to find the answer on the basis of one or at most two citations. However, there were those in both groups who said that by the third session they had changed the way they worked with the program to make things easier for themselves.

The evidence from the Session Histories and from feedback from the teachers seemed clear enough to warrant a revision of the program to encourage users to work sensibly and productively with it from the start. The largest change was to change the program flow, so that from the Top screen the program would always present Show once a file had been chosen, and Quiz would only be available from the Show screen, thus encouraging users to investigate the data before testing themselves on it. The version as trialled and the revised version can be compared by means of the

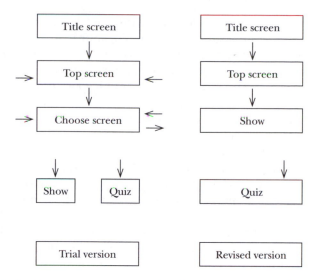

Figure 7.2 Screen sequences in trial and revised version of Contents

following, simplified, diagrams. The option of changing the number of items in Quiz available from the Choose screen in the trial version is, in the revised version, presented in a Window that opens at the start of Quiz together with basic information on how to use Quiz (see Figure 7.2).

The second change is to print a message in Quiz reminding the user that there are more contexts available for an item.

Other planned changes include training sessions for our in-session overseas students in the use of the program, and (based on what we learn in the course of those sessions and on further logging of the program) a revision of the student brochure describing the program to bring out more clearly the methods that can be used to obtain maximum benefit from it.

4 Conclusion

To date, Contexts has proved a modest but useful adjunct to our teaching: it could also in other teaching situations be a convenient way of introducing concordance-based methods and as preparation for using a full concordancer.

Whether the program deserves further elaboration is for the moment an open question. For example, at present selection and editing of concordance data is time-consuming and requires fine linguistic and pedagogic judgement, and it is tempting to consider the construction of a program that would operate directly on a corpus, applying selection criteria (a) to (c) already described (see page 104). For example, to mimic criterion (a) one might in software identify the main collocational patterns present in the data, and ensure that the automatically selected citations reflected those patterns. To mimic criterion (c) software might measure the average frequency of the words in the key item on the simplistic assumption that more common words are easier to understand than less common words. The automatic selecter could also check that the sentence containing the key item is complete within the 80-character horizon of the KWIC citation on the assumption – again simplistic – that short, complete sentences are easier to understand than longer, truncated ones. Selection of the items to be included could also be automated, using the criteria of frequency and the range of texts covered to distinguish between 'common-core' vocabulary and that characteristic of specialized genres and subject areas. In other words, using computing methods that are by now reasonably familiar, one might attempt to create, automatically, learning materials from any corpus that one might throw at it – an ambition that has attraction both for the computer expert and for the lazy teacher. That this is not, at present, the direction in which I see Contexts evolving stems from my obstinate belief that even the most refined expert system would here, at best, come a poor second to the teacher's imperfect human system in selecting examples that truthfully reflect the patterning of an item in the corpus, and that students can work with and learn from.

Acknowledgements

I am grateful to members of the CALL group at the Language Centre, University of Malaya, Kuala Lumpur, for many useful suggestions as to how Contexts could be improved: to the 1993–94 Malaysian teachers' course for their assistance in the workshop trialling of Contexts; and to Ian Upton of the University of Birmingham Centre for Computer-based Learning for helping with the implementation of the program on the campus high-speed network.

Note

1   The program descriptions in this article relate to a development version of Contexts, demonstrated at the TALC94 Conference, Lancaster University, 10–13 April 1994.

8

The Automatic Generation of CALL Exercises from General Corpora

EVE WILSON

1 Introduction

This chapter discusses three areas where computer tools can assist the production of computer-based learning programmes: teaching materials, presentation and user adaptability. It considers the derivation of exercises for Computer-assisted Language Learning packages from two different corpora: a computer readable version of the *Oxford Advanced Learners' Dictionary of Current English* (*OALD*) and the Susanne Corpus, a fully tagged subset of the Brown Corpus. A comparison of the advantages and disadvantages of the two corpora as a source of exercises is followed by a discussion of the pedagogic shortcomings of using randomly selected sentences and passages to illustrate linguistic features and how more cohesion in teaching material can be introduced into the automatic generation process.

2 Computer-based learning

A problem which in the past has retarded the advance of computer-based learning (CBL) has been the high cost of program development; it takes an average of 500 hours to produce one hour's instruction (Merrill 1993). One way to achieve a more efficient *production time/instruction time* ratio is through computer-based tools to facilitate program development. Such tools can assist in three areas:

(a)   Materials on which to base teaching.
(b)   Techniques on how to present teaching material.
(c)   Adaptive interfaces to adapt materials and presentation to the needs of individual students.

2.1   Teaching materials

In language course design there are two major problems:

(a)   How to provide a range of materials to meet the needs of students with different abilities.
(b)   How to provide at every ability level enough exercises to ensure that a student is confronted by a different set of examples whenever he or she uses the language-learning program.

To this end corpora present a unique and unexploited resource. Large general corpora aim to represent in microcosm the genres and styles that comprise English in its various constituencies, hence providing material appropriate to every level of linguistic competence. Such corpora should relieve teachers of the need to prepare special material and leave them with more time to devote to the social problems of learning: encouragement, motivation, and fostering group activities and learning through collaboration.

2.2   Presentation

The presentational techniques used with examples described below have, by design, been restricted largely to selection techniques which are fully described in Wilson *et al.* (1992).[1] What I wish to emphasize here is that the *content* of a presentation should be independent of the *format.*[2] This is needed to ensure that

- the material can be used for a multiplicity of purposes;
- the presentational techniques can be used with a variety of materials: that is, a presentation format might be considered as a frame with slots for variables.

2.3   User-adaptive interfaces

Once learning materials have been divorced from the means of presentation, a student profile can be used to ensure that the exercises presented are commensurate with student ability. The profile records student attainment in each of the linguistic skills that the language-learning program can support. When a student has decided which linguistic skill to practise, a text suitable for current proficiency in that skill is selected as the vehicle for the exercise and converted to match the appropriate exercise template.[3]

3   Deriving teaching material from corpora

3.1   *The corpora*

The corpora initially available to this project were a machine-readable version of the *OALD* and the Susanne Corpus, a fully tagged subset of the Brown Corpus of American English.

3.1.1   *OALD*

The *OALD* consisted of the published text of the third edition (1974) augmented by SGML tags. The tags that were of greatest significance in finding exercise material include:

- the headword tag, for lexical searches
- syntactic function tags, particularly those that classify verbs and how they can be used
- specialized vocabulary tags denoting words that are specific to certain domains, e.g. law, architecture
- tags for colloquial expressions
- tags for example sentences.

While this may sound like largesse for linguists only the structural components of a dictionary entry were tagged; the linguistic structure of the content was not tagged and this was to prove a major defect. It was a defect not shared by the Susanne Corpus.

3.1.2   Susanne Corpus

The Susanne Corpus (Sampson 1992) is a collection of 64 texts from four genres of the Brown Corpus:

N18:1070w	–	PPHS1f	She	she	OSNas:s.Nas:s]
N18:1080a	–	VVDt	raised	raise	[Vd.Vd]
N18:1080b	–	AT1	a	a	[Ns:o.
N18:1080c	–	VVGv	protesting	protest	[Tg[Vg.Vg]Tg]
N18:1080d	–	NN1c	hand	hand	Ns:o]
N18:1080e	–	IW	with	with	[P:h.
N18:1080f	–	AT1	a	a	[Ns.
N18:1080g	–	VVNt	startled	startle	[Tn[Vn.Vn]Tn]
N18:1080h	–	NN1n	air	air	.Ns]P:h]S]
N18:1080i	–	YF	+.	–	.O]

Figure 8.1 Example of tagged data from the Susanne Corpus

A: press reportage
G: belles lettres, biography, memoirs
J: learned (mainly scientific and technical writing)
N: adventure and Western fiction.

For details on the source publications of the texts, see Francis and Kucera (1989).

Each text in the Susanne Corpus contains more than 2000 words and every word generates six tag fields. The tags are based on the Lancaster set listed in Appendix B of *The Computational Analysis of English* (Garside *et al.* 1987). The four most pertinent to the task were:

- Word tag: this gives the syntactic category of the word.
- Word field: this often coincides with a word in the orthographic sense but is occasionally only part of a word or a punctuation symbol.
- Lemma field: this gives the dictionary headword of which the lemma is a form. (These forms are from the *OALD*, so the two databases form a coherent whole.)
- Parse field: this field is what distinguishes Susanne from other corpora. It gives the grammatical structure as a labelled tree. The tree is represented as a bracketed string.

These proved invaluable in designing algorithms for multiple tag searches. An example of marked-up text from the Susanne Corpus is shown in Figure 8.1.

It will throw light on the merits of the corpora as sources of CALL exercises to consider some examples. In this chapter the exercises are classified by the complexity of the search needed to derive the material for the exercise, rather than by the purpose of

```
.Nl
Complete the following sentences by choosing the appropriate participle:
.Nl
.Nl
1.
.Bu a l n
startled do shyly; Delete-to '. '; Type startled
.bU
.Bu a l n
startling do shyly; Delete-to '. '; Type startling
.bU
.Bu a l n
wrong word do shyly; Delete-to ' '; Type ......
.bU
.Nl
.Nl
   a.   She raised a protesting hand with a ...... air.
.Nl
.Nl
.Nl
```

Figure 8.2   Text from Figure 8.1 with Susanne mark-up transformed
to Guide mark-up

the exercise. However, the reader should bear in mind that exercises fall into three main groups:

- *Lexical*: primarily concerning topics such as word use, idioms, irregular plurals, and so on.
- *Syntactic*: dealing particularly with sentence level features, e.g. use of prepositions, verb forms, pronouns, agreement.
- *Discourse*: how to structure text so that it is cohesive above the sentence level.

The objectives of the project were:

- firstly to create a computer model of student competence based on ability in each linguistic skill covered
- secondly, to select automatically texts that matched student competence in a skill
- and finally, from these, to generate exercises *automatically without human intervention at any point.*

Figure 8.2 shows the text from Figure 8.1 stripped of the Susanne tags and embedded in a template tagged for the Guide hypertext system. The completed exercise as it would appear in Guide is shown in Figure 8.3. Human teachers could undoubtedly produce

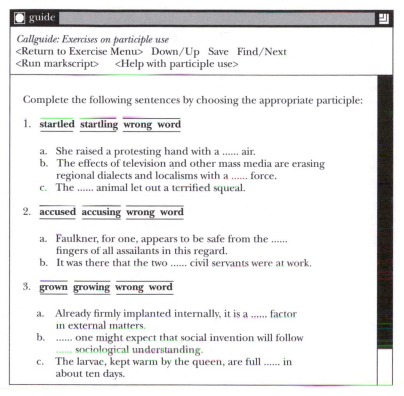

Figure 8.3   Text from Figure 8.2 displayed as a Guide file

better and more comprehensive examples of a finite number of exercises for a predefined ability level, or even for a discrete number of ability levels. However, could a computer program working with a large general-purpose database of texts produce an effectively infinite number of examples for a continuously variable ability range?

3.2   Searches involving a single search term

Fortunately, a single search term is adequate for many simple lexical and syntactic exercises, particularly lexical exercises on the use of specific words or word classes. The search term may be orthographic, i.e. a search for a specific word or word form or for a single syntactic tag. For many orthographic searches, the *OALD* is

Complete the sentences by choosing the appropriate word.

affect   effect

She ....s an American accent.

His death ....ed us deeply.

Punishment had very little .... on him.

The hotel-keeper seized her personal ....s because she could not pay her bill.

The plans will come to be carried into .....

Will the changes in taxation .... you personally?

Figure 8.4   Distinguishing between *affect* and *effect*

Complete the sentences by selecting the appropriate relative pronoun:

who   whom   whose

But there seemed to be some difference of opinion as to how far the board should go, and __ advice it should follow.

Despite the warning, there was a unanimous vote to enter a candidate, according to Republicans __ attended.

God 'gives to both North and South this terrible war, as the woe due to those by __ the offence came'.

He will be succeeded by Rob Ledford of Gainesville, __ has been an assistant more than three years.

Figure 8.5   Part of exercise on relative pronouns from the Susanne Corpus

an excellent source and Figure 8.4 shows an exercise on the words *affect* and *effect* derived from the *OALD*.

Even when a syntactic class is well defined a single word search is often preferable when the number of instances in that class is small or when the teacher or learner wishes to concentrate on only a subset of the category. For example, an exercise on the relative pronouns *who, whom* and *whose* is most easily found and balanced by searching for the words themselves rather than their syntactic class. Figure 8.5 shows an exercise so derived from the Susanne Corpus.

3.3   Searches requiring two or more tags

There are two reasons for requiring two tags: to remove ambiguities and to find more complex syntactic constructs.

Complete the following sentences by choosing the correct pronouns:

I	**me**	**myself**	**he**	**him**	**himself**
we	**us**	**ourselves**	**she**	**her**	**herself**
you	**you**	**yourself**	**it**	**it**	**itself**
		yourselves	**they**	**them**	**themselves**

Occasionally, __ may come across one or two bumblebees in the cold season, when __ are turning over sods in your garden, but __ have to be a really keen observer to see __ at all. __ keep their wings and feet pressed tightly against their bodies, and in spite of their often colourful attire __ may very well mistake __ for lumps of dirt.

Once __ has made up her mind, the queen starts out by constructing, in her chosen abode, a small 'floor' of dried grass or some woolly material.

But let __ return, after this gruesome interlude, to our willow catkins in the spring; there are other wild bees that command our attention.

Figure 8.6   Part of exercise on pronouns derived from J10, readability grade 10.07

3.3.1   Removing ambiguities

Some exercises that ostensibly require only a single tag can be immeasurably improved by using a second tag to avoid ambiguity in the sentence. For example, unlike most referents for relative pronouns, those for ordinary pronouns do not necessarily appear in the same sentence as the pronoun. When sentences are selected automatically it is difficult to ensure that the referent has been included. Consequently, it is impossible for the user to determine what pronoun was used in the original text. A way of overcoming this is to use a second tag to avoid the ambiguity. Figure 8.6 shows an exercise on pronouns. It has been derived by selecting only sentences that contain a pronoun and a possessive adjective that agree in number and person. Replacing only the pronoun and leaving the possessive article (or vice-versa) results in an example with a single correct answer.

3.3.2   Finding more complex syntactic constructs

A similar technique can be used with verbs but, of course, exercises on verbs frequently require two tags simply to obtain a basic set of sentences. Fortunately, the tag sets required are easily defined:

> Complete the following sentences by choosing the *to*-infinitive or the gerund (*ing*)
>
> **infinitive   gerund**
>
> After they had finished [**EAT**], Melissa took Sprite the kitten under her arm . . .
>
> He wanted [**KNOW**] if my father had beaten me or my mother had run away from home to give me an unhappy childhood.
>
> I kept [**CIRCLE**] the block hoping [**SEE**], from the street behind it, the rear of the hall.
>
> It is one that most try [**AVOID**], as long as they can see an alternative approach to the problem.

Figure 8.7   Part of exercise on gerunds and infinitives

> passive: be + past participle
> progressive: be + present participle
> perfect: have + past participle
> modal: modal + infinitive

Obviously yet more complex verbal exercises can be derived by combining two or more tag sets to select the original basic set.

Figure 8.7 shows an exercise from the Susanne Corpus on the use of gerunds and infinitives as the objects of verbs.

3.4   Increasing the specificity of exercises

The aim of many exercises can be refined by increasing the complexity of the initial search. So far the skills discussed have ranged from straightforward skills of good grammar through lexical skills to increase vocabulary and improve word usage. These are among the simpler in the spectrum of skills involved in writing good English. Greater subtleties are required to produce coherent and cohesive text that sounds natural. The more subtle the skill, the harder it is to evaluate how well an author has engineered his text to demonstrate that aspect of language use; the harder, too, to define by algorithm how to recognize it through a sequence of tags. However, two simple skills that add greatly to the natural rhythm of a text are the ordering of adjectives and the positioning of adverbs. Figure 8.8 shows an exercise on positioning of adverbs of frequency. This was done by searching explicitly for frequency adverbs and then checking sentence type to ensure that a mixture of interrogative, affirmative and negative cases were chosen. This exercise contrasts with others covered so far: here students do not

---

Select the appropriate position for the adverb:

always

He will not be indisposed.

Do you navigate like this?

There has probably been a bridge of some sort at the southeastern corner of the city.

Had he wished to be a conductor?

Lincoln was willing to concede to each 'slave state' the right to decide independently whether to continue or end it.

Figure 8.8   Part of an exercise on adverb positioning

simply have to choose a word to fill a blank – the normal Cloze procedure. Instead, they must choose where, in the sentence, the adverb should be placed. This demands the provision of a different exercise template and increases the complexity of the computer program.

3.5   Selecting coherent passages of text

Explicit signposting with adverbial conjuncts is not the only way to attain cohesion. The advantage of this method over other techniques is that it can be easily recognized automatically; more subtle techniques are less easy to find by algorithm. Recognizing cohesion in discourse by computer is an area where much research is still needed. One simple measure of cohesion is to count, for each sentence, pronouns, adverbial conjuncts, and content word, roots in common with the preceding sentence. While this is a useful rough guide, it is not an accurate measure because it ignores cohesion introduced by synonymy, lexical attachment and ellipsis.

After a coherent paragraph has been selected, a rudimentary exercise to improve the student's logical ordering strategy can be devised by displaying the sentences in random order. The student's task is to reassemble the paragraph to match the original text. In this exercise it is particularly important to choose a text which has a level of difficulty commensurate with the student's reading ability, because reordering demands a deeper understanding of the text than many of the other exercises.

Even when good cohesive passages can be found it is still not easy to devise for the student interactive exercises that can be both generated and assessed automatically. While benefits will accrue to the student from reading coherent texts, passive appreciation is not so effective a learning strategy as active involvement. More complex exercises can be formed by combining two different exercises in a longer passage of text; for example, pronoun exercises and conjunction exercises. While this will cause the student to concentrate on cohesive devices, it can be laboriously slow and take much of the spontaneity out of reading.

4   Comparison of the strengths of *OALD* and Susanne sources of CALL exercises

4.1   Word searches

For word searches the dictionary is to be preferred where it can be used. There are two reasons for this:

(a)   The coverage is exhaustive: every accepted sense of the word is explained.

(b)   The usage shown is always accepted: idiosyncratic usages, or usages that are simply errors on the part of authors, have been excluded by the dictionary compilers.

The Susanne Corpus is not nearly so suited to word searches because

■   word coverage is erratic: some words occur frequently, while others occur rarely or not at all

■   there is no guarantee that the word usage is sound.

4.2   Tag searches

When the search involves usage of even a single syntactic class of function words, the balance tilts more in favour of fully tagged corpus texts. This type of exercise covers the common function words: such as articles, pronouns, prepositions, verb particles. There are two main reasons for this:

(a)   For some exercises the number of example sentences in the dictionary is inadequate for the production of a variety of exercises.

(b)   Authors are less likely to misuse function words.

4.3   Multiple tags

When multiple tags are needed, the Susanne Corpus (a fully tagged corpus) has a clear advantage over the *OALD*. The *OALD* makes little use of multiple tags. It does occasionally use single tags to denote co-occurrence of attributes but even when it does this the association between tags and examples is often poor. For example, it tags verbs that can be followed by an infinitive or by a gerund. However, all syntactic tags are given together at the start of the entry for that sense, while all the example sentences are given at the end of the entry without an explicit connection between tag and usage. This means, of course, that examples showing a specific feature cannot be selected using tags alone.

Nevertheless, the dictionary is a convenient source for compiling exhaustive lists of verbs that can be followed only by a gerund, or only by an infinitive or by both. Exhaustivity is one of the great strengths of the dictionary: with the corpus it is impossible to state that a feature never occurs, merely that there is not an instance of it in the corpus.

4.4   Concise examples

The Susanne Corpus is also at a disadvantage to the *OALD* when sentence length is a consideration. Probably because space was at a premium in the printed version, the dictionary compilers have ensured that all examples are as concise as clarity of usage will allow; indeed, many examples consist merely of phrases. Authors in the Susanne texts laboured under no such constraint and some sentences are convoluted and tedious, particularly when read out of context. While reading extraneous material may improve a student's overall command of English, it could well be argued that this time would be better spent doing more interactive exercises. There are two ways of reducing the length of the text that appears on the screen:

(a)   When material is plentiful, discard all sentences longer than a predefined number of words.

(b)   When material is in short supply, use the structural analysis in the Susanne text to take only the relevant phrase or clause.

4.5   Paucity of good examples

A shortage of good examples afflicted both corpora from time to time. The original plan was to generate sets of examples on line so that students were given different exercises every time they used the system. However, if large quantities of material need to be searched, the system response time will be unacceptably retarded for on-line work. It would seem sensible, therefore, to leave some of the more advanced exercises already prepared for the student. When there are only one or two sets to be found, it is tedious and wasteful to search and regenerate every time the system is used.

5   Shortcomings of corpora for CALL

It is possible to summarize some of the main points already covered to highlight the shortcomings of the use of corpora in CALL:

(a)   The linguistic quality of some texts is not acceptable for a language-learning program.
(b)   Long and complex example sentences may inhibit the learning process.

Of course, the use of unconnected sentences to illustrate lexical and grammatical uses was once a feature of many general language-learning courses and is still the dominant technique in dictionaries. However, in these circumstances the sentences used had been specially chosen or devised with the aim of providing an unambiguous illustration of a precise linguistic feature as concisely as possible. Texts in general corpora have no such aim: the linguistic attributes are incidental to the text's content – not the object of its content. Consequently, contextual complexity can easily obscure the linguistic purpose which the sentence has been selected to illuminate. Language learners may be deprived of linguistic focus as well as content coherence and risk becoming disoriented in the learning environment.

A consistent and predictable learning environment is particularly important in a computer-based learning program because such programs are often impoverished socially and culturally. Social interactions support and enhance learning: teacher interactions help to explain concepts, clarify context and applaud student endeavour

– peer group collaborations can help students develop understanding through discussion and negotiation; even classroom competition can increase motivation and promote confidence. These kinds of interaction are absent from computer-based learning, which tends to be solitary. Many computer-based learning programs have sought to redress the balance between burgeoning student numbers and teacher shortages by providing packages which allow students to rehearse skills individually. Few have addressed the problem of social isolation. Some social estrangement is inevitable when services hitherto rendered by a human being are provided by a machine. However, it is likely to be further exacerbated by an erratic journey through a linguistic universe of random components. Even if full comprehension of a textual passage is not strictly necessary to determine the correct answer to a language exercise, some students may feel the need to understand. This is not a need that current computer programs can meet and this deficiency is likely to induce uncertainty and insecurity in the learner. Fortunately, there are a number of improvements that might ameliorate the situation.

6   Conclusion: improving the learning environment

In conclusion, I will concentrate upon enhancements to the computer-based learning environment. These will be discussed with specific reference to materials, as it is here that corpora have their main impact, though this does not indicate that improvements in terms of presentation and user adaptivity are not also possible.

The original motivation for this project was to help undergraduate and graduate students who already have a good command of English hone their skills to a level appropriate for writing dissertations and theses. Ideally, machine readable texts from within the students' academic discipline should have been used as vehicles for such exercise generation. However, even in computer science, texts locally available in a machine readable form were frequently stylistically poor and consequently unsuitable for the task. Even where texts were adequate, they were not tagged and tagging to the required level was beyond the project's resources. The Susanne Corpus, a comprehensively tagged database, and the *OALD* were subsequently chosen as compromise test databases solely for their linguistic attributes.

A major objective of the project was to select automatically by algorithm material appropriate for a range of exercises, so that the degree of difficulty and the content could be varied to suit an individual student's needs. Firstly, it must be emphasized that the passages so chosen were sound examples of the required linguistic feature. Secondly, the content of many passages, while it might not reflect a student's personal interests, was suitable for a general language-learning course. However, it was not possible to ensure automatically that content was appropriate to purpose. This was a disappointment, although it might have been expected because the Susanne Corpus had not been assembled with CALL in mind and consequently had none of the quality control for style and linguistic coverage that good CALL demands.

Naturally, the more complex the exercise, the more demanding were the selection criteria and the rarer were appropriate texts. More complex exercises rapidly exhausted the resources of both databases: frequently, there was a paucity of examples and this was sometimes coupled with poor stylistic quality in the retrieved text.

It seems that, ideally, texts for a CALL database ought to be pre-selected from a corpus with great discrimination. Teachers should be satisfied that all texts are models of good practice in word usage, syntactic constructions and cohesive discourse. Texts must be graded according to readability but must also be classified by distribution of linguistic features to ensure that the database coverage is adequate for the task. Whenever possible linguistic properties should not be the only criteria for inclusion in the database: language learning is inseparable from activity, and learning in any subject should take place through interactive communication.

To realise this end, the database should contain texts that relate to students' tasks and interests in other disciplines. In other words, a student's goals in the language-learning program should coincide as far as possible with the student's wider goals. It seems true, therefore, that corpora are of use as sources of material for CALL programs in so far as they can attain this goal.

Notes

1   As this chapter discusses the exploitation of textual corpora, I will not discuss the merits of multimedia approaches to CALL here.
2   For a more detailed discussion of this point, see Wilson (1993a).
3   For further details see Wilson (1993b).

9

Exploiting a Corpus of Written German for Advanced Language Learning

BILL DODD

1 Introduction

My purpose in this chapter is to demonstrate that a computer-supported investigation of language corpora provides a powerful and simple tool for language learning. It can be exploited with little or no adaptation in the advanced stages of learning a foreign language, and certainly at undergraduate level.[1] I will review some of the recent work done in this field in the Department of German Studies at the University of Birmingham, and suggest further ways in which corpus material and data-driven learning might be exploited to give students a richer language-learning experience in the FL environment (see Johns 1993: 3). The major advantages of a corpus-based approach are of course two-fold: the authenticity of the examples, and the opportunity for students to make their own discoveries.

The largest and most varied selection of corpora of German has been assembled by the Institut für deutsche Sprache (IDS) in Mannheim, and other corpora are being developed by academic institutions and commercial organizations.[2] Thus, while relatively little is readily available for teaching purposes at present, it is likely that the situation in English today offers a view of the future in German and other languages. In any case, huge corpora are not necessary for language-teaching purposes. A modest corpus of a million or so words is certainly enough to make a valuable teaching aid, and is realistically within the reach of most teaching institutions. At Birmingham, work began in 1993 preparing one of the

Mannheim corpora, the Bonner Zeitungskorpus ('Bonn Newspaper Corpus', henceforth BZK) for teaching applications, and from September 1994, BZK has been accessed using MicroConcord (Scott and Johns 1993) on a computer network in the School of Modern Languages. BZK has just over 3 million words of running text systematically extracted from East German and West German national and local newspapers over the period 1949–74. Since we were primarily interested in researching and teaching grammatical patterns, codes added to the text by the compilers to indicate 'start of paragraph', 'proper noun', etc., were stripped out using a program especially written for this purpose by Tim Johns. This makes it more difficult to extract certain kinds of information from the data (such as the provenance of the text) but has the advantage that the corpus data appears as natural text, which makes it more accessible for students. It also maximizes the amount of text which can be viewed or printed out in a line of a KWIC concordance.

Programs such as Contexts (see Johns, this volume) have an obvious appeal in FL teaching, and it is likely, in the early stages of learning, that working with carefully edited data files in this kind of closely controlled environment will greatly enhance the learning experience. In this chapter, however, I wish to explore the possibilities of using unedited corpus data as a language-learning resource for advanced students. I will discuss three ways of exploiting 'raw' (unedited) data: firstly, as an informal resource for students to browse through; secondly, as a resource for formulating explicit grammatical knowledge; and, finally, as a resource for student-led projects on grammatical or sociolinguistic topics. At this level, several teaching aims are likely to coincide. These include improving the practical proficiency of the learner, improving the learner's formal knowledge about the language (and about language in general), and giving the student an insight into the work of the descriptive grammarian.

2   Browsing through 'raw' corpus data

I should perhaps preface my remarks by saying that 'raw data' is not the same as 'raw text'. By 'raw data' I mean a concordanced file in unedited form. Working with 'raw' corpus data will probably be of limited benefit to beginners and intermediate learners until they reach a point at which they are not unduly worried if they do not recognize every language item in the context. But depending on the exercise, this point may come relatively early. A case in point may well be vocabulary building, and a file such as that illustrated in Figure 9.1 (overleaf), though it may contain much that the student does not recognize, offers an interesting way of building students' vocabulary and knowledge of word formation.

This is the kind of data file which can easily be made by students, especially where they have open access to a corpus, and German is of course a language which lends itself well to this kind of morpheme-based work. Groups of students might be given the task of looking up different suffixes (e.g. *-freundlich, -feindlich, -nahe, -fern, -fähig, -gerecht*) and reporting back with six words which they had not known previously and which they explain to the rest of the group. The 'incidental' nature of the lexical combinations captured in the corpus may actually prove a stimulus to learning: no textbook would come up with such a range of examples, nor with the kind of contextual clues as to usage (the collocation of *kündbar + Vertrag*, for instance, or *sofort + lieferbar, telefonisch + erreichbar, Grundstück + bebaubar*). It is often possible to extend the learning experience, for example by comparing the *-feindlich* file with *-freundlich*, or by replacing the instances of *-nahe* with *-fern*.

With guidance from a teacher, students wanting to check on a particular language feature ought to be able to make a concordance file. For example, students wanting to explore the syntax of modal verbs can search for *h*tte* within three words of (for example) *sollen*. In BZK this produces the data shown in Figure 9.2 (overleaf).

Since this is a 'raw' text file, part of the students' task is to decide which of the citations captured are to be discarded as 'rogue' examples (nos 5 and 6). Having done this, students can observe the way this construction functions in main and dependent clauses, and see that the second subjunctive form *hätte* is involved in most of these examples.

The information on frequency given by most concordancers is also a feature which can be exploited quite simply. For example, three of the common translation equivalents of 'complete/ly' occur with very different frequencies in BZK: there are 24 citations of *total*, 70 of *absolut* and 409 of *völlig*. This immediately says something about usage. It shows that they are not absolutely interchangeable, and suggests that looking at the contexts in which they are used might be an interesting exercise. The potential for students to 'browse' through structures is practically infinite. Initially they will

z Hofheim / Taunus 13027 qm: Prs. DM 55, -, auch **teilbar**. 2-1/2Geschossige Bebauung, Staufen-Imm., 6 geschrieben hat, und doch ist seine Handschrift **unverkennbar**. Auch in diesen lose aneinandergereihte uftkurortes Hoffmannsthal sind in 10 Gehminuted **erreichbar**. Beste Verkehrsverbindung nach Köln! Sof. hrittmacherimpulses in bestimmten Zeitabständen **unabdingbar**. Bislang mußte der 'Träger' zur Kontroll riften sind dokumentenecht, fotokopierfähig und **mikroverfilmbar**. Color-Spot sollten Sie näher kennen er und Kenner. Cheverolet Corvette Sportcoupe m. **abnehmbar**. Dachteil, Radio, Autom., elektr. Fensterh ein gegenläufiger Zug der sowjetischen Politik **bemerkbar**. Die sowjetischen Politiker werden nicht m zu. Daß die Lage Berlins nicht normal ist, sei **unbestreitbar**. Eckardt sagte: 'Ich glaube nicht, daß t, etwa um eine Rente, kämpfen muß, machen sie **versicherbar**. Eine weitere gute Gelegenheit zur Werb db, die Entscheidung des Kanzlers sei für viele **unfaßbar**. Er glaube, Brandt habe mit diesem Schritt 4 E DM 17950, - (statt 22600) inkl. Mwst. Sofort **lieferbar**. Erfragen Sie Einzelheiten bei Volvo Vertr in Rossmarkt 15. Wir sind jederzeit telefonisch **erreichbar**: Ffm. (0611) 20056. Firmenzeichen. Fabrik nlichkeit mit dem 'Jungvolk' zur Hitlerzeit ist **unverkennbar**. Foto: Keystone. Blick über den Schlagb n überreden kann'. Das Vorgehen der Polizei ist **unberechenbar**. Griechische Häftlinge klagen die Junt raße 30. Keine Vertreter-Besuche. Alle Verträge **kündbar**. - Hierdurch bitte ich um Zusendung von Band egante Hanglage, ca. 1500 qm, 1-1/2 - 2 gesch., **bebaubar**. Kaufpreis DM 32, - pro qm. Heinz Leue K.G., s Anwesen lastenfrei, Grundstück 6000 qm, teils **bebaubar**, Komfortvilla, massive Halle, passend für M stische Maßnahmen, die niemand will, wären dann **unanwendbar**. Manchem mag es jetzt schwerfallen, poli

Figure 9.1   Concordance of * bar (words ending in -bar)

1 ischen Monumentalwerks 'a study of history'. Man **hätte** meinen **sollen**, daß das Erscheinen der letzten vier Bände dieses Werke
2 h blickte ihm nach. Als er davonging. Ich **hätte** ihm antworten **sollen**, daß ich nie von selbst dorthin gehen könnte. Nie würde
3 iligtümer, denen auch die verhinderte Revolution **hatte** dienen **sollen** : Der totalen Politisierung und Egalisierung der Gesell
4 erwarten. Allein das Beispiel des 30. Juni 1934 hätte warnen **sollen**. Der Streich glückte, weil, wie an so vielen Fronten, i
5 hn- und Einkommensteuer; die am 1. Januar 1975 wirksam werden **sollen**. Der Bundesrat **hatte** den Beschlüssen des Bundestages ni
6 fe auf Häuser, Geschäfte und einzelne Personen erlaubt **hatte**. **Sollen** die Sowjetbehörden Anspruch auf bestimmte Grenzstreifen
7 auch der Instrukteur des Landesvorstandes. Er **hätte** anleiten **sollen** und den Funktionären praktische Ratschläge erteilen müs

Figure 9.2   Concordance of hätte/hatte in close proximity to sollen

need advice on how to use the concordancer and how to search for particular structures, but they will quickly begin experimenting on their own.

3   Comparing corpus evidence with reference works: two procedures

The importance attached to metalanguage when discussing corpus data is largely a matter for the course designer. Formal grammatical description will usually play a secondary role, the main emphasis being on observing text patterns in order to improve students' accuracy and extend their competence in the language. But on a slightly different level, it is possible to bring in a second focus, on formal grammatical description. This kind of approach may have applications in advanced grammar courses and courses in linguistics, where corpus data can be used with the twin aims of improving language competence and sensitizing students to issues in the kind of language description known to them from standard reference works. There seem to be two obvious ways of doing this: by moving from textbook to data, and vice versa. Moving from textbook to data entails having students gather information on the way a particular language feature is described in one or more reference books, before gathering or consulting the corpus data on this feature. Obviously, it is preferable to have students do their own interrogation of the corpus and obtain a print-out from which they can work, since this is likely to increase motivation and also teamwork: when a group of students work together, the learning experience is likely to be enhanced, and this kind of exercise works best when it stimulates a collaborative brainstorming session. Having summarized the description offered by the grammatical 'authorities', they then proceed to test these grammatical explanations against the data, matching examples to categories and checking them off. This is an exercise which can strengthen a student's insight into formal grammar while promoting language competence, and it is not uncommon to have the situation where, having 'checked off' the types, the students are left with a residue of problematic examples. These will either have to be accommodated to the received grammar or new descriptions will have to be found, and this process obviously has the potential for forming new insights into the structure of the language. My experience of

working with a corpus is that this is a more common phenomenon than one would expect, and certainly provides a positive
learning experience for students with the confidence to handle
authentic data.

Moving from data to textbook is more demanding, but potentially very productive as a learning experience for a particular kind
of student because it offers the challenge of writing one's own
grammar and comparing it with a published authority. This is 'first-
hand' grammar (as opposed to the norm of 'second-hand' grammar). Students start with corpus data and formulate their own
grammatical description(s), attempting to cover all the examples
with the minimum of categories and the maximum of generalization. They then consult the published grammarians to see how
the experts have tackled the question, noting where the received
description is better than their own (more comprehensive, perhaps,
or more concisely formulated) and, occasionally, where they have
found something which does not appear to be covered in the
textbook. While both procedures lend themselves to teamwork,
moving from data to textbook is perhaps best regarded only as a
collaborative task. Whichever way round the procedure is tried,
there is a very real chance that students will discover some new
aspect which was unknown to them, and it is quite possible that
they will find features which have been inadequately covered
by traditional grammars. Exploiting a corpus makes this kind of
discovery-centred approach possible.

I would like to offer two illustrations of the kind of language
work which could be tackled by advanced learners. The first relates
to a syntactic problem and is about to be tried out on a final-year
undergraduate group taking the option in Linguistics of German.
The second relates to a semantic problem and recounts what
actually happened when corpus evidence was used in last year's
Linguistics of German course.

3.1   From textbook to data: an example

It has been my experience that even advanced learners of German have difficulty with the complex 'consecutive' conjunction
als daß. For many students it is a source of error, and they may
tend to avoid it completely. Grammars at the beginning and intermediate level tend not to cover this construction, dealing only with

als and *daß* as discrete items. This may encourage the perception that the grammar of *als daß* is simply an aggregation of the two, with *als* being associated with the comparative construction (e.g. *mehr als,* 'more than'). Corpus evidence is likely to be illuminating here because it will provide the kind of wider contextual information unlikely to be contained even in the more comprehensive grammars of German such as the Duden *Grammatik* or *Hammer's German Grammar and Usage* or Durrell's *Using German.*[3] The *Hammer* states: 'with a change of subject, the conjunction *als daß* is used after *zu* or negated *genug*' (Durrell 1991: §13.2.5a), and indeed nearly all the examples in these three works show different grammatical subjects in the two clauses linked by *als daß*. On the basis of the descriptions offered in these reference works, we would expect *als daß* to be used only after adjectives modified by *zu, nicht genug* or *nicht so*; to find a high incidence of the second subjunctive in the *daß*-clause, and we would expect to find *als daß* used in 'negative contexts'. Let us now turn to the *als daß* file from BZK (see Figure 9.3 (overleaf)).

The corpus evidence suggests a number of refinements to the received grammatical accounts:

(a)   Almost one in three *daß*-clauses has the same grammatical subject as the preceding clause (3, 6, 7, 8, 14, 15, 24).

(b)   The significant determining word in the left co-text is not always *zu* or a negative: note *eher* in examples 6 and 16 and possibly in 15 (two of these examples have shared subjects). However, this *eher* can plausibly be fitted in to the received accounts by interpreting it as a negative ('not this . . . but that').

(c)   Nevertheless, the combination '*nicht* + comparative adjective' seems to be indicated by example 14 (*nicht mehr . . . , als daß*).

(d)   As line 23 shows, *kein* is also possible in the negative preceding clause.

(e)   The incidence of the indicative in the *daß*-clause is probably higher than the grammars would lead one to expect (nine clear examples).

The relative frequency of the types of significant item in the left co-text may also be of interest. Here, the intensifying '*zu* + adjective' is almost exactly as frequent as the negative *nicht, nichts* or *kein*. If we include *eher* as a comparative (though there may be

1 n fällt zur BDR-Intendantenkrise nichts anderes ein, **als daß** sie auch gern mitreden, auch gern ihre Finger im Pfründenkuchen haben
2 ift, dann bedeutet das praktisch gar nichts anderes, **als daß** man es in Paris vermieden hat, sich mit der veränderten Taktik Moskau
3 ich ist Johnson zu erfahren im Geschäft der Politik, **als daß** er sich schon heute – öffentlich oder privat – festlegen würde, aber
4 mödchen von Neil Simon. Passieren tut weiter nichts, **als daß** ein blutjunges Paar eben geheiratet hat. Sie ziehen in ihrer Liebe un
5 erden könne, das kann nicht anders ausgelegt werden, **als daß** der Kanzler bei seiner Meinung als Wirtschaftsminister geblieben ist,
6 älderischen Gesinnung, auf die sie eher stolz sind, **als daß** sie sich ihrer schämen: Schließlich müssen sie aus der Not eine Tugen
7 e er die Motive komponiert, das alles ist zu subtil, **als daß** es naiv genannt werden könnte. In einigen Landschaften blieb noch ein
8 hten, weil wir in zu viele Probleme verstrickt sind, **als daß** wir noch an ein 'eindimensionaled' Weltbild glauben könnten. Gisela F
9 ddi (etwa sechs Sekunden Vorsprung) war zu weit weg, **als daß** Meißner sich in diesem Rennen noch eine Siegchance hätte ausrechnen k
10 en in den einzelnen Ländern zu unterschiedlich sind, **als daß** sich Patentrezepte für eine Bevölkerungspolitik finden lassen. Brück.
11 tsenden. Der Unterschied im Spielniveau ist zu groß, **als daß** für die Gäste mehr als ein Schaukampf erforderlich gewesen wäre. Die
12 zur Kohle stehen, das aber bedeutet nichts anderes, **als daß** der bergbau mit steigendem Angebot von Heizöl und Erdgas automatisch
13 Bildungssteuer, nach einem 'Bildungspfennig' nicht, **als daß** sie als romantische Träumerei Bildungsbesessener abgetan werden könnt
14 e beantwortet wäre. Heute kann man nicht mehr sagen, **als daß** man die Zukunft Berlins mit unerschöpflicher Geduld verhandeln will,
15 önigs von Sachsen aud seinen Hof zurückziehen würde, **als daß** er sich zwingen ließe, das Gesicht zu verlieren. Am Donnerstag nimmt
16 erhauswahl erklärt hatte, eher werde 'Blut fließen', **als daß** etwas am Wahlrecht für die Stadträte geändert werde. Die Bürgerrechts
17 ichen Mittelmeer, die 'zu gut synchronisiert' seien, **als daß** es sich um einen Zufall handeln könne. Im ganzen gesehen will die sow
18 en und – objektiven, kriegsbedingten – Hindernissen, **als daß** man diesem neuen Ansatz reiche Vorschußlorbeeren auf den Weg geben mö
19 e automobilrevue? Autofahren ist zu teuer geworden, **als daß** man auf umfassende Informationen verzichten könnte. Deshalb gibt es d
20 ld. Nichts anderes braucht es zum Triumph des Bösen, **als daß** gute Menschen gar nichts tun. Edmund Burke. Wie viele Schultern ohne
21 ift, dann bedeutet das praktisch gar nichts anderes, **als daß** man es in Paris vermieden hat, sich mit der veränderten Taktik Moskau
22 opa. glt, was für Attika. galt: Zu viele kluge Köpfe, **als daß** die Klugheit siegen kann. Stern. Große alte Männer haben große alte G
23 ein könnten, aus keinem anderen Grunde zu schließen, **als daß** sie keinen Müllplatz hätten, führte zu Aktivitäten. So wurde auf Init
24 itische Bindung der SPD/FDP ist noch viel zu intakt, **als daß** sie ein Scheel-Votum der Union erschüttern könnte. Erschüttern könnte

Figure 9.3 Concordance of als daß

reasons for not doing so), then a comparative is found in the left co-text in about 16 per cent of the citations. The use of *als daß* in 'negative contexts' (Hammer) or in constructions with a 'negative consequence' (Duden) is generally borne out by the data, though in confirming these descriptions we also become aware of how much more subtle the real examples are. It is interesting to note how difficult it can be to locate the negative aspect of the context. A semantic negative can be found either in the adjective/adverb (*zu weit weg*, line 9) or in the consecutive clause (*erschüttern*, line 24). In this last example, the adjective (*intakt*) is prima facie a semantic. (Lines 13 and 18 do not contain enough contextual information to allow a judgement, and in this case the concordancer allows the user to view the larger context on screen. This can also be printed.)

On a purely descriptive level, it is possible to distinguish between cases where *als* is part of a (negative) comparative construction (such as *nicht/s anders als* (e.g. in lines 1, 2, 5, 6, 12, 14, 16, 20, 21, 23), and cases where it follows the intensifier *zu* plus adjective and is part of a complex conjunction. If we take this observation further and try to unify these two patterns in some kind of grammatical description, we might be tempted to say that the construction is found where contrast (or unequal comparison) is centrally involved in linking two clauses – and that the language treats these particular logical relations as in some sense the same phenomenon.

3.2 From data to textbook: an example

The second illustration relates to cognitive synonyms and more particularly to the interference of L1 patterning in L2 learning as evidenced by so-called 'translation synonyms'. Following an introduction to the theory of synonymy and a discussion of the contextual approach to meaning, the group of ten students was asked to come up with the difference in meaning between the words *Unterschied* and *Differenz*, both of which are typically rendered in English as 'difference'. Without access to dictionaries, much of their response was inevitably based on intuition. At the end of this discussion, during which the teacher simply made a list of the ideas produced by the group, they were given two print-outs (produced by the teacher) from a concordance of each word and asked to study these and report back in the next seminar. This led to another discussion during which the initial ideas about meaning and usage were in part confirmed, in part refined, and in part added to. It was only at this stage that dictionary definitions were consulted.

In the first discussion, the group arrived at a consensus: (i) the two words are not interchangeable in all contexts; (ii) they may not in fact be interchangeable in any contexts, though there was uncertainty on this point; (iii) the main distinction between them is that *Differenz* 'has to do with numbers and money'. A sample from each file is reproduced in Figures 9.4 and 9.5.

Having had time to study the corpus data, the following points emerged from the group: (i) *Differenz* can also mean 'disagreement/difference of opinion'; (ii) *Unterschied* applies to difference of quality, *Differenz* to difference of quantity (which led to a discussion as to whether the German for 'difference of opinion' was *Meinungsdifferenz* or *Meinungsunterschied*, and why it was the latter rather than the former); (iii) both are used with *zwischen*, although there are differences in the collocation with other prepositions. At this point the teacher wanted to look at whether the use of singular and plural forms might reveal differences between the two words, but instead the discussion focused on an issue raised by one of the students. Line 53 in the *Unterschied* file had not been explained; in fact it contradicted the 'grammar' they had worked out so far, which predicted that *Differenz* would be used in the context 'five goals difference' between two teams. This gave rise to a stimulating discussion which lasted for the remainder of the hour. One course of action was to suppress the example, to ignore it or label it an anomaly, but this was proposed only as a joke. One student who had been an avid reader of sports pages during his year abroad confirmed that *Unterschied* was normal in such a context, and the group was then forced to reconsider the quantity/ quality distinction. What emerged was a tentative proposal that in this context the difference between the two teams' scores was also a difference in the quality of the teams. This was accepted reluctantly by some, who asked whether they hadn't just made up this explanation in order to 'save the theory'. The 'anomalous' collocation was not found in any bilingual dictionary, and consulting dictionaries added little to their analysis, though dictionary examples did suggest that the two items overlap and that the use of singular and plural forms of these nouns may be relevant to a full description of their use.

This experience suggests that corpus evidence, in addition to being of interest to grammarians, also has a great potential value

```
29 Prinzipien Lenins bleiben ausschlaggebend. Der  Unterschied  zwischen früher und heute liegt lediglich
30 le überwunden werden können. Das ist der große   Unterschied  zur Lage in Westberlin. Wer heute noch gl
31 ben es dem Philosophen offen eingestanden. Der   Unterschied  zwischen Wissenschaft und Stammtisch: Der
32 e die Demokratie überhaupt ablehnen und keinen   Unterschied  mehr sehen, der die Diktatur der Mehrheit
33 eßende werden vom ganzen deutschn Volk, ohne     Unterschied  der Parteien, als ein Versuch der wirtsch
34 Erfüllungsgehilfen für ihre Politik. Welch ein   Unterschied  zwischen August Bebel und dem jüngsten Pa
35 erletzte insg. (In den Jahren vorher wurde ein   Unterschied  zwischen Leicht- und Schwerverletzten gem
36 deutscher Wissenschaft' gesprochen, als ob ein   Unterschied  zwischen der deutschen Wissenschaft und d
37 chtern: 'Meine Mannschaft ist ausgebrannt. Der   Unterschied  zwischen Regional- und Bundesliga ist rie
38 ist durchaus verdient. Es drückt deutlich den    Unterschied  zwischen beiden Mannschaften aus. 'Hat es
39 erwarten, daß westdeutsche Schriftsteller den    Unterschied  zwischen Peter Hacks und Harald Hauser, z
40 , ergeben sich manche Ähnlichkeiten. Der große   Unterschied  besteht aber darin, daß die Kapitalisten
41 werden. Für Einlagenzinsen gilt folgendes: Der   Unterschied  zwischen Sichteinlage in provisionspflich
42 en Kommission von Gewerkschaftsvertretern ohne   Unterschied  ihrer politischen Richtung und religiösen
43 n irischen Witz bei Johnson hat äußerlich den    Unterschied  gewählt, daß er seine Konferenz nicht in
44 e am größten und im Apogäum am geringsten. Der   Unterschied  kann dabei sogar sehr betrachtlich sein.
45 h der zurzeit geltenden Regelung. Ein weiterer   Unterschied  besteht darin, daß die bisherigen Beihil
46 häften für jedermann zu kaufen sind. Mit einem   Unterschied  allerdings. Sie werden gegen 60 Pfennig W
47 ie Heimat allen gehört, wo allen Menschen ohne   Unterschied  der Rasse und des Geschlechts das Recht a
48 rarfinanzierung so teuer geworden ist, muß der   Unterschied  zwischen Eigeneinnahmen und Finanzbedarf
49 schen K 700 mit 220 Pferdestärken. Das ist ein   Unterschied  wie Tag und Nacht. Das sind die Früchte d
50 existierten? Worin besteht der grundlegende      Unterschied  gegenüber solchen 'demokratischen' Staate
51 bezeugung gemeint, dann ahnt man erst, welcher   Unterschied  hier zur Rede steht: 'Leckts mi...!'. Gu
52 ten Aufwertung, bis heute nichts geändert. Der   Unterschied  ist anderswo zu suchen. Vor dem kabinetts
53 lich hätten die Hannoveraner mit fünf Treffern   Unterschied  siegen können. So überlegen spielten sie.
54 rachempfinden bereitet es Schwierigkeiten, dem   Unterschied  zwischen 'Sieger' und 'Gewinner' einen gr
```

Figure 9.4 Concordance of Unterschied

7 zahlen eine 'Vergönnungsmiete', bei der die	**Differenz**	zwischen alter und neuer Miete um 40 Prozent
8 egen nur 27, 65 D-Mark. erläutert wurde diese	**Differenz**	mit dem Hinweis, die Tarifbedingungen lägen u
9 den. Allein im Kreis Gardelegen bestand eine	**Differenz**	von 1000 Hektar. Die Regierung hat daraufhin
10 k mehr wurden Langspielplatten verkauft. Die	**Differenz**	zwischen Angebot und ständig wachsender Nachf
11 r allem einen klaren Hinweis darauf, daß die	**Differenz**	zwischen Kaufpreis und Tilgungswert bei Regie
12 mäßig wurden 6, 9 Prozent mehr abgesetzt; die	**Differenz**	resultiert aus der Entlastung der Preise durc
13 erwettbewerbs knapp mit 79:82. Eine minimale	**Differenz**	also, die den TSC-Spielern am Donnerstag um 1
14 cke von rund 385 Millionen DM. Eine so große	**Differenz**	hat es in keinem Jahr zuvor gegeben. Hoppe wi
15 der deutschen Frau. Von dieser anatomischen	**Differenz**	lebt eine ganze Industrie. Foto. Der große Hu
16 Aufkommen zwischen 320000 und 360000 t. Die	**Differenz**	wird durch Importe gedeckt. Der Durchschnitts
17 tig, jedoch nunmehr mit der Maßgabe, daß die	**Differenz**	von 80 Prozent, die früher beim Exporteur – i
18 zugenommen. bemerkenswert ist dabei, daß die	**Differenz**	zwischen realer und nomineller Entwicklung –
19 'über Nacht'. 200 DM wert geworden sein. Die	**Differenz**	von 190 DM wird zur Hälfte von der Gemeindeka
20 niger gestiegen sind als zuvor, hat sich die	**Differenz**	zwischen der Zunahme der Arbeitsentgelte und
21 zahlen. Die Unternehmer haben lediglich die	**Differenz**	zwischen der Unterstützung und den üblichen L
22 usgelaugt wurde. Groß-Gerau. – 0, 6 Pro mille	**Differenz.**	Bei der Untersuchung einer Blutprobe kamen d
23 ng soziale Reformen'. Von den prinzipiellen	**Differenzen**	zwischen SPD und Jusos, von Ausschlußverfah
24 anischen Gebiete westlich des Jordans mag es	**Differenzen**	zwischen den verschiedenen Parteien geben.
25 politischen europäischen Union, die nur der	**Differenzen**	zwischen den Weltblöcken in der Zeit des po
26 astungen ausgesetzt. Die EWG werde durch die	**Differenzen**	über den Getreidenpreis gefährdet. Die EFTA
27 s 20. Juli 1969 in Stuttgart. Spannungen und	**Differenzen**	werden dabei deutlich werden. Aber erst die
28 Schmidt angesprochen, die 'trotz bestehender	**Differenzen**	grundsätzliche Solidarität in dieser Partei
29 tegration verbunden ist. Noch nie haben sich	**Differenzen**	der europäischen Konjunktur- und Geldpoliti
30 tzenden Mao Tse-tung trotz der ideologischen	**Differenzen**	eine Neujahrsbotschaft, in der von neuen Er
31 uar 1973 und am 1. Januar 1974 eingefügt, um	**Differenzen**	zwischen der auf atomaren Vorgängen basiere
32 in Treffen auf höchster Ebene nur die tiefen	**Differenzen**	der arabischen Welt offenbaren. Ägypten sch

Figure 9.5 Concordance of Differenz (-en)

as an aid to language competence and language sensitivity in advanced learners. Even if their analysis is not as sophisticated as the ones offered above, they are likely to gain two benefits from this kind of exercise: competence in using the structure appropriately, with the confidence that comes from having a range of authentic examples to work from; and a greater, critically informed sensitivity to the problems of linguistic description.

4 Student-led projects

A corpus-based language module is offered as part of the Department's MA in Modern German Studies. Students are trained in corpus techniques and basic linguistic concepts such as collocation and 'semantic prosody' (see Louw 1993) before drawing up their own corpus-supported research project. In 1993/94 five students chose this module and presented dissertations. Three of these used corpus data to critically evaluate grammatical descriptions in reference books: these were studies of the distribution and frequency of the translation equivalents of 'complete/ly' (*total, absolut, völlig, vollständig, ganz, gänzlich* and *restlos*); 'decide' (*[sich] entscheiden, sich entschließen, beschließen* and *bestimmen*); and 'at least' (*wenigstens, mindestens* and *zumindest*). All three of these studies came up with interesting critiques of the accounts found in Farrell's *A Dictionary of German Synonyms*. Two students chose sociolinguistic topics. A study of the use of *nuklear, Atom-* and *Kern-* in the language of the nuclear debate largely bore out observations by sociolinguists that 'an antagonistic relationship exists between *Atom-* and *Kern-*, in which *Atom-* carries negative and *Kern-* positive connotations' (see Townson 1992: 222). And a study of selected lexical items in East German and West German newspapers surprisingly failed to produce enough data to support a critical analysis of the secondary literature on this subject. The relatively meagre data, however, was rightly seen by the student as a significant finding which, in turn, led to an analysis of the way the BZK was constructed and a possible explanation for the unexpected finding. (It is sometimes useful to realize that unexpectedly finding nothing or not much can itself be a finding. A colleague recently told me of a disagreement among political scientists about the way the Federal Government talks about the German national interest. The phrase *national* Interesse* was found just six times in BZK – surprisingly rarely – and of these six, four related to countries other than Germany. The remaining two were from an East German source. A 'non-finding' such as this is potentially significant.)

In addition to the kind of morphemic, lexical-semantic and syntactic investigation outlined in the main part of this chapter, there is scope for investigating any number of language features. For example, we might look at features of register (by comparing the relative frequency of a German verb with its related deverbal noun: *anordnen* vs *Anordnung*); or of lexical borrowing (by noting whether an imported word appears in marked form – italics, quotation marks; whether it is morphologically productive; whether its syntax follows the pattern of the lending language: *checken – durchchecken – Checkliste*); or of its sociolinguistics (is *Führer/*führer* used in postwar German? If so, in what contexts?).

In fact, the greatest constraint on the uses to which this resource can be put is probably the intellectual resourcefulness of the investigator, and the ideas contained in this chapter by no means exhaust the possibilities for exploiting corpora with advanced learners. I hope to have shown that this is an exciting and many-faceted tool for foreign language learning, whether we understand by that improving the learner's linguistic competence or promoting the analytical and descriptive skills associated with learning *about* the language.

Notes

1 I am indebted to the Institut für deutsche Sprache, Mannheim, for permission to use the Bonner Zeitungskorpus for teaching and research purposes at Birmingham; and to Professor John Sinclair, Philip King, and especially to Tim Johns for their practical support.

2 The following corpora of German are held at the Institut für deutsche Sprache: Mannheimer Korpus 1 (*c.* 2.2 million word forms); Mannheimer Korpus 2 (*c.* 300,000 words); Bonner Zeitungskorpus (*c.* 3 million); Freiburger Korpus (spoken language, *c.* 300,000 words); Dialogstrukturkorpus (*c.* 200,000); Pfeffer-Korpus (spoken language, *c.* 650,000); four Handbuchkorpora (*c.* 11 million); Limas-Korpus (1 million); Thomas-Mann-Korpus (*c.* 3.4 million); Goethe-Korpus (*c.* 1.4 million); Wendekorpus (*c.* 3.3 million); Marx-Korpus (*c.* 500,000). Further information can be obtained from Dr Irmtraud Jüttner, e-mail: juettner@ids-mannheim.de. In addition, see the chapter in this volume by Randall Jones. Many newspapers and journals are now

commercially available on CD-ROM, but those which incorporate pictures and graphics (such as *Der Spiegel*) may not be amenable to text-processing. Known projects involving building a corpus of German include a corpus of legal German at the University of Central Lancashire and a corpus of business and economics German (currently 500,000 words) at the University of Birmingham. The newly founded Institute for German Studies at the University of Birmingham will be building a bank of authentic machine-readable text from a variety of German sources.

3   See Durrell (1991, §§13.2.5a, 16.4.5a, 19.4.3), Durrell (1992: 214, 241) and Duden (1984: §§669, 1236).

10

Creating and Using a Corpus of Spoken German

RANDALL L. JONES

As a teacher of German I have long been interested in the relationship between the language contained in instructional materials and the language that is actually used in authentic situations
by native speakers. As I studied this relationship I soon became
aware of two interesting facts. First, much of the selection process
of vocabulary items used in American textbooks for the learning
of German is based on frequency lists, some dating back to the
last century. And second, it is very difficult to speak of *the* German
language when there are so many variations, ranging from local
dialects to very formal literary German. Many of the frequency
lists used in selecting vocabulary for German language instructional material are based on literature or newspaper texts, while
the goal of language learning is often to develop conversational
fluency.

Between the extremes of German dialects on the one hand and
the formal standard language on the other lies the vast territory
of colloquial German or *Umgangssprache*. This is the German language used by native speakers in most situations: in shops, business offices, restaurants, at the workplace, on the street, among
acquaintances, etc. It is the language used by the tourist from
Berlin when he visits Vienna, or the businesswoman from Freiburg
when she is in Hamburg. It reflects regional linguistic colouring
but it is comprehensible anywhere in the German-speaking world.
There is no standard *Umgangssprache* and there is no single grammar to describe it, but the numerous varieties seem to be mutu-
ally comprehensible. In my opinion the colloquial language or
Umgangssprache should serve as the model for at least some of the
vocabulary used in the German classroom.

As a graduate student I became aware of the work done by J. Alan Pfeffer with his Grunddeutsch project (Pfeffer and Lohnes 1984). In 1960–61 he recorded approximately 400 interviews with native speakers in the Federal Republic of Germany, the German Democratic Republic, Austria and Switzerland. The informants were carefully selected in order to reflect a rational sample of native speakers, the topics for the interviews were chosen from a list of approximately 25, and the recordings were all made under ideal conditions. The material in this corpus of spoken German became the basis for numerous publications dealing with the modern German language, especially vocabulary studies (Pfeffer 1970).

In the early 1980s Brigham Young University (BYU), Utah, obtained a computerized version of the spoken Grunddeutsch material. For several years it was accessible via a mainframe computer for use in German language research, and was later converted to a DOS ASCII format for use with the text retrieval program WordCruncher. As the age of the language in the Grunddeutsch Corpus began to approach thirty years, I began to be concerned about its currency. Language does not change significantly in that sort of time period, but changes do occur. For example, I was interested to find that nowhere in the Grunddeutsch Corpus did the word *Computer* occur, and there were very few occurrences of the word *Umwelt* (environment). There had been a great deal of social, political, technical, and demographic change in German-speaking countries during the period since 1960, and such changes often have a major impact on the language. I decided to work on a new corpus of spoken German, based on the Pfeffer model but with interviews that were current.

In the summer of 1989 I began the work in Austria, Switzerland and southern Germany. Most of the recordings in what was then the German Democratic Republic were done under the direction of Professor E. Hexelschneider, former director of the Herder Institute in Leipzig. (It will probably not escape the notice of the reader that the year 1989 was a year of significant political change in Eastern Europe. The first interviews in the GDR began in September of 1989, but the work was not completed until after the fall of the Berlin Wall in November of that year. Needless to say, these events had an effect on the content of some of the interviews in both parts of Germany.) The remainder of the recordings were done as time and funds would allow during the next three years. In some cities in Germany the local *Volkshochschule* (Adult Education

College) was kind enough to arrange for the interviewing. I was present at all other interviews, although they were conducted in all but a few cases by local native speakers.

The format for the new corpus is similar to that of the Grund-deutsch Corpus: approximately 400 interviews (totalling about 80 hours of speech) from 60 localities in Germany, Austria and Switzerland; consideration of demographic factors such as age, gender and educational background; interviews which last approximately twelve minutes and which are on a variety of topics such as family, school, work, leisure time, politics, etc.

Before a typical interview I would first spend a few minutes explaining to the person being interviewed about the nature of the project. We would discuss possible topics and select one that was comfortable to him or her. I would ask that they speak as naturally as possible, for example as though they were speaking to someone at a bus stop or on a train. There were no prescribed questions that were asked, just an informal beginning with a typical opening question such as, '*Würden Sie bitte etwas über*. . .' ('Would you please say something about. . .') or '*Erzählen Sie bitte*. . .' ('Please tell me . . .'). The interview – perhaps better described as the conversation – would then take its natural course. There was no attempt to restrict the conversation to the original topic or to move from one topic to another, except as would occur naturally. The interviewer might for example refer to something mentioned earlier in the conversation, then ask for additional information. Lavaliere microphones and a high-quality Sony cassette recorder were used to record the interviews. The beginning of a sample interview is illustrated in Figure 10.1.

The 400 interviews were transcribed using WordPerfect. The transcriber was a native speaker of German living in Provo. She was instructed to make a lexical transcription, i.e. ignore prosodic features as well as phonetic variations, unless they could be represented in conventional orthography. For example, the vowel in a word such as *ja* can be pronounced in a variety of ways, but the word was always written as *ja*. However, when distinct varieties of words were used, e.g. *ni, nich, nit, net, ne* for the word *nicht*, they were transcribed as such. Also, cases of apocope and syncope were recorded in words such as *ghabt* for *gehabt* and *hab* for *habe*. In the latter examples both the full lexical form as well as the actual form were recorded (*habe [hab]*) in order to have an accurate lexical frequency count.

BA02_Würzburg
ǀtF
ǀs1   Darf ich zunächst um deinen Namen bitten?
ǀtA
ǀs2   Inge W.
ǀtF
ǀs3   Und du kommst aus der Umgebung von Würzburg.
ǀs4   Wie heißt das Dorf noch, wo du herstammst?
ǀtA
ǀs5   Riedenheim.
ǀtF
ǀs6   Vielleicht könntest du etwas von dem Dorf erzählen oder von deinen Erinnerungen daran, wie du dort aufgewachsen bist.
ǀtA
ǀs7   Mhmh.
ǀs8   Mh ja Riedenheim, das ist ein Bauerndorf in Ochsen vor der Gau, und hat ungefähr sechshundert Einwohner, und die Bevölkerung ist also zu neunundneunzig Prozent katholisch, und auch das Dorfleben ist stark kirchlich geprägt, auch heute noch.
ǀs9   Und mh ja so wichtige Erlebnisse in der Kindheit waren dann auch die erste Kommunion und die Firmung, und uh ich ging auch die ersten paar Jahre im Dorf zur Schule, in die Volksschule, und dann mh – wir wurden später dann mit dem Bus in Nachbardörfer gebracht, wo wir dann abwechselnd zur Schule gingen.

Figure 10.1   (Beginning of) sample interview

As one might imagine, the transcriber made errors, especially with words and phrases not familiar to her. For example, in an interview that was conducted in Villach, Austria, the speaker used the word *Ringelspiel*, which is the common Austrian word for 'merry-go-round' or *Karussell*, as it is known in Germany. The transcriber was not familiar with the word and simply wrote *Regelspiel*, even though it didn't make any sense. In a second reading a native of Austria caught the error and corrected it. In other cases the first transcriber simply did not understand some words, and simply wrote a '*[?]*'. The second listener was able to make out some of these, but not all. I fear that even after numerous readings there will still be errors and words that were not comprehensible. That is the nature of working with spoken language.

The resulting corpus has about 600,000 running words. The files were indexed using WordCruncher, a text retrieval program developed at BYU. WordCruncher provides immediate access to words, lists of words, phrases, word combinations and parts of words in the indexed file. The retrieved information is presented in its context, which can be enlarged as needed. Figures 10.2 to 10.6

Is166   Uh Bibliotheksarbeit ist immer Sissifußarbeit, und unsere Aufsichtskräfte machen ja **neben** ihrer Aufsichtszeit auch noch Regaldienst, das heißt, sie gehen die Regale durch und schauen nach, welche Bücher verstellt sind und stellen die wieder an den Platz.   (BA03 Würzburg A: 166)

Is130   Und dann sagten Sie noch die Schweiz, glaube [glaub] ich, nicht, oder, **neben** Österreich?   (BD01 Nürnberg F: 130)

Is109   In der Schule **neben** meines Studiums, habe ich mich dann sehr schnell eines Besseren besonnen, und bin dann sehr schnell im Studium noch umgestiegen.   (BD06 Nürnberg A: 109)

Is41   Sie wissen ja, daß wir **neben** den Professoren Lehrbeauftragte haben, die stundenwise hier Unterricht halten.   (BJ03 Karlsruhe A: 41)

Is21   Das andere waren Bauern, die voll auf der Landwirtschaft waren [ware] oder noch ein [e] bissel **neben** [nebe] ihrer Berufstätigkeit her hatten [hatte]?
                                (BL03 Ludwigsburg F: 21)

Is70   Und dann trommelt er mit der Faust auf den Tisch **neben** dem Mikrophon {Husten}, und das was den Toningenieur auf die Barrikaden gebracht hat, uh wenn so was geschah, das war uns als Interviewer natürlich recht lieb.
                                (BM02 Tübingen A: 70)

Figure 10.2   Examples of *neben*

Is4   Vielleicht können wir damit beginnen, daß Sie uns etwas **über** Ihre Familie ezählen.   (BA01 Würzburg F: 4)
Is39   Aber wenn doch der gesundheitliche Zustand meinetwegen dann so schlecht wäre, daß sich der alte Mensch nicht mehr selbst bewegen kann, also aus'm Bett rauskommt, dann kommt er aber **in** diese andere Abteilung sicherlich?   (BA01 Würzburg F: 39)
Is71   Da ist man also **auf** die Hilfe von Ihnen, beziehungsweise Angehörigen angewiesen.   (BA01 Würzburg F: 71)
Is105   Freut sich also **über** Besuch wahrscheinlich, wenn Sie dann kommen, daß sie auch Unterhaltung hat?   (BA01 Würzburg F: 105)
Is128   Mir han –, **in** dem Alter hat man das [ma des] net so gemerkt.
                                (BA01 Würzburg A: 128)
Is8   Mh ja Riedenheim, das ist ein Bauerndorf im Ochsen **vor** der Gau, und hat ungefähr sechshundert Einwohner, und die Bevölkerung ist also zu neunundneuzig Prozent katholisch, und auch das Dorfleben ist stark kirchlich geprägt, auch heute noch.   (BA02 Würzburg A: 8)

Figure 10.3   Examples òf Accusative/Dative Prepositions

illustrate the results of searching for the German preposition *neben,* the nine German accusative/dative prepositions, the phrase *von mir aus,* various forms of the verb *werden* but only if it occurs with *von, mit* or *durch* in the same context, and the suffix *-mäßig.*

ls160   Und wenn ich den eben haben will, dann werde [werd] ich schon selber **von mir aus** den ersten Schritt tun müssen, indem ich den Leuten zum Beispiel sage, daß ich irgendetwas sprechen kann in ihrer Sprache, und sei es noch so falsch.
(BM01 Tübingen A: 60)

ls78   Ich kann, **von mir aus**, wenn mal eine ['ne] Kette runtergesprungen ist order mal einen ['nen] Reifen wechseln oder so was, solche Kleinigkeiten.
(BM04 Tübingen A: 78)

ls62   Im Gegenteil also ich kann das **von mir aus** sagen, ich habe [hab] eine nette Nachbarin, die immer uh auf meine Katze aufpaßt, wenn ich verreise, und die füttert.   (BS06 Frankfurt A: 62)
ls110   Ich meine [mein], ein Autor wise Grass und andere können ja frei schalten und walten, und **von mir aus** uh Sätze bilden.   (BS10 Frankfurt F: 110)

ls12   Aber **von mir aus** hätte es [hätt's] nicht sofort eine Wiedervereinigung geben müssen, also in dem Punkt ja kann ich mich leider nicht anschließen.
(RC08 Bonn A1: 12)

ls36   Ja, aber wie gesagt, Wiedervereinigung, **von mir aus**, hätte [hätt] sie nicht unbedingt sein müssen.   (RC08 Bonn A1: 36)

Figure 10.4   Examples of *von mir aus*

ls31   Daß sich das [des] einmal ändern mußte, das war schon vorauszusehen, aber der Zeitpunkt jetzt, also wie das jetzt 1989, glaube ich nicht, daß der von irgendjemand **vorausgesehen wurde**.   (BD05 Nürnberg A: 31)

ls75   Uh, würden Sie sagen, daß uh ihre politischen Grundauffassungen von den großen Parteien auch immer **berücksichtigt werden?**
(BD05 Nürnberg F: 75)

ls51   Uh, doch, notgedrungen **wurde** ich von meinen Eltern zum Reiten, zum Balletunterricht, in diverse Sportgruppen **geschickt**.   (BD06 Nürnberg A: 51)

ls164   Der Posteinlauf, der **wird** auch von mir **erledigt**.
(BE07 München A: 64)

ls84   Also bisher gab es uh eigentlich, ja das einzig größere Kollektiv, was **untersucht wurde**, waren die Opfer von Hiroschima und Nagasaki.
(BH04 Freiburg A: 84)

ls106   Es **werden** einem uh Fragebögen **zugeschickt** mit je sechzig Fragen, nee?   (BE04 München A: 106)

Figure 10.5   Examples of passive voice

Even though the corpus is not yet in final form, it is still very usable and has already provided much valuable information for me as well as for students and colleagues at Brigham Young University and elsewhere. In the remainder of the chapter I would like to describe briefly some of the applications.

Is4   Altersmäßig, oder spielt das keine Rolle?   (BT05 Gießen A: 4)
Is149   Und zwar hatten die an ihren Häusern, die haben so Torbogen gehabt, und das ging dann so, so fächermäßig so, nicht, und wo diese Rundbogen oben so waren.   (RK08 Braunschweig A: 149)
Is151   Und mich mit, nicht nur mit der Geschicklichkeit nur, mit der Fähigkeit öh, also jetzt bewegungsmäßig was umzusetzen, und ja dann auch ja mit Leuten was zusammen zu machen, nö?   (RM04 Göttingen A: 151)
Is129   Ich werde [werd] bald eine Funktion haben, die mich arbeitsmäßig auch ausfüllen wird, und in so fern äh bin ich also mit dieser, mit diesem Ergebnis zufrieden.   (RN05 Hannover A: 129)
Is33   Das Arbeitsamt hat mir angeboten, eine {'ne} Umschulung als Stenokontoristin, das ist für mich ein Job, ich kenn den Job so im Einzelnen nicht, aber äh unterqualifiziert also so abschiebemäßig [?] mach was, [?].   (RP06 Berlin-W A: 33)
Is91   Und des weiteren auch berufsmäßig mit eingeflossen die Malerei.   (DI01 Wismar A: 91)

Figure 10.6   Examples of words with -*mäßig* as suffix

I have long been interested in German word frequency. However, all frequency lists that I am familiar with have significant limitations. Either they are based on written material, or they have problems with lemmatization and disambiguation, or they do not provide adequate information about the function of the words in the list. If the word *denn* appears high on a frequency list it usually isn't clear whether it is a conjunction or a modal particle. The word *liebe* can be a verb form, an adjective or, if capitalization is ignored, a noun. Unfortunately, the BYU Spoken German Corpus does not have the tools to do an automatic grammatical and semantic analysis of all words, but it does provide the necessary information to make such an analysis a much simpler task. Figure 10.7 shows a lemmatized word frequency list based on the corpus. The entry *sein* for example represents all forms of the verb *sein*, i.e. *bin, bist, ist, sind, gewesen*, etc. This was easily accomplished by adding up the frequency of the various forms. The entry *denn*, on the other hand, represents examples of both the conjunction and the modal particle. In order to distinguish between the two it will be necessary to analyse each case individually. The frequency list in Figure 10.7 thus represents an intermediate stage.

Even without further refinement the word frequency list contains quite a bit of interesting information. Note, for example, that the indefinite personal pronoun *man* appears in 15th position, ahead of such common words as *aber* and *oder*. Many American

Rank	Frequency	Word	Rank	Frequency	Word
1	58320	die/der	36	3217	dies-
2	52573	er/sie	37	3063	sagen
3	27082	sein	38	2943	müssen
4	25184	und	39	2836	auf
5	15392	haben	40	2788	mal
6	15113	ja	41	2712	an
7	14335	ein-	42	2673	als
8	11357	in	43	2583	eigentlich
9	10308	so	44	2444	hier
10	10218	auch	45	2431	weil
11	9674	also	46	2299	geben
12	8953	nicht	47	2289	all-
13	8682	dann	48	2191	Jahr
14	8460	da	49	2175	immer
15	6552	man	50	2137	zum
16	5941	daß	51	2124	eben
17	5730	zu	52	2062	ganz
18	5622	was	53	1935	mehr
19	5330	mit	54	1883	aus
20	5248	oder	55	1874	bei
21	4806	aber	56	1849	nur
22	4280	werden	57	1793	nach
23	4242	können	58	1686	halt
24	4046	wie	59	1678	viel
25	4009	machen	60	1651	wo
26	3971	jetzt	61	1590	ander-
27	3966	im	62	1499	gut
28	3940	von	63	1376	doch
29	3906	noch	64	1345	natürlich
30	3883	sehr	65	1331	wissen
31	3708	für	66	1311	wieder
32	3692	sich	67	1307	denn
33	3614	mein-	68	1284	vielleicht
34	3464	wenn	69	1280	über
35	3324	schon	70	1271	Kind

Figure 10.7   Lemmatized frequency list: first 70

textbooks for the learning of German treat *man* superficially, if at all, yet it is one of the most commonly used words in colloquial German. Another interesting observation is the high frequency of particles such as *eigentlich, mal, eben, halt* and *doch*. These are rarely used in the written language, and therefore do not appear in frequency lists based on literature or journalism. Yet they do occur with high frequency in the colloquial language, together with numerous other similar particles.

One of the most fruitful applications I have experienced with the BYU Spoken German Corpus has been with students in seminars dealing with modern colloquial German. At the beginning of the seminar we discuss differences between written and spoken German, as well as between dialects, formal spoken German and *Umgangssprache*. Students are assigned to read selections of German literature and newspapers, then to watch German television (*Deutsche Welle*) and listen to a recording of one of the interviews made for the spoken corpus. They are to make notes of the differences between spoken and written German. They are then assigned to analyse a printed version of an interview, looking for such features as the use of modal particles, hesitation words, *Ausklammerung*, passive voice, subjunctive mood, future tense, the indefinite pronoun *man*, syncope and apocope (especially in verb forms), repetition of words, incomplete sentences, sentence repair and grammatical errors. They then listen to the recording of the same interview and find that in real time most of these features pass by them without being noticed.

The remainder of the semester is spent using the corpus with WordCruncher in order to analyse a variety of words and phrases. The corpus is available to students in the student computer lab through the college network. At first all of the students are given the same assignment, which is usually a single word. They make an analysis of the word as it occurs in the corpus, then compare that analysis with a German–English dictionary, a standard German reference grammar and with a beginning and intermediate textbook for learning German. Often the results are quite revealing. Students have found grammatical functions of words that are sometimes not explained in reference grammars. In all cases it is useful to learn the relative frequency of the various functions of the word. For example, the verb *werden* has the lexical meaning 'to become', it is an auxiliary verb used in forming the future tense, it is an auxiliary verb used in forming the passive voice, and it is commonly used in its subjunctive form – *würden* – plus an infinitive as a substitute for a conjugated subjunctive verb. All of this information is found in reference grammars, but what is not found is the relative frequency of each function. In the BYU Spoken German Corpus the use of *werden* with the passive voice constitutes almost 50 per cent of the cases.

Perhaps even more revealing is a study of the German prepositions that can be used with either the accusative or dative case. Students learn very early that there is a simple rule which can assist them in deciding when to use which case. By examining examples in authentic speech, however, it is soon learned that the rule is usually not terribly useful. Most examples provided in text-books show spatial relationships: *Die Lampe steht **neben** dem Tisch. Das Auto steht **hinter** dem Haus. Das Kind wartet **vor** der Schule.* In real language these prepositions are most commonly used in figurative meanings: *Was ist denn **neben** Deutsch dein zweites Fach? Also zwei Wochen haben wir schon **hinter** uns. Doch, **vor** allem im Sportverein sind die Jugendlichen immer noch stark engagiert.* Again, students are able to calculate the relative frequency of each meaning.

As was mentioned earlier, colloquial spoken German contains a high number of modal particles, e.g. *denn, doch, eben, eigentlich, halt, ja, mal, wohl, zwar,* etc. It is very difficult to give a translation for these words, and most reference grammars only begin to discuss their complicated use in the language. By analysing a spoken corpus, however, students are able to develop a better feel for their function in the language and how to use them correctly. Students have learned that in most cases these particles may be left out without altering the basic meaning of the sentence. However, their use definitely does carry some meaning, even though it cannot be translated easily. They are sometimes referred to as 'flavouring particles', suggesting that without them the language is a bit less savoury.

Towards the end of the semester students broaden their perspective and study larger topics, e.g. the difference between modal verbs in expressing possibility as in *das könnte sein, das kann sein, das mag sein, das dürfte sein, das müsste sein,* etc. One student is studying the use of the genitive case by searching for the genitive prepositions as well as genitive determiners such as *des, eines, meines,* etc. The use of the grammatical future tense with the verb *werden* as opposed to the use of the present tense to express the future has also become an interesting topic. By searching for forms of *werden,* examples of the grammatical future can be located. By searching for time adverbials such as *morgen, nächste Woche, bald,* etc., examples of the present tense expressing the future can be found, e.g. *Nächste Woche fahren wir nach Berlin; Bald bin ich mit dem Studium fertig.* It is important to point out that for certain kinds of searches WordCruncher has limitations. It will often find only some of the desired examples and frequently it will find more than is needed. It is a tool that can be used to retrieve data which then must be refined by the user. What it can do it does extremely fast, usually in less than a second. When compared to a manual search of 400 interviews for examples of one or more words there is no question that it saves a great deal of time. The user must be prepared to make his or her contribution by continuing the analysis.

A collection of authentic speech examples such as the BYU Spoken German Corpus can be a valuable tool for studying colloquial German. With approximately 600,000 words it is a relatively small sample, and the fact that the language was elicited in the context of an interview restricts somewhat how it reflects modern spoken German in general, but overall it is probably a good sample. In addition to its use for studying individual words and phrases it can be used to make comparisons of language among the speakers, e.g. male vs female, north vs south, younger generation vs older generation. Together with the Grunddeutsch Corpus it can be used to compare German of the early 1960s with German of the early 1990s. My observation has been that only recently has *Umgangssprache* been the object of serious linguistic study. With a collection of speech samples and a useful computer text retrieval program the door to future studies should be wide open.

11

The Role of Corpora in Studying and Promoting Welsh

KHURSHID AHMAD AND ANDREA DAVIES

1 Introduction

The Welsh language is currently enjoying a revival. There are dictionaries and written grammars of Welsh that are used in the teaching and learning of the language, but a typical learner of Welsh does not appear to have ready access to the many different ways the language is used, for example, in newspapers, in magazines, in scientific journals, and so on. The compilation of Welsh dictionaries and written grammars relies extensively on hand-crafted phrases and sentences rather than on authentic naturally occurring data. It is now possible, especially as a result of developments in corpus linguistics and in software engineering, for a large number of teachers and learners to use text corpora to understand what is acceptable to other speakers and writers of Welsh at a given time or what is acceptable to them when, for example, they write scientific texts, describe historical events, talk about politics, and so on.

Welsh, a lesser-used language, is regarded by many as the everyday language of particular and well-defined communities and has an extensive textual heritage, dominated by literary and religious texts. There are newspapers, youth magazines, scientific and technical journals, bilingual official documentation (Welsh–English), road signs in Welsh, Welsh as the medium of instruction in primary schools, and the acceptance of Welsh by the legal establishment in Wales. The compilation of an *OED*-on-historical-principles equivalent for Welsh, *Geiriadur Prifysgol Cymru* (1987) ('Dictionary [of the] University of Wales') and an initiative for organizing a corpus of contemporary Welsh texts and for building an electronic lexicon for Welsh, will certainly help in the creation of an infrastructure for promoting Welsh as a language.

An infrastructure for a language can be specified at a number of linguistic levels, for example, at the level of vocabulary, grammar, semantics and pragmatics. The vocabulary infrastructure includes the provision of dictionaries, both historical and contemporary, as well as term banks. The grammar infrastructure requires access to a contemporaneous description of the language, in other words, a record that reflects the usage of the language among the community, balanced by the view of the grammarians and other language experts. At the semantic level, the requirement is to access and disseminate neologisms, lexical semantic relationships, and semantic field data that are idiosyncratic to the language. The pragmatic infrastructure concerns the data related to the current and preponderant vocabulary and grammatical resources of the language across the social divides, and indeed data related to the arcane, obsolete and less frequently used items in the repertoire of the language.

The advent of machine-readable text corpora on networked computers will help to free authors and readers from the tyranny of paper-based methods of information dissemination. Machine-readable texts cover the entire spectrum of texts, from ephemeral text fragments to literary landmarks, and from myth and legend texts to scientific and technical texts. This has eased the logistic bottleneck faced by the writers and readers who use English. The distribution of machine-readable texts then depends on the availability of computer networks and there is talk of transmitting texts through satellite links. The texts can be reproduced almost indefinitely.

Here is an opportunity for Welsh: not only is there an enthusiastic people involved in enriching the textual heritage of their language, an electronic means for disseminating this heritage is also available. There are two important uses of this textual heritage. First, it can provide the raw material for building a useful corpus of texts that can be used for creating dictionaries and written grammars that reflect the state of Welsh as it is used by its speakers and writers. Second, textual heritage can be used in the creation of terminology data banks, especially by examining the ways and means in which authors of scientific and technical texts have harnessed the lexicogrammatical resources of Welsh to create neologisms that either increase the population of loan words in Welsh or use an extant word in an entirely different manner. In the long term, it is possible to envisage a situation where children and second-language learners of Welsh are being routinely asked to explore a text corpus for investigating aspects of vocabulary, facets of grammar, semantic constraints and pragmatic conventions of Welsh.

In this chapter[1] we elaborate on these two major uses of the textual heritage of Welsh, showing how methods and techniques of corpus-linguistics can be used for enriching dictionaries and written grammars, and for constructing terminology data banks.

2 Welsh grammar and lexicography

Recent developments in English lexicography and grammar can be compared with those in Welsh, to which we return below. Recent methods chosen to codify English stress that language is not a uniform whole and that it is continuously changing. Synchronically, differences manifest themselves across the varieties of English, across registers and so on. Diachronically, changes are indicated by the renewal of the stock of words and phrases in English (e.g. neologisms, borrowings), and the rejection of other sets of words and phrases. Acceptability is therefore relative to social, regional and chronological factors.

Quirk *et al.* (1985), in *A Comprehensive Grammar of the English Language,* have argued that the 'assessments by native speakers [of British and American English] of relative acceptability largely correlate with their assessments of relative frequency' (1985: 33). In addition to the native-speaker assessments, Quirk *et al.* have also drawn on data related to 'the frequencies of language phenomena' based on their analysis of three major corpora of the English language: the Survey of English Usage, the Brown University Corpus and the parallel Lancaster–Oslo/Bergen Corpus. Geoffrey Nunberg's introduction to 'usage notes' in the *American Heritage Dictionary* (1992) refers to the crucial role of the *AHD*'s usage panel, a body of 173 leading academics, writers and public speakers who comment on how a given word in the dictionary should be used. The *AHD* records the differences between the members of the panel by recording a voting figure for those in favour of a given usage and those against it. John Sinclair, in his introduction to the *Collins Cobuild English Language Dictionary*, supports the 'noble tradition in lexicography', founded by Dr Johnson and Murray, of using citation from *actual* texts, and he has criticized the use of the 'made-up' examples in traditional dictionaries: 'These examples have no authority apart from the thoughts of the person who creates them and they are quite often unnatural' (*Cobuild Dictionary*: xv).

The use of corpora and native-speaker assessment may have been motivated in English by its international nature, its status as the language of science and technology, its position as the main language of the United Nations and the European Union, and its dominant position as the language used in international litigation and patent law. But what the frequency studies cited above, often supported by text and speech corpora, are stressing are the twin notions of acceptability and frequency, and above all what is acceptable to some or most of the native-speakers and writers of a language. The teachers, the learners, and the promoters of a language have to be aware of, and indeed themselves decide, what words, phrases and grammatical constructs are central, and which of them are marginal to the speech and writing of the language community.

The discussion of grammatical categories and features of words and phrases in Welsh, although quite detailed, and often peppered with references to regional variation in Welsh, references to literary Welsh and so on, appears to be intuitive and introspective. We look at the citations in four grammatical texts in Welsh: Awbery (1976), Jones and Thomas (1977), Williams (1980) and King (1993). The authors rely extensively on introspection and intuition when they make judgements about the Welsh language. There are no references to native-speaker assessments or to any modern Welsh text. The text used most widely is the Welsh Bible and there are no citations of newspaper or magazine texts or references to scientific or technical texts.

This is not to say that there is no tradition of using native-speaker assessment and corpora in other areas of Welsh language studies, particularly sociolinguistics and clinical linguistics. Perhaps, due to the very nature of their work, the sociolinguists and the clinical linguists have to collect and analyse speech and text fragments from language users at large, rather than rely on their own linguistic intuition.

2.1 Theoretical studies of Welsh

2.1.1 Awbery's treatment of voice in Welsh

Awbery (1976) discusses passive sentences in Welsh within the transformationalist paradigm proposed by Chomsky (1965). Her emphasis is on relating passive sentences to other constructions in Welsh: 'The rules which appear in the derivation of the passive, with the exception of the rule removing the subject of the embedding, are also required in the derivation of other forms' (1976: 221). She discusses a variety of 'phrases and sentences' in order to highlight the transformational properties of the active and passive sentences. She appears to rely either on informants who are linguists working in related areas (not necessarily Welsh) or 'from the intuitions of my Welsh-speaking friends and relations' (1976: vii).

Awbery concludes her discussion of active sentences by remarking that there is 'a lack of simple tie-up between semantics and syntax' (1976: 46). She cites about 97 phrases and sentences, over 40 of which relate to the description of 'a man (with a stick)' and 'a (disappearing) dog', while the other 40 sentences/phrases relate to a 'girl reading a book' or a 'book being lent or borrowed'. The overall vocabulary in these sentences/phrases is less than 100 words, not counting inflected verbs and noun plurals or proper nouns. It is instructive to note here that Jan Svartvik compiled a corpus of over 300,000 English words, made up of eight texts in five genres, including both speech and writing, to point out that passive constructs in English cannot just be regarded as simple transforms of active sentences. Furthermore, Svartvik shows systematic and statistically plausible differences between non-agentive and agentive passives in English (see Svartvik 1966).

2.1.2 Jones and Thomas' study of Welsh syntax and semantics

Morris Jones and Alan Thomas' study of the syntax and semantics of Welsh distinguishes between 'formal written Welsh' and 'spontaneous speech' systematically throughout their Chomsky-inspired description of Welsh syntax which is 'primarily concerned with categorical matters and transformational possibilities' (1977: 6). The authors comment on dialect variation and its influence on Welsh syntax. The work contains a useful appendix on exemplar inflected verbal forms that describes 'traditional written', and 'northern' and 'southern spontaneous spoken' variants of the verb inflection *mae* ('is'), and paradigms for 'traditionally written' and 'spontaneously spoken' commonly used verb inflections like *oedd* ('was'), *bu* ('was'), *buasai/byddai* ('would be'), etc. However, it is not clear who the informants are or whether or not a corpus of relevant (representative) texts was used: the references at the end of the book are mainly on transformational grammar.

Despite the apparent paucity of data relating to the acceptability of grammatical categories, Jones and Thomas appear quite certain about the stylistic usage of certain grammatical categories in Welsh. The authors, for example, talk about the 'stylistic usage of pre-sentential particles'. A particle, according to Jones and Thomas, is determined by the stylistic context, especially when usage in 'spontaneous spoken Welsh' is contrasted with 'traditional written Welsh'; they conclude that the preverbal particle is eliminated in the spoken language. This may be true, but we are presented with no evidence here. For example, are the authors suggesting that this is the case for all the regional variants? If this is the case, then the elimination of the preverbal particle may be deemed as an important feature of standard Welsh.

2.1.3   Williams' study of Welsh grammar

Williams' study of Welsh grammar (1980) is exhaustive with regard to various parts of speech and considers the effects of the Welsh orthography reforms of the late nineteenth and early twentieth century. It is aimed at readers 'desiring to become acquainted with standard literary Welsh'. Williams' examples comprise colloquial and dialect words and expressions in order either to compare 'spoken and written forms' or to 'draw attention to debased colloquial usages' (1980: v).

Williams relies extensively on introspection on the one hand and, on the other, refers to over 40 works in Welsh, including the Bible, hymns and songbooks and classic Welsh written grammars (*c.* 1909–60). The most recent of his citations is a Bible translation by Henry Lewis – *Yr argraffiad newydd o'r Beibl* (1955) – and a hymn book, *Y Caniedydd* (1960). There are no citations explicitly quoted from post-1950 literature.

However, this does not appear to deter Williams from making judgements of acceptability concerning current usage. For instance, while discussing the verb *cael* in the context of the verb–noun category in Welsh, he suggests that 'the use of *cael* with the verb–noun to express the possessive is shunned by the best writers if possible' (1980: 119). This may indeed be the case in post-1950s Welsh literary texts, but a citation from post-1950s literature will be more convincing here than introspection.

2.1.4   King's treatment of verbs

Gareth King's grammar (1993) covers typical grammatical categories like articles, verbs, prepositions, etc., together with a brief section on complex sentences and a note on English words which may pose particular translation problems. His work is prefaced by a description of the Welsh mutation system with the focus on differences of usage in northern and southern Welsh dialects, together with a brief commentary on Welsh word order and sentence structure. King's treatment of Welsh grammar is substantially more detailed than the other grammars we have referred to and the bibliography covers some recent work on Welsh verbs and mutations together with some classical references like Rowland's grammar (1876) and Fynes-Clinton's treatment of the vocabulary of the Bangor district (1913).

King distinguishes between 'literary' and 'written' Welsh (1993: 3). His remarks on literary Welsh are not kind; he regards literary Welsh as an 'artificial' form of Welsh (1993: 3). In contrast, he claims that his grammar describes 'for the most part written colloquial Welsh' (*ibid.*). King goes on to further distinguish between the Welsh used in his grammar and that of standardized colloquial grammar which is regarded by some in Wales controversially as *Cymraeg Byw* ('Living Welsh'). King does not elaborate on, for example, linguistic differences between literary Welsh and living Welsh. His comments on variants of Welsh notwithstanding, the examples in the grammar are sentences which reflect modern-day reality, such as *(Fe) glywes i'r newyddion ar y radio bore 'ma* ('I heard the news on the radio this morning') (1993: 138) and *Mae llaeth yn yr oergell* ('There is milk in the refrigerator') (1993: 144). There are a number of paradigm tables used to illustrate the use of words that belong to different grammatical categories: for nouns there are paradigms for number and gender and there are inflectional paradigms for the tenses of verbs. There are a number of paradigm tables for what is perhaps the most frequently encountered verb in Welsh – *bod* ('to be') – with variations on fields of meaning like *identification, existence* and *description*. King uses no less than 11 paradigm tables and 163 sentences to illustrate the use of *bod* but like his peers – Awbery (1976), Jones and Thomas (1977) and Williams (1980) – we are not given the source of his examples. Some are distinctly artificial examples such as *Mae'r teigr yn yr ardd* ('The tiger is in the garden') (1993: 162) while others have been devised to illustrate comparative uses of the verb 'to be' in English and Welsh. Furthermore, the distinction is not made between what one might encounter in speech as opposed to written text (cf. King's examples of elliptical constructs such as *Fydd dim geiriaduron 'da chi* – 'You won't have (any) dictionaries').

2.2   Empirical studies of speakers in Welsh

Although there are no examples of the use of corpora in the description of Welsh grammar, the situation with regard to other aspects of the Welsh language is somewhat different. Ball (1988) has produced an edited collection of papers in sociolinguistic, dialectal and clinical linguistic topics specific to Welsh. These papers refer to field data that includes, for instance, the linguistic output of adults on radio and television, the linguistic output of language-disordered children in clinical situations, and linguistic output collected for studying child language development. These studies are described briefly below.

Ball *et al.* (1988) have analysed a news bulletin, a religious broadcast, and a popular music-and-chat programme, with a view to studying language variation by looking at three linguistic variables: nasal mutation after *yn* ('in'), the aspirate or spirant mutation, and the use of personal pronouns. The authors conclude by remarking that 'on radio, the type of Welsh used varies in much the same way as styles of Welsh vary in the speech community' (1988: 198) and that 'radio Welsh is not [...] an externally imposed variety that native speakers cannot understand' (1988: 190). The authors report that they have 'listened' to the tape recordings of these programmes.

There are a number of studies of Welsh dialects also reported in Ball (1988) that are based on the analysis of tape recordings from carefully selected groups of speakers of Welsh. One can also see some evidence of the use of introspection, references to the works of well-known sociolinguists such as William Labov, and one can argue about the lack of details concerning experimental and analytical methods. Furthermore, one-hour speech samples are perhaps rather short. It would also be useful if the transcripts of the speech samples or the raw input to the questionnaires were available to colleagues studying Welsh. However, one cannot doubt the objective nature of these studies in that the experimental data is field data, not data based on what the author thinks or wishes the language to be. It is easier to separate *comments* from *facts* in a field-based study, than in a purely intuitive, introspective and limited-data theorization.

Hatton's questionnaire-based study (1988) of the development of the nasal mutation among schoolchildren is perhaps more quantitative and closer to the current notion of using corpora. The author indicates that this developmental study was based on the output of 26 schoolchildren in the Swansea area over a period of two years – 1978 to 1980. There are two major conclusions in Hatton's paper. First, 'mutating in some situations is more established than in others' (1988: 256). Second, 'the development in the use of the nasal mutation between the ages of seven and eleven is indisputable' (1988: 256).

Munro (1988) has studied phonological disorders among Welsh-speaking children, and has produced 'complete phonemic inventories' of two children.

The above examples of work from fields as diverse as sociolinguistics, clinical linguistics and language development show that archiving language samples, and subsequently analysing these samples, can be undertaken.

3   An account of the Surrey Welsh corpora: their creation and uses

In this section we demonstrate how corpora of general and special language can be used to create language resources easily and efficiently. The role of *representative* and *contemporary* corpora has been cited as a major one in the development of dictionaries, especially learners' dictionaries (see for instance, Cobuild and Rundell and Stock 1992).

3.1   The Surrey Welsh corpora

We are currently developing special and general-language corpora of Welsh[2] that can be used to explore models of language and language usage, and to produce language resources (Ahmad and Davies 1992a). The general-language corpus comprises approximately 200,000 words of contemporary text, while the special-language corpus has approximately 60,000 words from the domains of science and technology. We regard our general-language corpus as contemporary in that the texts in the corpus were published during the period 1968–92. The special-language corpus covers roughly the same period.

The general-language corpus has five different text types: advertisements, books, magazines, newspapers and official documentation. For the special-language corpus, two additional text types have been incorporated, namely journals and manuals. The special-language texts include extracts from textbooks in Welsh published by the Welsh Joint Education Committee and papers on radiochemistry by Jones (1985).

The design of our Welsh corpora of special- and general-language texts is similar to that of various corpora of English outlined in Aijmer and Altenberg (1991: 315–18). Our coverage is not exhaustive, and the selection of text is partly intuitive. The intention is to demonstrate what can be achieved with what would be regarded as two small corpora totalling 260,000 words in a world of 20 million, 30 million, or now, 100 million word corpora.

3.2   Analysis of general-language texts in Surrey's Welsh Corpus: preliminary results

A word frequency list of a general-language corpus of Welsh created at Surrey (comprising approximately 200,000 words) showed that the 25 highest frequency words are overwhelmingly closed class words. An analysis of the Lancaster–Oslo/Bergen (LOB) general-language corpus of British English (Johansson and Hofland 1989) shows that similar results are to be found in English. An analysis of the contexts of the closed class words in Welsh shows that they occur very frequently in phrases and collocations and are worthy of extensive coverage in dictionaries. Figure 11.1 shows a selection of phrases which incorporate the closed class verb[3] *cael*

Welsh Phrase	English Equivalent
ar gael	available
cael a chael	touch and go
cael amcan	have a (rough) idea
cael blaenoriaeth	take precedence
cael cip	glimpse
cael cyfle	have the opportunity
cael digon	have enough
cael dylanwad	influence
cael gafael ar	get hold of
cael gair gyda	have a word with
cael gwared o	get rid of
cael hen ddigon ar	be fed up with

Figure 11.1   Selection of phrases which include the high-frequency closed class verb *cael* ('to have')

('to have') and its inflections, of which there are 1191 instances in the corpus.

In the concordance from which the phrases were taken, 1191 was the absolute frequency of the verb *cael*. Of the sample in Figure 11.1, only *cael a chael* and *ar gael* can be found in the Welsh/English part of the Welsh dictionary *Y Geiriadur Mawr* (1986). Similarly, it was found that many of the other phrases are not documented in this and other standard Welsh dictionaries.

Evidence to support the claim that corpora can enrich language resources can be found by comparing information stored within entries of the University of Wales's *Geiriadur Prifysgol Cymru* ('Dictionary of [the] University of Wales') with information gleaned from a concordance of Surrey's general-language corpus. We take the word *iaith* ('language') as an example. In the *Geiriadur* ('Dictionary', Vol. II, 1987), nearly a whole page is dedicated to the word *iaith* and its associated information (definition, collocational information, etc.). *Iaith* occurs 266 times in Surrey's Welsh general-language corpus. A comparison of the dictionary entry and the 266 concordanced instances of *iaith* in Surrey's Corpus shows that there are several facets of the word which have not been covered by the dictionary, despite its extensive coverage of the word. The collocations of *iaith* are particularly interesting; for instance, the phrase *trwy gyfrwng ei briod iaith* subsumes two collocations: *priod iaith* ('main language') and *trwy gyfrwng iaith* ('by means of language'), neither of which is included in the dictionary. Both collocations are used frequently but, while the collocation *priod iaith* may be created by a language learner by analogy with *ail iaith* ('second language'), *mamiaith* ('mother tongue'), etc., the collocation *trwy gyfrwng iaith* is not so easily inferred.

3.3   The creation of a special-language terminology

The pedagogic overheads of teaching and learning science and technology in a second, or in some cases third language, are considerable. This is especially true of the children learning the methods and techniques of science at a formative age. The child has to deal not only with the complexities of abstract concepts and novel artefacts, but also has to understand a language which might be typologically different from his or her first language.

Moreover, the teaching of science and technology in a second language creates an impression that the first language has somehow a *lower status*. So, while the first language helps the learner to talk to grandparents and to talk about everyday things, when it comes to things like high-technology artefacts, the first language is unable to cope.

The twin overheads of pedagogy-related and status-related problems that may impede the growth of a language can be overcome by encouraging the scientists and the technologists of the language community to write about their disciplines in their first language. The teaching of science and technology in the European Union and the former Soviet Union relies to an extent on translating texts from English into the respective first languages. However, this was made possible by substantial investment in subjects like language for special-purposes, technical writing, translation studies and documentation. This investment included support for technical dictionaries and terminology data banks. This investment was channelled through the national standards organizations and terminology associations and there is substantial private sector interest in such dictionaries and terminology data banks. The existence of multilingual terminology data banks, essentially electronic lexica in which the emphasis is on the semantics of the lexical entries (e.g. synonyms, antonyms, hyponyms) and various pragmatic aspects like language variety, encourages not only the translation of documents but also for scientists to coin terms in their own language. Terminology data banks can facilitate the teaching and learning of science and technology.

There is a substantial literature in science and technology in Welsh and terminologies have been compiled in a range of subjects.[4] However, the compilation of terminologies is costly: it has been estimated that the cost of acquiring and elaborating each term can be as much as 1000 ECU.

Corpus-based methods can be of help here. Scientific texts have a distinct texture when compared with general-language text: there is a profusion of nominals, relatively more passives, more plurals, fewer pronouns and shorter sentences, when compared with newspaper text, works of fiction, magazine texts, and so on. And, scientific and technical texts contain neologisms. Therefore, the comparison of the frequency-ordered list of words in a scientific text with, say, a list of words from a corpus of general-language texts, can be used to find neologisms and other terms. An alphabetically ordered concordance of scientific texts will reveal the grammatical environment of terms.

We have created a prototype dictionary of radiochemistry in Welsh, comprising 200 entries, from a text of 7660 words in Welsh and its English equivalent. The prototype Welsh/English dictionary of radiochemistry was created with a view to demonstrating the speed with which specialist dictionaries can be compiled using machine-readable corpora of specialist text.

As a first step, John R. Jones's text *Cemegion Ymbelydrol* (1985) was rendered machine-readable using an optical character reader. System Quirk, a text and terminology management system developed at the University of Surrey (Holmes-Higgin *et al.* 1993), was then used to semi-automatically identify term candidates in the text. The system can be used to compute the *ratio* of the relative frequency of the words in the special-language text and its relative frequency in a general-language corpus of the user's choice. The computed *ratio* of a given word is defined as the relative frequency of that word in the special-language text (or text corpus) divided by its relative frequency in the general-language corpus. So, for instance, if the Welsh word *cemeg* ('chemistry') has a relative frequency of 1.4 in the general-language corpus and a relative frequency of 0.05 in the special-language corpus, the ratio of the word *cemeg* is: 1.4/0.05, or 28. The higher the ratio of a word, the more likely it is that the word is a term candidate. System Quirk can also produce concordances, word lists, collocations, and can be used to configure corpora according to user-defined text typologies.

amledd radio
domain: Chem
grammar: NOUN + ADJ masc
abbrev: rf. RF (enGB00003)
English Definition: A frequency between 3 kilohertz and 300 gigahertz.
(enGB00003)
bib ref: cyGB00001
context: Cynhyrchir yr ymbelydredd gan osgiladur o amledd radio ac mae'n
taro'r sampl a astudir, sydd gan amlaf yn bresennol ar ffurf hylif.
English: radio frequency (enGB00001)
bas (basau)
domain: Chem
grammar: NOUN masc
Welsh Definition: Sylwedd cemegol. (cyGB00004)
English Definition: A chemical compound that combines with an acid to form
a salt and water. (enGB00003)
bib ref: cyGB00001
context: Medr asid, bas, metel neu oleuni weithredu fel catalydd i'r adwaith yma.
English: base

Figure 11.2   Typical entries of terms in the Welsh/English term bank
of radiochemistry

adwaith – reaction	defnydd elfennol – elementary
amledd radio – radio frequency	substance
asid amino – amino acid	dylif magnetig – magnetic flux
bioleg folecylaidd – molecular biology	hydrid metel – metal hydride
bromoethan – ethyl bromide	nitradiad – nitration
cemegion ymbelydrol – radio chemicals	nwy tritiwm – tritium gas
cyseiniant magnetig niwclear – nuclear	osgiladur amledd – beat frequency
magnetic resonance	rhif cwantwm – quantum number

Figure 11.3   Selection of terms from the glossary of Welsh/English
radiochemistry terms

Those term candidates which were considered to be bona fide
terms were entered into a term bank and the terms were elaborated. Figure 11.2 shows an extract from the term bank. The terms
were elaborated using a variety of means including the source text
and its English parallel text, reference works and expert advice.
Once the term bank was complete, it was validated by a domain
expert (in this case, the author, Professor John R. Jones, University of Surrey) and printed in a variety of dictionary formats (see
Figure 11.3).

The corpus of radiochemistry texts (11,900 words in total) proved
to contain sufficient data to create a term bank of 200 Welsh terms
and their associated data at an average rate of 34 fully elaborated

terms per person day. More details of the corpus-based approach to terminology management that has been used successfully in creating terminology data banks for a variety of specialisms, in English, Catalan, Dutch, French, German and Spanish, can be found in Ahmad and Davies (1992b).

4 Conclusions

In this chapter we have described our attempts to identify ways and means of studying and promoting languages spoken by a numerically small community of people. Language is a community asset and one can, and in many respects should, seek evidence to either substantiate or reject hypotheses related to, for example, the syntax, semantics and pragmatics of the language.

We are continuing to build our general-language corpus of Welsh texts and have been fortunate in finding a collection of Welsh texts that will help us in having full-texts that have been published at roughly ten-year intervals from 1890 to 1990. This will allow us to investigate further the diachronic changes that may have taken place in Welsh over a century, copyright problems notwithstanding. We have also been successful in obtaining substantial amounts of texts from Welsh newspapers. The stock of special-language texts has been increased albeit more slowly than that of the general-language texts. We intend to produce an up-to-date frequency list of words in phrases in due course for free distribution to Welsh language researchers and teachers.

We believe that the principal result of our study has been to outline a methodology for extracting terminology semi-automatically based on the differences in frequency distribution of terms in general language and in special language.

In conclusion, we hope to have shown that advances in computer-based corpus linguistics, together with the strong social and cultural heritage of Welsh, can be harnessed to promote the language, especially in the area of teaching and learning through the compilation of lexical resources based on authentic texts.

Notes

1   The authors are grateful for helpful comments by Margaret Rogers, University of Surrey.

2   We have also collated a modest corpus of Middle Welsh (16,000 words) and a corpus of spoken Welsh specifically for linguistic analysis. The Middle Welsh Corpus is the tale of Peredur (from J.G. Evans and Sir John Rhys's nineteenth-century compilation: *The Text of the Mabinogion and Other Welsh Tales from 'The Red Book of Hergest'*, Oxford 1887) The speech corpus was recorded using digital sound recording techniques and comprises four hours of discourse between a fieldworker and five different informants: senior citizens whose first language is Welsh and who seldom use English. The topics covered include flora and fauna, home and buildings, education and kinship. (Our intention is to transcribe the speech corpus, to render it machine-readable and make it available to bona fide researchers.)

3   Quirk *et al.* (1985) regard the primary verb 'to have' as a closed class verb. We have adopted Quirk *et al.*'s word-class categorization for our Welsh research.

4   Consider, for example, the terminologies produced by the Welsh Joint Education Committee, which include terminologies of computing, biology, chemistry, etc.

Section C

Teaching Linguistics

Introduction

The contributions to this third section challenge some of the basic assumptions underlying the conventional teaching of linguistics. Not only are questions raised concerning what should be taught and how it should be taught, but even the basic facts upon which the teaching is based prove to be contentious.

Two of the major themes of Section B are continued into this section. In order to teach linguistics using corpora, it is essential to pay attention not just to what the teacher does, but to what the student is doing. The student's agenda when faced with historical or prosodic data (Knowles, Chapter 14; Wichmann, Chapter 15) may be very different from the teacher's agenda, and what the students are actually learning may be very different from what the teacher believes is being taught.

The roles of teacher and student are altered in the corpus-based approach to style (Jackson, Chapter 16) and literary appreciation (Louw, Chapter 17). It is difficult for the beginner to make useful generalizations in these areas, particularly when the language used is not the mother tongue. Jackson shows how concordancing techniques can enable students to make comparative studies of style, and Louw outlines a means of relating words used in literary texts to their use in the language at large. It may seem obvious to the native speaker of English that *hail* is frozen rain: it may be less obvious that the term is more frequently used of a shower of bullets.

Secondly, the boundary between teaching and research is productively blurred. Students examining acquisition data (Kettemann, Chapter 13) may be overtly aiming only to understand what researchers have already found out; but by recapitulating the steps of researchers, they take on the role of apprentices, and learn the techniques required to do this kind of research themselves. Training students to search written texts effectively (Peters, Chapter 12) may teach them something about written language, but also gives them an understanding of problems in natural language processing. Understanding how phoneticians annotate the prosody of spoken texts highlights current research problems which can be tackled by students trained in this way. The enormous difficulty of generalizing about historical periods as a whole (Knowles, Chapter 14) makes it almost inevitable that a study of a text from earlier centuries will raise questions which can only be answered by research.

A number of the major points made in these chapters, while they may be new, are also rather obvious. It is obvious that orthographic conventions should be taken into account in morphology (Peters), and that our understanding of historical change will alter radically as more texts are investigated (Knowles). It is obvious that students should study prosodic transcriptions undertaken by experts before being expected to do it themselves (Wichmann), and that the use of words in special contexts should be related to their general usage (Louw). The question to ask is: Why have these things not been said before in the conventional teaching of linguistics?

12

Micro- and Macrolinguistics for Natural Language Processing

PAM PETERS

1 Introduction

The title of this chapter is also the name of a course newly launched in Macquarie University's degree program: 'Micro- and Macro-linguistics'. Those terms express some of our ambitions for the course: that it should bring together small-scale, highly focused approaches to linguistics and ones which are large-scale, broad-ranging and quantitative. As in micro- and macro-economics, the course should relate small subsystems (of language) to the aggreg-ate system; or, to borrow a metaphor from another discipline (mathematical physics and chaos theory), it should show how the flutter of a phonetic feature may affect a universe of discourse. The course is specifically geared towards computational linguistics and the requirements of natural language processing rather than conventional descriptive linguistics.

Like most linguistics departments, the one at Macquarie separ-ates the teaching of phonetics/phonology from that of grammar, semantics and discourse; and the divide is bridged only in pass-ing in applied subjects, such as communication disorders and ESL teaching. 'Micro- and Macrolinguistics' is designed to draw on and draw in all structural levels of language – to integrate the various elements of the discipline as a kind of finishing course for stu-dents in the third year of a Linguistics major. The 'learners' for whom this course in Micro- and Macrolinguistics is designed are investigating linguistics rather than a particular language.

'Micro- and Macrolinguistics' has the strategic purpose of intro-ducing students to the various linguistic databases held in or under development in the department. We have an unusually rich range: structured speech databases (one analogous to the American TIMIT database, and another like the European ACCOR); termbanks of health and social welfare terminology like those developed for EU translators; text corpora built on the Brown/LOB model, such as ACE (Green and Peters, 1991), as well as the ICE model; a large (20 million-word) corpus of Australian literary classics attached to the *Macquarie Dictionary*; and other corpora of specialized types of discourse such as legal cross-examinations, high school students' writing, and mother-and-child talk. We are duly proud of all this, but at the same time we want to educate students to appreciate both the scope and the limitations of computer databases. They are an enormous resource for many kinds of linguistic inquiry, yet ultimately they constrain the answers. Users must know what's inside the database or corpus if they are to properly interpret the data drawn from it. 'Know thy database' is our late twentieth-century commandment to students. Don't be dazzled by its sheer size, and be sure you critically evaluate its appropriateness for the task in hand.

The course interleaves a series of seminars on speech databases and termbanks with others on text corpora and their exploitation. During a thirteen-week series we can hardly go far into the software for each; rather we focus on the linguistic search points in each system, and the extent to which its structure or annotation facilitates particular kinds of investigation. The marking of syllables and stress in the speech databases, grammatical tagging of the corpora, and identification of speech acts in some of the specialized discourse corpora, have of course been set up for different projects, but we raise questions about how to interrelate them in the quest for fuller understanding of natural language processing.

The seminar series is integrated through a good deal of emphasis on morphology – i.e. the morphology of words – as the pivot between phonology and the semantics of discourse. This subdiscipline of linguistics tends to slip between the stools of phonology and grammar, and is hardly picked up when the latter becomes 'lexicogrammar' in Macquarie's systemic-functional courses. The morphology encountered in 'Micro- and Macro-linguistics' is geared towards computational linguistics rather than language description *per se*. But in this context we can make something of older word-based morphology as well as the recent 'a-morphous morphology' of Anderson (1992).

The processing of large amounts of written text requires a slightly different approach than the one taken in conventional linguistics.

In computational linguistics we have to work with conventional orthographic representations, and this affects our view of such things as

- inflectional morphology
- homonymy
- 's forms
- marginal words such as *hmm* and *ugh.*

These will be investigated in the following sections.

2 Morphology

Although morphology is the interface between items of the linguistic code and their meaning, the relationship isn't necessarily one-to-one. Polysemy is the normal condition of words, as a glance at the dictionary would confirm. Most strings of sounds or letters (take *tank* or *wax*) carry more than one meaning, because of:

- lateral development of a single morpheme (so *tank* has a far-flung set of polysemes, as a container for anything from water to military personnel); and
- the coincidence of two separate morphemes (coinciding on *wax* there is a verb 'grow' and a noun referring to the substance out of which candles are made).

Other morphological issues emerge with words which are divergent reflexes of the same morpheme, e.g. *bring* and *brought, sing, sang, sung.* Despite their different forms, they embody the same lexical meaning. These two kinds of mismatch between form and meaning (the many to one and the one to many) – as well as sheer indeterminacy of form – are among the morphological facts of life to challenge the student in devising search routines for the corpus. They also challenge one of the basic premises of morphology, that phonology is the starting point for analysing any formal variation among words. Let us proceed to explore this, using the three conditions just mentioned under which forms and meanings may be related:

Condition 1: many to one
Condition 2: one to many
Condition 3: indeterminate relationship between forms and
meanings.

3   Variability within the lexeme

The problem of multiple forms for the same lexeme (Condition 1) is at its worst with English verbs – most notably the verb *be*, with eight manifestations of the paradigm:

be   am   is   are   being   was   were   been

In searching for passive constructions (or any others based on *be*), our students must anticipate all those forms of the verb. The verb *be* is, of course, unique in its variability, and other irregular verbs confine themselves to five forms or less:

cling	clings	clinging	clung	
cut	cuts	cutting		
drive	drives	driving	drove	driven
strike	strikes	striking	struck	(stricken)
take	takes	taking	took	taken
write	writes	writing	wrote	written

Regular verbs typically have four forms:

admit	admits	admitting	admitted
grin	grins	grinning	grinned
reply	replies	replying	replied
splice	splices	splicing	spliced

Looking first at this regular set, we notice a number of intriguing orthographic alternations to the stems of those verbs, involving the doubling of a final consonant, the substitution of *i* for *y*, and the dropping of final *e*, all of which impinge on computational work. Yet traditional morphological analysis focuses instead on points of variation among the underlying sounds:

/ədmɪt	ədmɪts	ədmɪtɪŋ	ədmɪtəd/
/grɪn	grɪnz	grɪnɪŋ	grɪnd/
/rəplaɪ	rəplaɪz	rəplaɪɪŋ	rəplaɪd/
/splaɪs	splaɪsəz	splaɪsɪŋ	splaɪst/

In phonological dress, the variation in the stems disappears, while variation in the inflections for present and past tense is featured, with three different forms (allomorphs) for each. These are (in Australian pronunciation):

(present)	/s z əz/
(past)	/t d əd/

This morphophonemic variation illustrates certain phonological principles very nicely, but impinges not at all on the computer – or on mature readers, who work with the orthographic/visual form of the word. (If they didn't, they could never achieve the reading speeds they do!) What both they and the computer do register are morpho-orthographic variations in words. The orthographic principles are mostly taught to us as spelling conventions early in life, and are often regarded as trivial. Bolinger (1946) was one of the few linguists to argue for the importance of the visual form of words, postulating 'visual morphemes' where others then and now restrict the term 'morpheme' to one which is phonologically determined. The reasons for this restriction (apart from linguistic tradition) are unclear. Visual morphemes and their morpho-orthographic allomorphs are certainly the ones which impinge on computational linguistics. And in a literate society we have to reckon with both written and oral codes of communication working in parallel, rather than one (the written) dependent on the other.

The orthographic conventions of English (such as those concerning doubling of consonants, the alternation of *y* with *i*, and the dropping of final *e* before suffixes) repay close attention. They help to describe common patterns of variation in regular verbs derived from French and Latin as well as Anglo-Saxon sources, and to anticipate the conjugation of verbs newly derived from within the language. Their finer points also shed light on apparent eccentricities among the irregular verbs: the doubling of a consonant such as *t* in *written* but not *v* as in *driven* (*v* never doubles in standard English words, being a late arrival in the orthography). The doubling of *k* (with *c*) takes place after a single-letter vowel (as in *struck*), but not after a digraph (as in *took*). (Compare *regretted* with *repeated*.) Orthographic regularities among the irregular verbs tend to be downplayed in the context of the individual lemmas which are the basis of standard verb classifications, like that of the *Comprehensive Grammar of the English Language* (Quirk *et al.* 1985). The verb classes shown there are phonologically based (a legacy of both philology and modern linguistics), and there would be fewer classes and subclasses if based on orthographic criteria instead. (By my estimate the number would come down from 28 to 12.)

Emphasizing visual morphology thus helps to make better sense of the variant forms within standard lemmas, and to cope with variable elements in them. Most of these 'pressure points' can be seen as spots where usage is resisting extra changes to the form of the word, replacing *shorn* and *shore* as the past forms of *shear* with just *sheared*, and tending to prefer *shrunk, sunk* and *stunk* (instead of *shrank, sank* and *stank*) for the past tense as well as the past participle – so that such verbs undergo only one vowel change, as has already happened with *fling, cling* and *sling*. Other, regionally differentiated parts of verb lemmas can be better appreciated through the orthographic filter: the preference of British English for *chiselled/swivelled* and *enrol/fulfil* (where American English has *chiseled/swiveled* and *enroll/fulfill*) certainly suggests a stronger endorsement for orthographically stable forms in North America. Australians are heirs to both traditions, and students must be competent at formulating the more elaborate orthographic specifications required for British English. Such competence will also enable them to evaluate commercial lemmatizers, and to supplement them where necessary to capture the full array of variant forms for the same lexeme.

4 Homonymy

The condition in which alternative meanings can be mapped onto the same word form or string (Condition 2 above) is the essence of homonymy, which our students must also confront for its effects on the reading of computerized data. The English language is notorious for its homonyms, and its rich endowment is less than fully documented among the 1200 listed in the *Dictionary of American Homophones and Homographs* (1966) – even when you allow for dialect differences affecting the tally of homophones. Our interest is more particularly in homography, whether or not the homographs are homophones as well. Thus *bear* (as the animal, or the verb 'carry') is as important as *lead* (as a metal, or the verb 'conduct'). The latter, sometimes called 'heterophones', are often the more surprising, as when one discovers the homography of *minute* 'very small' and *minute* 'fraction of an hour', both of which embody the same Latin stem, though they come into English by quite different paths.

This incidentally confronts students with the linguistic question as to where to draw the boundary between homonymy and polysemous developments of the same stem. How separate do the etymologies of two words have to be for them to qualify as homonyms? The answer *is* ultimately arbitrary, and a matter of how many linguistic parameters (phonological, syntactic, stylistic) and what time threshold (OE, ME, EME) one wishes to invoke.

The more pressing question in accessing computerized data is how many homographs there are among the high frequency words of English. In the top 1000 words in the Australian ACE Corpus there are just under 50, if we include only those which have led separate etymological lives since Middle English, such as:

bank   can   fine   last   like   means   rest   rose

The dual or triple roles of such words help of course to raise their overall frequency, even when the frequency of one is much greater than the other. *Can* appears as a modal verb over 1700 times in the corpus, whereas its appearances as a noun amount to only a few. (The same applies to *must* and *will*.) But the ratio between lexical verbs and their homographic nouns is more even (as with *felt, ground, saw* and *shot* – helped by the fact that they are past tense forms). A grammatically tagged corpus would of course separate homographs of this kind.

The difficulty with other homographs is that their roles are grammatically identical as well, at least as far as a typical word-class tagger might show. The noun *race* has two very different meanings 'ethnic group', and 'competition', the second of which is rather more frequently used in the ACE Corpus (by about 3 : 1). The two could perhaps be separated by probabilistic means, but we prefer to encourage students to differentiate them in terms of finer syntactic detail. With corpus evidence they would note that when *race* means 'ethnic group', it often functions as a mass noun, often flanked by other abstracts such as *age, sex, class;* or is particularized by a premodifying adjective, as in *the Aboriginal race, the Asian race.* In contrast the sporting uses of *race* are premodified by plain nouns such as *boat, horse, rat,* or proper nouns as in *Hobart race, Saturday's race.* This exercise in syntactic discrimination engages them with the frontiers of Eric Brill's rule-based tagging techniques (Brill 1993) and with the development of what he calls 'patches' to cope with tagging ambiguities.

5   Clitics and *'s*

The Brill technique can also be usefully applied to differentiating homographic inflections and clitics. The apostrophe *'s* embodies much more than the possessive case of English nouns and names, as corpus evidence will readily show. It appears on odd occasions as a plural inflection (not, I hasten to say, as in the roughly drawn signs at the markets, saying 'prawn's for sale') but in edited texts in ad hoc words such as *do's* in *do's and don'ts,* and in older house style where strings of capitals or numbers were made plural, as in *the 60's* and MP's). Training the computer to recognize the latter is simply a matter of registering the change of font (to upper case, or to numerals) which precedes them.

The more difficult items to identify in the corpus are those where *'s* is a clitic form of the verbs 'is' and 'has' (and occasionally 'does'); and where it serves as an abbreviated form of the pronoun 'us' in *let's.* The last is a fixed and easily recognized form, whereas the contracted verbs are more of a challenge to specify. All of them can be distinguished from the possessive inflection, which is characteristically followed by a noun, with or without a premodifier: *Adelaide's streets, Adelaide's Mediterranean climate.*

Among the verbs, the clitic form of 'has' is relatively distinct because it is normally followed by a past participle: *She's been impossible.* An adverb (especially an intensifier or negative) may intervene, but they are specifiable as closed class items. The rather uncommon clitic form of 'does' (in *What's it matter?*) most characteristically follows an interrogative, and precedes a pronoun subject and infinitive form of the verb. The clitic form of 'is' can precede adjectives, prepositional phrases, adverbs, present participles, noun phrases, i.e. a wide range of grammatical structures, but still one which is predictable. The disambiguation of *'s* requires students to make the most of the immediate syntactic context, and to formulate it in terms which a standard tagger could implement.

This exercise also serves to acquaint students with some of the generic facts of texts. The distribution of the various types of *'s* depends on whether the texts are fiction or non-fiction, and relatively formal or informal. Figure 12.1 shows remarkable differences in the ratios between possessive and clitic uses of *'s* in different genres.

The Australian ACE Corpus is structured like the LOB and Brown corpora, except that category S (Historical fiction) compensates for the shortfall in samples available for other fiction categories such as L (Mystery), N (Adventure) and P (Romance). In extracting data from ACE or Brown or LOB, one is constantly reminded of the generic source, and the effect that text-type has

Category	possessive	is	has	let's	Total
A (Press)	645	125	10		780
H (Government)	169	2			171
N (Adventure)	26	34	1	4	65
S (Historical fiction)	210	210	16		436
Total Non-fiction	814	127	10		951
Total Fiction	236	244	17	4	501

Figure 12.1   The distribution of *'s* in various corpus genres. (Note that the numbers of samples used were: A(40), H(30), N(4), S(26); total 100)

on the distribution of linguistic items, which is excellent both in training students, and in spurring them to a discriminating reading of data presented by others.

6   Marginal words

Under Condition 3 above (the indeterminate relationship between forms and meanings), we may be confronted with words or strings of letters which dictionaries have hardly begun to codify in terms of form and meaning – items such as *uh-huh, hmm* and other such 'words' which we have been endeavouring to transcribe, out of samples of conversation for the Australian component of the ICE project. Though very common, their morphology has been little researched and they seem even to lack a grammatical name. The term 'interjection' is sometimes stretched to cover them, more (one suspects) because they are non-lexical noises with no grammatical status than because they satisfy the standard definition of interjections as being 'expressions of sudden emotion' (= *Collins English Dictionary* 1991). The *Comprehensive Grammar* (Quirk *et al.* 1985) refers to them under two headings: as 'interjections' and elsewhere as 'reaction signals', a term which points to their most vital function in spoken discourse, that of responding to another speaker's utterance. While registering a reaction, such 'words' avoid making an articulate response, or interrupting the other speaker before he or she is ready to relinquish the conversational ball. The term 'backchannel' used by Tottie (1991) and Stenström (1994) registers this backgrounding role which also seems characteristic.

If that is the interpersonal function of these reaction signals, they certainly embody quite specific kinds of reaction ranging from affirmation to negation. In our data they often alternate with *yes* or *no* in a series uttered by the listener:

Yeah . . .   Yeah . . .   Mmhmmm . . .   Yeah . . .   Uhhuh . . .
Uhhuh . . .   Mmm

Collins English Dictionary (1991) describes a couple of the back-channels as less emphatic versions of 'yes' or 'no'. Yet they often embody other shades of reaction: the *Macquarie Dictionary* (1991) notes for the handful listed that they may express such things as surprise, disbelief, dissatisfaction and contempt, and *Collins* adds hesitation and doubt. These are harder to demonstrate without a lot of context, but they seem to correlate with certain phonological properties. Unfavourable reactions are expressed through short, abrupt syllables, while sympathetic and thoughtful consideration goes with a prolonged syllable: compare *hm* with *hmmm* (or *yep* with *yeah,* and *nuh* with *no*). The length of the pitch change also seems significant, and with the shortfall of *uh-uh* the listener puts distance between herself/himself and the speaker; whereas the more accommodating *uh-oh* with its substantial pitch fall signals recognition of a shared dilemma.

  In transcribing reaction signals, our research assistants have been grappling with variability in the actual speech sounds of back-channels, and how far the roman alphabet can or should encode them. If *Oh* is prolonged by a speaker into the more reflective *Oooh* (with extra *o*'s) it coincides orthographically with *Oooh*, a much more engaged and emotional reaction signal (homography again). But it's also clear that *mmhmm* and *uhhuh* are very similar in function, in spite of looking different. Both express affirmation, and the phonetic differences may be no more than the result of one speaker having lips closed and the other a mouth open. They are simply allomorphs of each other – oral and nasal versions of the same signal. Several pairs seem to complement each other in this way (see Figure 12.2).

  In each set there are some with no counterpart in the other, and those with final fricatives *h(u)mph* and *ugh* express quite different kinds of negative reactions (disbelief and disgust, respectively). The nasal set with its range of vowels seems to have more expressive potential. American researchers also register a dental/alveolar reaction signal *unhunh* which has not apparently been heard by their British counterparts, and we have yet to hear it in the Australian material. Whether this constitutes a kind of regional

Oral variant	Nasal variant	Interpretation
ah	mm	recognition or acknowledgement
aha		affirmation of understanding
eh		request for confirmation or repetition
huh		contempt
oh	hm	moderate surprise or discovery
ooh	hmm	thoughtful consideration
	humph	disbelief, dissatisfaction
ugh		distaste, disgust
uhhuh	mmhmm	affirmation
uh-oh		dramatization of discovery
uh-uh	mm-mm	negation

Figure 12.2   Oral and nasal backchannels

difference, or is simply an idiosyncrasy of a few speakers, we shall see. It is one of the many points of comparison which we hope the ICE collections will illuminate.

To avoid pre-empting the question as to how many reaction signals/backchannels there are, we have been transcribing with the full array of word forms just listed. This is after all a frontier of morphology, where neither the signifier nor the signified seems to be encoded in the classic Saussurean fashion. It is indeed an area of 'a-morphous morphology', where the meaning of the sign has to be distilled from the surrounding discourse and the inter-action between the participants. The sign itself is amoeba-like in form, but within certain limits which suggest the threshold of lexicalization.

7   Conclusion

With extensive amounts of transcribed speech, our students have macrolinguistic resources in which to examine microlinguistic questions such as the status and distribution of backchannels. They will be able to contextualize them, quantify them, and correlate them with other interactive features of conversation. But amid the business of describing backchannels or homographs or variation within lexemes, they will, we hope, become more conscious of the independence of form and meaning, and the extent to which both readers and computers depend on visual morphology to decode the meanings of texts.

13

Using a Corpus to Evaluate Theories of Child Language Acquisition

BERNHARD KETTEMANN

This paper argues that the use of corpora in the teaching of linguistics is rewarding and necessary. It describes how to use the Polytechnic of Wales (POW) Corpus of child language in a course on linguistic theory in order to determine the importance of quantity and frequency factors in the acquisition sequence of grammatical morphemes in English, thus using corpus-driven research to decide on the respective explanatory power of, for example, universal grammar and parameter setting (UG) vs cognitive constructivism and self-organization (CC).

For the last thirty years much psycholinguistic research has focused on how children acquire grammatical morphemes such as inflections. Brown's (1973) longitudinal investigation of the order of acquisition of 14 of these morphemes in three children between the age of about 1 and 5 is probably the best known of these studies. 'Order of acquisition' means that those children who use the later morphemes 'correctly' always use the earlier ones 'correctly' also, but not vice versa. The acquisition sequence of the 14 grammatical morphemes Brown (1973: 281) investigated is as follows:

1 present progressive *-ing* (mommy runn*ing*)
2 preposition *in* (*in* the box)
3 preposition *on* (*on* the chair)
4 plural *-s* (two book*s*)
5 past irregular (baby *went*)
6 possessive *-s* (daddy*'s* hat)
7 uncontractable copula (*is* it nice)
8 definite/indefinite articles *the/a* (take *the* truck)

9   past regular -*ed* (she walk*ed*)
10   third person singular present -*s* (she run*s*)
11   third person singular present irregular (*does*)
12   uncontractable auxiliary *be* (*is* she walking)
13   contractable copula *be* (that's a dog)
14   contractable auxiliary *be* (he's coming)

Later studies confirmed the basic order in early and late morphemes even though the internal relative orders may vary somewhat.

Now that an acquisition order has been established the question is: Why is it there and how is it to be accounted for? Is it the result of factors internal to the acquisition process, i.e. innate principles of Universal Grammar, or of external factors, such as experience of and exposure to language in use? In short, the problem I set my students is whether linguistic experience (henceforth 'input') affects the acquisition sequence.

The standard view is that there is no correlation between order of acquisition and input frequency and quantity. Brown (1973: 362), Burt and Dulay (1980: 265), Dulay *et al.* (1982: 38) and Lightbown (1983), for example, see no relation between parental or tutorial frequency and the child's order of acquisition. However, other findings, especially from L2 research – e.g. Larsen-Freeman (1976) and Long (1981) – seem to contradict this. As the distinctions between L1 and L2 acquisition and between acquisition and learning seem to be less clear cut than has hitherto been assumed (see, e.g. Felix 1982: 179), the evidence from L2 studies cannot be dismissed lightly, when discussing L1 acquisition order (cf. Lightbown and Spada 1993: 59).

Let us then have our students approach the problem on a very tentative but empirical basis. This is an important and interesting question and relatively easily approached, if not answered by using the appropriate research tools. One of these tools is the machine-readable corpus.

The choice of corpus depends very much on the questions being asked. The Polytechnic of Wales Corpus contains samples of children's natural language production both in play sessions and in interviews. The data is thus potentially suited for an investigation of input frequency in young children.

Note that I am assuming that the natural production of one child immediately becomes communicative input for another child during play. This is the justification for the use of production data to assess the role of input frequency. There has been, to my mind, too much emphasis on adult and tutorial input. We know that input does not equal intake (e.g. Krashen 1985). Production data then clearly provides evidence for previous intake. I assume that production data reflects intake and therefore constitutes a much better basis for the discussion of the contribution of frequency factors to language development.

Machine-readable corpora representing possible input in a very narrow sense (e.g. parent–child interaction) are not yet readily available. Also very few children of that age read newspapers or novels, the text types covered by the LOB Corpus, for example.

The Polytechnic of Wales Corpus was compiled by Robin P. Fawcett and Michael R. Perkins between 1978 and 1984 and contains approximately 65,000 words of informal English spoken by 120 children from Pontypridd, South Wales. The children are divided equally according to sex, age (ages 6, 8, 10, 12), and four socio-economic classes. Each file contains a transcribed (SEU) and parsed (systemic) sample of a single child's speech in a play session or interview.

First we computed the relative token frequencies of selected morphemes for each age group separately. The morphemes selected were taken from the beginning and the end of the acquisition sequence: the present progressive (with and without auxiliary), plural, past irregular, genitive or possessive, past regular and third person present tense. This yields data presented in Figure 13.1.

A note of caution to my students was called for here. Brown's (1973: 281) list represents the order of the appearance of the respective morphemes in 'correct use' in three children between the age of roughly 1 and 5, and is not frequency related. We are looking here at frequency-related data of children aged 6 to 12. We do this under the assumption that frequency of use does not change dramatically in the use of these morphemes over different ages but over different functions and situations, etc.

Figure 13.1, which shows that frequencies over different age groups after the age of 6 do not vary significantly but basically remain stable, seems to justify our assumption, but with the one exception of Brown's first morpheme.

Note that the use of the progressive without a form of *to be*, e.g. in such sentences as 'Now you busting it up!' (6CBPSGH) or 'I'm doing mine you doing yours!' (6DGPSUT) is already very limited with the 6-year-olds. In most cases (except in certain dialects and

Morpheme	Age 6	Age 8	Age 10	Age 12	Total
Genitive	0.11	0.12	0.12	0.06	0.10
3rd Person	0.53	0.46	0.62	0.55	0.53
Past regular	0.41	0.63	0.70	0.52	0.56
Full Progressive	0.76	0.56	0.54	0.36	0.55
Progressive	1.33	1.30	1.46	1.25	1.34
Plural regular	3.31	2.27	2.76	2.86	2.76
Past irregular	3.62	4.21	4.14	4.68	4.08

Figure 13.1   Mean relative token frequencies for seven selected morphemes in the Polytechnic of Wales Corpus

sociolects) this non-standard form will be used even less as the children grow older. Its high frequency in early acquisition is a clear case of simplifying the full progressive and collapsing it with genuine participial uses. Instead, the majority of occurrences of *-ing* consist of, e.g. present participles and verbal nouns in various syntactic functions.

The frequency figures in this table are the result of the corpus being loaded into a concordancing program. The students then extract these morphemes and compute their relative token frequencies. To do this they have to produce concordances. A concordance is a list of contextualized examples, drawn from a corpus, of a particular word, part of a word or combination of words. The most common way of displaying a concordance is by a series of lines with the Key Word In Context ('KWIC' format). The KWIC concordances produced by the students are set out in Figures 13.2 and 13.3.

In Figure 13.2 students are looking for main verbs with -ing as full progressive, this means in the context of a form of *to be*, tagged as OX in POW and ignoring *going to* as an expression of future time. In Figure 13.3 they are looking for the regular past tense of main verbs by searching for 'M + *ed' and ignoring past participles and adjectives with OX and any verbs of the *need, breed, feed, sled* type.

Concordancing by itself is already a source of fruitful discussion on different linguistic topics and approaches (cf., e.g. Johns 1988, 1991b; Tribble and Jones 1990; Windeatt 1987). One could, for example, note the overgeneralizations of the past tense rule in the second concordance in order to enter on such topics as strategies for rule formation. But let us concentrate on the interpretation of the frequency table in Figure 13.1.

OH-GAWD 1 CL 2 S NGP 3 DD MY 3 H FINGERS 2 OX ARE 2 M   ACHING 212 Z CL 1 OM CAN 1 S NGP HP I 1 M HAVE 1 C
P 19 DD THE 19 H END 17 S NGP HP THEY 17 OX WERE 17 M   BASHING 17 CM QQGP AX UP 17 C? ? 33 Z CL 1 S NGP HP
[HZ:WELL] Z 1 CL 2 S NGP 3 DQ A 3 H DOG 2 OX WAS 2 M   BITING 2 C NGP 4 DD HIS [NV:UM] 4 H TAIL 1 CL 5 &
NGP 2 DQ A 2 H LADY 14 Z CL 1 S NGP HP I 1 OX 'M 1 M   BUILDING 1 C NGP 2 DQ A 2 H CAR 15 [NV:OH] Z CL 1 S
1 0 1 0 50 6BGIHJ 1 Z 1 CL 2 S NGP HP I 2 OX WAS 2 M   BUILDING 2 C NGP 3 DQ A 3 H HOUSE 1 CL 4 & AND 4 S
L F YAH 1 CL 2 & BUT 2 S NGP HP I 2 OX 'M 2 N NOT 2 M   BUILDING 2 C NGP DD THAT 1 CLUN & AN' 124 Z CL 1 S
A NGP 3 DQ EVERY 3 H TIME 2 S NGP HP HE 2 OX WAS 2 M   CHASING 2 C NGP HP IT 1 CL 4 S NGP HP HE 4 M WENT 4
] 2 S NGP 3 NGP 3 HP SOMEBODY 3 MOC ELSE 2 OX WAS 2 M   COMING 28 [NV:MM] Z CL 1 (S) 1 (OM) 1 (M) 1 C CL 2
& AND 11 S NGP HP THEY [RP:THEY] 11 OX WAS [NA] 11 M   COMING 11 C PGP 12 P TO 12 CV NGP 13 DQ A 13 H HOLE
2 P LIKE 2 CV NGP DD THAT 71 Z CL 1 (S) 1 OX ARE 1 M   DOING 1 C NGP 2 DD THE 2 MO QQGP AX LITTLE 2 H BITS
P HP YOU 1 (M) 1 (C) 60 Z CL 1 S NGP HP I 1 OX 'M 1 M   DOING [RP:DOING] 1 C NGP 2 DQ A 2 H DOOR 62 [NV:OO
AVEN'T 2 M FINISHED 1 CL 3 S NGP HP WE? 3 OX 'RE? 3 M   DOING? 3 C NGP HP IT? 3 A QQGP AX SOON? 74 Z CL 1 S
3 DQ A 3 H BRIDGE 130 Z CL 1 S SWH NGP HWH WHO 3 OX ARE   DOING 1 C NGP 2 DQ A 2 H GARDEN 135 Z CL 1 (S) 1
SOME 2 H PEOPLE 2 Q CL 3 SWH NGP HWH WHO 3 OX ARE   [FS: DOING] 3 M PLAYING 3 A PGP 4 P IN 4 CV NGP 5 DD THE
E 1 CL 6 & AND 6 S NGP HN HELEN 6 OX 'S 6 AI JUST 6   DOING 6 C NGP 7 DQ A 7 H WALL [FS:AND-THEN]
CARS 1 CL 10 & AND-THEN 10 S NGP HP SHE 10 OX 'S 10 M   DOING 10 C NGP 11 DQ A 11 H HOUSE 10 A QQGP AX THEN
NGP HP IT 2 Z 1 CL 2 S NGP HN CHRISTINE 2 OX WAS 2 M   DOING 2 C NGP 3 DQ A 3 H BUS-STOP 1 CL 4 & AND 4S

Figure 13.2 Concordance for '*ing' (192 lines); Proximity match for 'OX' (97 lines); Text: 6ABICJ.DAT (etc.)

```
78 HP ONE [FS:A] [FS:AN] 5 CREPL NGP 6 DQ AN 6 MOSIT CL    M ATTATCHED 6 HP ONE 65 Z CL ? NGP 1 (DQ) 1 MOSIT CL
41 C NGP 3 DQ AN 3 H ACCIDENT 56 Z 1 CL 2 S NGP HP HE 2    M BANGED 2 A PGP 3 P ON 3 CV NGP 4 DQ A 4 H TABLE
42 8 CV NGP HN MR-PEARCE'S 1 CL 9 & AND 9 S NGP HP HE 9     M BANGED 9 C NGP 10 DD HIS 10 H LEG 1 CL 11 & AND 11
7 C NGP 3 DD THE 3 H CAR 1 CL 4 & AND 4 S NGP HP THEY4      M BASHED 4 C PGP 5 PM INTO 5 CV NGP 6 DQ ANOTHER 6 HP
37 S) 1 (M) 1 (C) 1 AL CL 2 B COS [NV:UM] 2 S NGP HP I 2    M BRINGED/BUYED? 2 C NGP 3 DQ QQGP AX THREE 3 MO QQGP
40 CAUGHT 2 C NGP HP HIM 1 CL 3 & AND 3 S NGP HP THEY 3     M BRINGED [NA] 3 C NGP HP HIM 3 A PGP 4 P WITH 4 CV
54 V NGP 3 DD THE 3 H TREE 47 Z CL F NO 48 Z CL 1 (S) 1     M CHASED 1 C NGP HP HER 49 [NV:ER] 50 Z 1 CL F NO 1
9 [FS:YOU-THEY] Z CL 1 S NGP HP THEY [NV:GLE] 1 X GET 1     M CHIPPED 1 A PGP 2 P IN 2 CV NGP HP THEM 1 ATG CL 3
61 NGP HN CHRISTMAS 2 Z CL 1 S NGP 2 DD MY 2 H FATHER 1     M CHUCKED 1 C NGP HP IT 1 CM QQGP AX OUT 3 Z CL 1 <S>
34 7 57 Z CL F YES 58 Z 1 CL F YES 1 CL 2 S NGP HP SHE 2    M COMED [NA] 2 A PGP 3 P WITH 3 CV NGP HP ME 1 CL 4 &
35 E 6 S NGP HP IT 6 M WAS 5 CL 7 B HOW 7 S NGP HP SHE 7    M COMED [NA] 7 A PGP 8 P WITH 8 CV NGP HP ME 59 Z 1
79 M ATTATCHED 6 HP ONE 65 Z CL ? NGP 1 (DQ) 1 MOSIT CL     M DETACHED 1 (H) 70 Z CL 1 & AND 1 S NGP HP ME 1 (M)
83 1 OM CA... 62 Z CL F YEAH 64 Z CL ? 1 (DQ) 1 MOSIT CL    M DETACHED 1 (H) 67 Z CL 1 S NGP HP YOU 1 OM CAN 1 M
62 N 3 CV NGP 4 DD THE 4 H WATER 16 Z CL 1 S NGP HP HE 1    M DIED 17 Z CL 1 (S) 1 (O) 1 M EAT 1 C NGP 2 HP HIM 2
33 L 2 A NGP 3 DQ QQGP AX ONE 3 H TIME 2 S NGP HP THEY 2    M DIGGED [NA] 2 CM QQGP AX UP 2 C NGP 4 DD THE 4 H
16 3 C? PGP 4 P ON 4 CV NGP HP HIM 1 CL 5 S NGP HP HE 5     M DIVED 5 C PGP P ON 1 CL 6 A QQGP AX NOW 6 (MP) 6 C
52 (S) 1 (M) 1 C CL 2 (S) 2 (OM) 2 C CL 3 B WHEN 3 (S) 3    M DROWNDED [NA] 34 Z CL 1 (S) 1 (M) 1 (C) 1 AL CL 2 B
4 6 DD THIS 6 HP ONE 4 Z 1 CL 2 S NGP HP I 2 AI JUST 2      M FINISHED 2 C NGP 3 DD THAT 3 HP ONE 1 CL 4 & AND 4
```

Figure 13.3   Concordance for 'M*ed' (744 lines); 'OX', breed, etc. Deleted; Text: PAST10.POW (etc.)

Acquisition Order	Mean Frequency in %
1. -ing (Verb + ing. Progressive)	1.33
2. -s (Plural)	3.31
3. Irregular Past	3.62
4. -'s (Possessive)	0.11
5. Regular Past	0.41
6. -s (3rd pers., in full verbs)	0.53
7. to be +ing (Full Progressive)	0.76

Figure 13.4   Acquisition order and mean frequency (%)

The students were then asked to compare the established acquisition order (Brown 1973: 281) with the general frequency percentages of the respective morphemes in the corpus of the 6-year-olds, i.e. the youngest group and thus the closest to the acquisition process. This is set out in Figure 13.4.

Note that acquisition order and frequency order do not correspond with each other, e.g. no. 3 should be no. 1, no. 1 should be no. 3, no. 4 should be no. 7, etc. This result at first sight does not falsify the UG hypothesis that the relative contribution of input is low, cf. Chomsky (1981: 38), 'There is always a contribution of both UG and experience, but the relative contributions may vary.' What then are the relative contributions?

We computed the Spearman correlation coefficient for the two rank orders in Brown (1973) and the POW and were surprised to find a moderate correlation of 0.5 with a significance level of $p < 0.12$.

On closer examination we note an interesting fact: the first three most frequent inflectional morphemes in the POW Corpus of the 6-year-olds together have an accumulated mean token frequency of 8.26 per cent compared to the last four least frequent inflectional morphemes with only 1.82 per cent. When we divide these figures by the number of morphemes concerned we get a relative mean frequency ratio of roughly 6 (for the early morphemes) to 1 (for the late morphemes). This overall positive correlation seems to override the negative correlations within the two groups of early and late morphemes.

- *Early morphemes:* 2.75 per cent
  Progressive (− *be*)
  Plural, regular
  Past, irregular

- *Late morphemes*: 0.45 per cent
  Possessive
  Past, regular
  3rd Person
  Full Progressive (+ *be*)

The correlation of the acquisition order with the accumulated mean token frequencies across the two groups of early (acquired before about the age of 3) and late (acquired after about the age of 3) morphemes is high. The early group has a considerably higher frequency than the late group in the natural production of the 6-year-olds.

The negative correlations within the two groups may partly be explained by specific factors in the data collection design of the POW study, e.g. the relative high frequency of the past irregular can be directly related to both text-types *play-session* and *interview* where the children talk about definite or indefinite past events or actions, or the relatively high frequency of the full progressive in the present and the past can be related to the *play-sessions* where the children comment more than three times more often on present and past activities than in the *interviews*.

One further explanation for the negative correlations within the first group has already been mentioned: the 6-year-olds do not now very often use the progressive forms without *be*. Instead, they use present participles and verbal gerunds in various syntactic functions.

Evidence such as the overall positive correlation between the two groups of early and late morphemes and high and low frequency of use of these morphemes, leads me to the conclusion that experience or input frequency and frequency of use are important factors in language acquisition and that the relative contribution of Universal Grammar might be smaller than has been assumed up to now, and perhaps only the reflection of our common cognitive abilities.

Cognitive constructivism sees rule-formation, and thus language, just like other cognitive systems, as the result of our selective stabilization ability and of the constructive activity of experience-dependent self-organizational processes. In this sense language acquisition is a creative construction process. It follows that Chomsky's later statement (1988: 174) 'acquisition of language is something that happens to you, it's not something that you do' cannot stand uncontradicted.

It seems that language is not something that happens to us (except in a trivial sense of 'happen'), but is actively constructed, just like other cognitive systems.

Please note that I am not claiming that frequency is the only factor that influences acquisition order, nor am I claiming that corpus analysis is the only way to gain linguistic insights. Other factors influencing acquisition are, e.g. semantic and pragmatic, situational and emotional relevance, or constructional complexity. Other ways of gathering data in linguistics include intuition, elicitation or experimentation.

What I am claiming is that corpus investigation constitutes a valuable classroom resource, and that it has many possible fruitful applications in linguistics teaching: in the course of this small project the students have been exposed to a basic theoretical debate, have been acquainted with an interesting empirical research question, have been introduced to methods of analysis of authentic data, and have been familiarized with linguistic argumentation and reasoning.

14

Using Corpora for the Diachronic Study of English

GERRY KNOWLES

1 Introduction

The aim of this paper is to discuss some fundamental questions which have arisen in the course of the development of a new degree scheme at Lancaster University which started in 1993. Historical courses in English Language were for many years taught by the department of English, but these have been laid down and the Linguistics department is taking them up as part of the new English Language degree schemes.[1] The course discussed here was previously taught in the context of the study of medieval literature but has now been redesigned to complement courses on the contemporary language. It was also decided from the beginning to experiment with the use of corpora in teaching. The introduction of corpora has brought with it far-reaching changes in the method of teaching and the method of learning.

1.1 Materials available

The course began with very modest materials and concentrated on the period since about 1500. In the first year the materials consisted mainly of a set of texts in WordCruncher form, including the Helsinki corpus, and versions of the King James Bible, the works of Shakespeare, some nineteenth-century American writers, and the LOB and Brown corpora. In addition to the corpora, the *Oxford English Dictionary* was available on-line. It is intended to use a wider range of texts as they become available, and for example some texts from the seventeenth-century Lampeter corpus have recently become available for 1994–95.

Although corpora are now thought of as essentially machine readable, there is an older tradition which also made use of large collections of natural data. In this tradition are the Scolar reprints of books in the *English Linguistics 1500–1800* series, and these were available in the library at Lancaster University.

Teaching took place in a specially designed room containing six computers, each with WordCruncher installed. Classes contained up to twelve students, so that there was a maximum of two students per computer. This enabled individuals or small groups to work independently.

1.2   Classroom activities

The basic activity involves the use of a concordance. The package used was WordCruncher, which first requires the user to select a corpus, and then displays a wordlist with the frequency of occurrence of each word. Students select a word or group of words and examine a number of examples in context. In texts before about 1700 it is common to find words spelt in more than one way, and using the wordlist the user can select the variants, e.g. when concordancing on the word *doctor* in the authorized version, one also has to include *doctour.*

When a word has been selected, WordCruncher displays all the examples in the corpus. For each example, the sentence in which the word occurs is presented with highlighting on the key word itself. If the user clicks on a particular example, WordCruncher then displays the whole text in which it occurs, again with highlighting on the selected word. In this way the user can very rapidly trace the use of a word in a large body of text.

The computer-readable *Oxford English Dictionary* was essentially used in the same way as the traditional hard copy, except that looking words up was much quicker. Since the dictionary entries are arranged historically, it is easy to check whether, in the view of the dictionary compilers, the form of meaning of a word in a text is typical of its period. For example, the spelling *doctour* is found from the fourteenth century to the nineteenth century, so its occurrence in a nineteenth-century text is unremarkable. On the other hand, the association of *meat* with corn rather than flesh (see 4.3 below) is not listed at all, and so this might well be a specialized use of the word. In this way students were able to use the dictionary to provide a useful check on their preliminary findings from searching the corpus.

Concordancing and dictionary look-up were used to tackle a variety of problems over the period seventeenth to nineteenth century. Here are some examples:

- Changes in the meaning of individual words – such as *lewd* or *nice* – were illustrated by concordancing in a range of corpora.
- By concordancing on affixes it was possible to investigate patterns of word formation.
- The distribution of *-eth* and *-s* verb endings, e.g. *saith* and *says*, was checked in seventeenth-century texts.
- In order to make students more aware of the connection between degrees of formality and the origin of words (especially Germanic, French or Latin), they were given sets of words such as *holy/sacred/consecrated; fear/terror/trepidation; fire/flame/ conflagration*; and *rise/mount/ascend*. They found the origin of the words and checked the relationships between them in different corpora from the seventeenth century to LOB.

1.3 Teaching with technology

When new technology becomes available for teaching, it is perhaps natural to start thinking of what the teacher can do with it. However, the technology does not of itself provide a goal. It must be emphasized that the goal must be clearly identified before the technology can be usefully employed. If the computer is not used as part of an overall teaching strategy, it will quickly become a classroom toy, much as the language laboratory did in the 1970s, and the opportunities it offers will be squandered.

It would in principle be possible to use corpus-based techniques to do what was done previously with blackboard and chalk. One could use a corpus of Old English, for example, to teach inflectional endings. But before collecting the materials and developing the new techniques, it would be wise to ascertain that it is indeed essential for teachers to teach inflectional endings and for students to learn them. It is all too easy for the teacher – and even the student – to be trapped by established custom and practice, so that however courses are rationalized, things are really done in a certain way because they have always been done that way.

In practice, there is little point in introducing corpus-based methods on their own – grafting new technology on to old pedagogy – and new methods almost automatically involve a radical rethink of what courses are trying to achieve. What is perhaps less obvious is that the range of possible objectives is expanded by the new technology. Old style courses (discussed below) were limited not only by the pedagogical theory implemented in them, but also by paper-and-pencil technology.

Course objectives are usually defined according to the teacher's agenda, i.e. what the teacher expects the student to have learned by the end of the course. Students, however, come from a variety of backgrounds, and have their own objectives, which may not be the same as the teacher's. Different students may learn very different things from the same course. The objectives must include what the students are doing, what is being learned in addition to what is being taught. When the course objectives have been defined, the question of how they can be achieved by computer-based methods can be raised.

One of the advantages of computer-based teaching is that it gives a fresh insight into the learning process. The emphasis in this chapter will be not so much on how corpora can be used to help teachers teach, but on how they can be used to help students learn.

2   The identification of problems

The historical study of English has recently begun a revival which makes it an exciting area in which to work. This is due to the combination of several factors. Apart from the new opportunities raised by computer processing, the climate in England has improved following the introduction of the new English Language A level, which is creating a new generation of teachers and students interested in matters of language. There is also an interesting new generation of textbooks which take an approach that is very different from those of textbooks written a few decades earlier. Leith (1983) applies insights gained from sociolinguistics to the study of language history. Freeborn (1992) and Burnley (1992) present a range of historical texts and accompanying exercises, and in this way anticipate the corpus-based approach. Bauer (1994) examines change in the present century. In these circumstances, it is worth considering why there was formerly a problem.

2.1 The student's academic background

As a result of changes in the national education system, a new generation of students has come to university without the traditional academic background. An understanding of a conventional history of the language requires a general knowledge of history, and some metalinguistic knowledge. The student has to relate linguistic changes to events in the real world, such as the Norman Conquest or the introduction of printing. An understanding of the internal development of the language is greatly facilitated by the formal study of other languages, and until relatively recently grammar school children studied Latin as a matter of course. Different ways of teaching history and languages, however, have made it more difficult for students to understand the world in which the language has developed, and changes in the language code itself. If the student is unsure whether the Danish invasions came before or after the Renaissance, any historical context is meaningless and the attempt to provide one is unlikely to be successful. Similarly, if the student has learned some French but does not understand terms such as *noun* or *tense* then the simplest linguistic explanations will remain opaque.

The issue here is not whether these educational changes are good or bad, for in any case the problems which students have must be recognized and taken into account in designing courses. There is no point in lamenting the decline of the education system, because even if it were true, that would not address the problem. Nor is there any point in designing crash courses in English history and linguistic terminology: the time for such things is afterwards, when the students perceive their lack of traditional knowledge as a problem. Instead of relating the course to a background the students lack, we have to relate it to one they possess.

2.2 Received information

Turning now to internal problems, history of the language courses traditionally involve a received body of facts. A conventional history of English course will examine the loss of inflectional endings in late Old English, inkhorn terms – the thousands of words borrowed from Latin and Greek – in the sixteenth century, the Great Vowel Shift (a set of changes which took place in the long vowels, so that a word like *mouse* – originally pronounced like modern *moose* – developed the modern diphthong), and prescriptive attitudes in the eighteenth century. The study of these things is justified on the grounds that they give an objective account of the development of the language. The central facts will in turn provide the justification for other aspects of the course. In order to study the loss of endings the student will be told about synthetic and analytic languages. In order to see the endings in context, students have to study Old English texts, and in order to show an understanding of the texts, they may be required to follow Classical precedent and translate them.

The study of the history of English itself goes back over 400 years, and the kinds of text selected for analysis, and the kinds of topic considered worthy of investigation, reflect the preoccupations (and, it must be said, the political views) of language scholars at different periods. The practice of normalizing old texts may simplify problems for the student, but they also provide Old English with neat paradigms that look like Latin. Textbooks of the second half of the twentieth century (e.g. Baugh 1951: 287–9; Pyles 1971: 183–9) still claim that the Great Vowel Shift began in Chaucer's time and ended in Shakespeare's, even though this is inconsistent with the kind of dialect information that has been available for over a century. Some northern English dialects have still not undertaken changes which are alleged to have been completed before the Norman Conquest. The long vowels of south-eastern dialects, on the other hand, are still shifting, but later changes are arbitrarily excluded from the Great Vowel Shift. Language history is not at all the objective study it might at first appear.

Received information belongs to a pedagogical world in which the goal of teaching is to transfer knowledge from the mind of the teacher into that of the student, so that successful students become near-clones of the teacher. It also belongs to a technical world with restricted sources of information. The teacher who trains students to examine large amounts of data and find things out for themselves runs the risk that the conclusions reached will conflict with what has usually been thought before.

This section has identified three major problems:

■ the relationship of a course to the students' intellectual background
■ the 'factual' nature of information
■ the role of the teacher.

Solutions to these problems will be considered in the next section.

3   Problem solving by corpus

The problems identified above have nothing necessarily to do with history or with language *per se*, and are general academic problems. It will be argued in this section that the use of corpora has an important contribution to make towards their solution.

The key factor in corpus-based teaching is the sheer amount of linguistic information made available to the student. This brings about a chain of consequences, not only for the roles of student and teacher, but for what goes on in the classroom and ultimately for the underlying objectives of the course itself.

3.1   The role of the teacher

If the content of the course is seen as a fixed set of information, then it seems reasonable to expect the teacher to know the information, and to transmit it to the students. It also makes it difficult for the teacher who has not made a specialist study of the topic, and who has consequently not mastered that information, to devise a course as there is too much scope for error in points of detail.

As more corpora become available, the amount of information grows and the proportion of the whole which can be mastered by a single person diminishes. Expert knowledge based on selected subsets of the data becomes less important, and the new skills required include the ability to handle large amounts of data and to teach students to do the same. The teacher's role changes from being the source of knowledge to being the leader in the investigation.

3.2   The role of the student

The student's role also changes. Instead of assimilating the information provided by the teacher, the student's role becomes one of investigating the data under the teacher's supervision. The student may be faced with the problem of finding something useful to do with the output of a concordance program; this can include making generalizations about the data, and setting up hypotheses to account for variation in the data, and for differences between historical and modern data. It is argued below that this process requires not a detailed knowledge of the language but general literacy skills which the students already possess.

3.3   Defining objectives

There may be many objectives for a course, and they can be roughly categorized as 'teacher-oriented' or 'student-oriented', and 'overt' or 'covert'. The traditional reasons given for studying the history of the language are typically overt and teacher-oriented. The philologist, for example, may want to understand how English relates historically to other members of the Germanic family. Or it might be argued that students need a knowledge of the older language in order to read early literature in the original. Such teacher-oriented objectives appeal to only a tiny minority of students, as has been shown in several universities when compulsory language courses are made optional.

Student-oriented objectives relate to choices that the student has already made. Students taking degrees entitled 'English Language' can be presumed to have as one of their goals a general understanding of the language they use, and some historical information certainly helps an understanding of the present state of the language. An appropriate goal for a historical course is therefore to use the past to explain the present.

Given an objective of this kind, it is no longer sufficient to teach historical facts for their own sake. Inkhorn terms are used not to illustrate sixteenth-century English, but to explain the structure of the modern lexicon; their distribution in different sixteenth-century texts can be used to explain the development of modern registers. The Great Vowel Shift helps explain the present pattern of accents and dialects.

In addition to these overt goals, there are covert ones. Students are increasingly coming to university with basic computer skills, and even those who do not have them are aware of the need for computer literacy. Whatever the actual content of the course, students learn the skills of information retrieval and processing. These are going to be useful whatever they do after leaving university. Computers and information technology are part of the student's world, much as Latin was part of the student's world a century ago. It is obviously essential to relate the history of the language to the student's world in this way.

4 Teaching and facilitating learning

Previous sections have dealt in general terms with teaching and corpora, but little has been said about what actually goes on in the classroom. This section will illustrate ways in which the activities of teachers and learners are affected by corpora.

4.1 Gobbets

In a conventional course, ideas are developed in a lecture and then confirmed in a follow-up seminar. If actual texts are used, the teacher will carefully select a short passage or 'gobbet' to illustrate the point at issue. For example, a lecture might deal with the wholesale use of Latin and Greek words by sixteenth-century scholars, to be followed by the study of a suitable passage from the works of Sir Thomas Elyot containing lots of examples. Given the technology available, there was nothing better a teacher could do: a gobbet could be reproduced on a handout, but there was no way the whole body of sixteenth-century scholarly works could be studied in a 50-minute seminar!

The difficulty with gobbets is that they tie students' learning to the teacher's existing views. Teachers can either take a directive approach and explicitly lead the students through their own patterns of thinking, or they can use a format in which the students are apparently learning by discovery. In the latter case there is, in reality, little the students can discover other than the teacher's own ideas. If they are studying a text carefully chosen to illustrate the use of Classical vocabulary, then – assuming they can actually recognize Classical words – it is difficult for them to conclude anything other than that it contains lots of Classical words.

It is not clear what generalizations are to be made from the study of a gobbet. The teacher may intend to use an extract from

Elyot merely to illustrate the difference between Germanic words and Classical words; but in that case it would be easier for the student to work on a twentieth-century passage. It is difficult for the student not to infer that the sample is a good example of its type. Not many students will ask how representative the text is, and representative of what. If the students were able to search freely through a corpus, on the other hand, and were to come across the sermons of Latimer, they would come to very different conclusions about sixteenth-century vocabulary. Since a lot more people in the sixteenth century could understand sermons intended for ordinary people than the scholarly language of Elyot, these conclusions would have a more general validity.

4.2   Using reference books

Gobbets can be used effectively for events that occur with high frequency in texts, such as Classical words in some sixteenth-century texts. To study low-frequency events with conventional technology, use has to be made of reference books. Consider, for example, change of word meaning. A traditional lecture on change of meaning (of the kind I have myself given!) will discuss different kinds of change, and students will then investigate words known to be good examples of their type, e.g. narrowing of meaning will be illustrated by words like *fowl*, *meat* and *deer*. The information is to be found in the *Oxford English Dictionary*, and in etymological dictionaries.

While this may appear to be a common-sense way of proceeding, it involves the teacher in perceiving an interesting theoretical problem and providing the students with a solution. Again, at best the students can only confirm the teacher's ideas. The dictionary contains a highly condensed account of the history of individual words, and a semantic theory which deals with changes of sense through time seeks to generalize about the history of large groups of words. It can be difficult, even for an experienced teacher, to reconcile the complex detail given by the dictionary with the neatness of the semantic theory. It must be much more difficult for students, unless they have sufficient experience of old texts, to understand that there is a problem to be solved. For example, students who have encountered the word *deor* in an Old English text referring to a wolf will be able to make sense of the information that *deer* formerly referred to animals more generally. If they are just told that *deer* has narrowed its meaning, that is just an isolated fact which corresponds to nothing else in the students' experience.

Unless the students have experience of the problem, the solution is unlikely to mean very much. As a result, students who are familiar with semantic change and who think about these things may retain the information about the actual examples. Others may learn that words change their meaning, and some may understand and learn nothing at all.

4.3   Exploring a corpus

Even a relatively small set of corpus materials, such as is described in 1.1 above, will provide sufficient examples for some low-frequency events. This section will discuss the use of corpora in the study of word meanings.

Studying change of meaning in a corpus draws on normal linguistic skills to the extent that it is part of our linguistic experience to cope with words used in a slightly unfamiliar sense. Visitors to Lancashire, for example, may be puzzled by local uses of the word *while*, as in *Don't open the door while the train's stopped.* Other examples, such as *She'll not be back while dinner-time* give the clue that it corresponds to standard *until.* Compare the experience of students concordancing on the word *meat* in the authorized version of the Old Testament:

(a)   Sacrifices, meat and burnt offerings
(b)   Ye shall offer no strange incense thereon, nor burnt sacrifice, nor meat offering . . .
(c)   he . . . offered upon [the altar] the burnt offering and the meat offering
(d)   no meat offering shall be made with leaven
(e)   meat offering . . . green ears of corn
(f)   when any will offer a meat offering . . . his offering shall be of fine flour
(g)   if thy oblation be a meat offering baken in a pan, it shall be of fine flour unleavened.

Example (a) gives no hint that the word does not have the modern meaning, but this is increasingly difficult to reconcile with (b)–(g). Students will make different interpretations of the historical senses at varying degrees of sophistication:

- *Meat* was adopted as a translation equivalent for a Semitic word.
- The range of meanings of *meat* could at one time include 'corn'.
- *Meat* used to mean 'corn'.

While the teacher's attention may be on the change of sense, the discovery made by the student may be of a quite different kind. At least one student in the course of the above exercise grasped the concept of semantic change itself, which is an obvious prerequisite to understanding the details of change of sense. A student who fails to get even this far may of course draw the wrong conclusions, and for instance infer that in the sixteenth and seventeenth centuries words could mean what you wanted them to mean.

Note that one conclusion that cannot be drawn from the corpus exercise is the original point to be illustrated, namely that the meaning of words can narrow over time. Generalizations of this kind can be provided by the teacher once the students understand the problem that is being solved.

4.4 Generalizing from corpus data

Gobbets and corpora both have problems with regard to the generalizations to be made, but they are of different kinds. The use of gobbets relies on the teacher's judgement, e.g. that the study of a passage of Elyot leads to useful conclusions about sixteenth-century English as a whole. The corpus study of *meat* does not support the conventional assumption that the word referred to food in general, and, at the least, conventional theory has to be modified, e.g. by adopting 'prototype' categories (Taylor, 1989). In other words, it is not possible to specify the meaning of *meat* as a single category which all examples fit. Examples cluster round typical meanings or prototypes, and the prototype can vary in the course of time.

If subgroups of students examine different data, they are likely to come to different conclusions. This was done in a study of the second person pronouns *thou* and *you*. The interest in these pronouns in the sixteenth and seventeenth centuries is that they were still sufficiently different to be used strategically to convey speaker meaning. In the corpus exercise, one group of students took examples from the book of Genesis in the authorized version, and discovered that *thou* was consistently singular and *you* plural (and that it was the oblique form corresponding to the subject form *ye*). Another group, looking through Shakespeare, found no pattern at all (and also no consistent pattern in the use of *ye* and *you*).

Now it might be argued that the corpus approach is actually inferior to the traditional approach since it merely produces confusion in the minds of students. However, the time for generalizing about the language as a whole – or even examining a special case in a Shakespearean gobbet – is afterwards, when the students already understand the nature of the problem. If some false generalizations are debunked in the process, then this is a gain rather than a loss.

As in the case of the semantic change exercise, the teacher cannot always be sure what the student is learning. The *you/thou* exercise is overtly about number in second person pronouns, but one student later confessed to having understood for the first time that the word *thou* is a second person pronoun.

5   What the students said

Corpus exercises, like other computer-based exercises, elicit feedback which is different in kind from that obtained in conventional classes. Students report what they are learning and describe problems as they perceive them, which may be different from the teacher's perception. In a conventional phonetics class discussing vowel reduction, for instance, a student may feel inhibited from asking what *shwa* means, but faced with examples on the computer screen, more than one student has triumphantly reported an understanding of the letter 'e' written upside down. For the teacher, shwa is a vowel sound, but if students come to phonetics thinking in terms of letters, then it is through letters that they are going to make their first discoveries. In the same way, in a traditional language seminar, a student is unlikely to ask about funny words. The teacher might think in terms of pronouns and paradigms, but the student has to become aware of funny words in old texts before attempting to classify them. Before responding to corpus data in the teacher's way, the students have to respond in their own way, relating the data to their previous experience. The teacher's initial reaction may be disappointment that students are learning at a level below the overt level of the seminar. And yet it is difficult to believe that such students do better in conventional seminars: students who get confused with upside down 'e's and funny words are more likely to switch off and gain nothing at all from the course.

This informal feedback is valuable, but in view of its spontaneous and sporadic nature it is difficult to collect. It is also difficult to present except in an anecdotal fashion, as in the present chapter. The formal kind of feedback contained in end-of-term questionnaires includes some perceptive remarks on the new style of teaching:

> The use of the computers has been a 'fun' alternative to boring classroom seminars, the sessions being presented in such a way as to make investigation interesting.

> The idea of doing your own research is a good one, it makes the student's part more active and involved and makes everything more interesting.

> [I would like] a greater explanation of how research can be compiled and conclusions made.

> The quantity of information can be overwhelming and it can be difficult knowing what to look for.

> All that is done is searching through and not finding anything specific.

> Time spent looking at corpora in seminars is often too short.

> I even look forward to seminars! ... Looking through corpora can be tedious.

> Looking up words week after week can get boring.

It is interesting to note that, just as teachers need to rethink their role as teachers in response to the new technology, some students need to rethink their role as learners. Students must have a clear idea of the problem they are trying to solve by searching the data; otherwise, as the negative comments reveal, just browsing through masses of corpus data can be a tedious and overwhelming experience.

6   Conclusion

When academic interest in the history of the language first developed in the last century, it was in a favourable environment. Students came from a Classical background, and learned to do with older English what they had already learned to do with Latin. A historical approach was taken in other subjects, including zoology and politics. Interest in the medieval period was reflected in painting, architecture and literature. All this has now gone. If the subject is to survive, it has to be recreated in an environment which is more favourable at the end of the twentieth century. Corpus linguistics – and its links to the world of information technology – provides such an environment.

The tasks set for students in this new environment have not necessarily differed greatly from those on more traditionally taught courses, and in addition to the studies discussed above have included morphology, affixes and word formation, and the relationships between near-synonyms. The difference is not in the topics themselves but in the way they are approached by the teacher and by the student.

The first indications are that this approach is likely to be successful. It is exciting and challenging for the teacher to discover that, far from having a subject in which all the work has long since been done and all problems solved, we are only just beginning to ask the interesting questions. Some of the basic ideas are not necessarily limited to the teaching of the history of the language, and could be modified for teaching modern languages.

However, this chapter has made only a superficial prima facie case for teaching with the new technology. What we have done so far at Lancaster seems to work, and on the whole the students seem to like it. But we have no hard evidence. We do not really know whether the first positive response is due to the technology, the use of corpora, the student-centred pedagogy, or just the enthusiasm of the teachers. Something interesting seems to be happening in terms of student–computer interaction, but the anecdotal evidence available so far is not a sufficient foundation on which to base a new kind of pedagogy. It will be essential over the next few years to base new teaching developments in this area on sound pedagogical research.

Note

1   Much of the course, including the corpus-based seminar tasks, was designed by my colleague, Jonathan Culpeper, whom I also have to thank for valuable comments on this chapter.

15

The Use of Annotated Speech Corpora in the Teaching of Prosody

ANNE WICHMANN

1 Introduction

The aims and objectives of the teaching of phonetics and phonology as part of a wider programme of study, such as a degree in Linguistics or English Language, are not, to my knowledge, widely discussed. Although traditionally much time is spent on training transcription skills (segmental and prosodic), we can perhaps assume that the principal aim, as in other areas of linguistics, is for learners to gain insight into a system, and understand how it relates to other systems. In comparison with lexical and grammatical systems, the prosodic system of English is still relatively unexplored, and there is much to be said about theoretical issues, particularly the continuing lack of general agreement about how to analyse it.

In order to understand theoretical issues, an element of practical data analysis is an important part of a phonetics course. There are considerable problems associated with this, however. Prosody is rather messy, and even if one adopts one particular system – in this case the British system of tones and tone-groups – transcription is neither easy to learn nor easy to teach. The component parts – tempo, pitch, loudness and voice quality – pattern in complex ways, some relatively easy to observe, such as pause, and others more elusive, such as pitch contours. It requires considerable training to transcribe prosodic patterns consistently. These patterns are particularly hard to identify in natural data. There is a great discrepancy between the neat simplified data used in textbooks for illustrative purposes, and the complex patterns found in naturally occurring speech.

An annotated corpus of speech can provide a bridge between textbook illustrations and natural speech. By using such a corpus, prosodically transcribed by experts, it is possible to deal with many practical issues despite the relative lack of expertise of the students. A corpus may also provide a secure foundation for teachers who themselves have only limited expertise in this area. It certainly provides a greater quantity of data, and a more reliable transcription than could be produced by the students themselves. In this way training in the skill of transcribing need not be the only practical element in a phonetics course.

2   Annotated speech corpora

There are several corpora of naturally occurring spoken language, but only few have been annotated prosodically. These include the London Lund Corpus (LLC), the Lancaster/IBM Spoken English Corpus (SEC) and the Corpus of Spoken American English (CSAE). The corpora vary in size: the SEC contains 50,000 words, the CSAE approx 200,000 words and the LLC approx 500,000 words. The LLC, the oldest of the corpora, is publicly available in its printed form only. For the other two the original recordings are also available. The transcription systems are not identical, but all are based on the British system of marking tone groups and tones. All use a more or less iconic set of symbols, which are relatively easy to understand. They indicate at least prosodic boundaries, pitch direction on prominent syllables and a variety of other features.

Although much can be learned about prosody on the basis of the written transcription alone, the availability of the original recordings, in whatever form, plays an important part in the teaching and learning process. When the course described in this paper was being developed, only the SEC was available with recordings, since the CSAE was still being compiled and the tapes of the LLC are not publicly available. Unlike the CSAE, which contains mainly face-to-face conversation, the SEC contains mostly prepared or semi-prepared British English speech (monologue). Each text is available in its orthographic form (unannotated) and also in its transcribed form. Figure 15.1 shows a sample of the corpus in its

the ˈfire ˈstarted | ˈjust after ⁻ten oˈˈclock | and within ˈminutes | ˈthick •black ˈsmoke was ˈbillowing out of ˈthree of the ˈfour entrances | to the ˈtube station ‖ it's ⁻thought the ˍblaze beˈgan | in a conˈtractor's ˈhut | on one of the ˈplatforms | where renoˈvation work | ↓was being carried ˈout ‖ more than •two ⁻hundred •firemen | with ⁻breathing apparatus | ⁻worked in ˈrelays | ↓going ⁻down ˈinto the •tunnels | to ⁻reach the ˈhundreds of ˈpassengers ˈtrapped ‖ visiˈbility | was ⁻down to ˈzero | ↓at •Oxford ˈCircus itˈself | so ⁻teams of ˍfiremen | •disˈpersed to suˈrrounding •stations | and ˈworked their way ⁻back down the •line | to the ˍcrowded ˈtrains ‖ Steve ˈAnnett | •talked to ˈsome of the •passengers | as ˈthey arrived | on the ⁻platform at Piccaˈdilly •station ‖ ˈthey'd been •stranded | for ˈtwo ˈhours | and had⁻walked about •half a ˈmile along the ˈtunnels ‖

Key: Tones (with pitch movement): [ˊˋˇˉ] fall, rise, fall–rise, level
       Stressed syllables (without pitch movement): [•]
       Boundaries: [| ‖]
       Marked pitch excursion: [↑ ↓]

Figure 15.1   Extract from Spoken English Corpus, prosodic transcription

prosodically transcribed form (see Knowles *et al.* 1996). The transcription captures features which include tone groups, accents (with associated tones) and marked pitch excursion.

3   Teaching a course on prosody

There is a lot more to be said and learned about prosody than can be incorporated into a 12-week course. It is therefore essential to limit what is taught to a few fundamental, and hopefully interesting, issues. Three basic issues which seem to be worth investigating, and which relate reasonably well to one another, are the demarcatory function of prosody (the division of speech into 'phrases'), the accentual function (its role in creating syllable prominence) and its discourse function (the effect of pitch movement, e.g. rise, fall).[1]

3.1   Boundaries: the demarcative function of intonation

Chunking is an essential element in the performance of spoken texts. However, it is no easy matter to identify boundaries in real data, as anyone who has tried to do so will testify. The 'common-sense' view, and students' most common initial assumption, is that all boundaries are marked by pauses. The first step is therefore to illustrate that this is not necessarily the case. There are two possible ways of doing this. One is to play recordings of small sections of the corpus, specially selected to illustrate clearly audible boundaries *not* cued by pauses. The second is to perform exaggeratedly simple examples oneself, in which the boundaries are cued by marked nuclear tones and syllable lengthening. If there is access to a speech workstation, it is possible to show by means of the waveform that there is no pause. The crucial point is that for illustration purposes the students must be able to identify the phrase boundaries easily. Once it is demonstrated to them that they are able to do this despite the absence of pauses, they acquire a degree of confidence that they are actually able to hear boundaries, even if they are as yet not sure how they were cued. At the same time it is important to warn them that not all boundaries are so obvious.

Students can then be given a section of the corpus in its unannotated form, asked to listen to the relevant tape and mark where they hear boundaries. They should be told to devise a symbol for 'not sure', and use it. They can then be encouraged to compare their results with those of other students and to identify, first, the boundaries on which they agree. They then consider the 'not sure' boundaries – the more interesting variety. The aim at this stage is two-fold: firstly, to demonstrate the phonetic variability of boundaries and the different degrees of boundary strength and, secondly, a more general pedagogical one, which is to inspire confidence to be 'not sure'.[2] Finally, students can be given the same text in its prosodically transcribed form and asked to compare it with their own tentative transcriptions.

The inevitable discrepancies between the published transcription and their own are (I hope) by this stage not perceived by the students as failure on their part. Instead it should become clear that the cues to boundaries vary, and that some are more obvious than others. This can lead to a discussion of why boundaries are perceived. There are clearly many phonetic cues. Some are segmental, such as an absence of simplification processes (assimilation and elision). Others are prosodic and include pause, pitch discontinuity and syllable lengthening. Further cues include changes in tempo (e.g. speeding up at the beginning of a tone group), and changes in voice quality (e.g. creaky voice as a finality signal) (see Knowles 1991; Chafe 1995). Once students have learned:

- that prosodic phrasing exists
- that they can recognize it themselves (up to a point)
- that there are many different phonetic cues to phrasing besides the obvious pause

there is a lot to be said about the relation between prosodic grouping and the structure of the text.

3.1.1   Prosodic and syntactic boundaries

Students can investigate the relationship between tone groups and syntax, discovering that (in the prepared speech contained in this corpus) the majority of prosodic boundaries co-occur with a syntactic boundary. An important caveat here: in his study of the phonetic correlates of boundaries in the SEC, Knowles (1991) found that some boundaries may have been cued not by any phonetic features at all but by grammatical structure. This of course means not only that we hear things that are not there, but also that systematic attempts to relate grammatical boundaries to perceived prosodic boundaries may in some cases be circular.

3.1.2   Boundaries and punctuation

An understanding of tone groups makes it possible to examine the relationship between prosodic segmentation and (particularly non-standard) punctuation. Students are given examples of writing which has been over-punctuated, and asked to comment on it. It is often possible to explain the non-standard use of punctuation as a reflection of prosodic intuitions. I feel that this is a useful insight for anyone concerned with, or likely to be concerned with, the teaching of writing.

3.1.3   Boundaries and speaking styles

Finally, there are stylistic issues to be considered, such as length and variability of tone groups. Although the stylistic variation in the corpus is in some ways narrow (all prepared or semi-prepared speech) there are none the less some interesting differences to be observed. A very rough measure can be made according to number of words per tone group; a more reliable measure would be (potential) syllables per tone group. In general, the more formal the text, the shorter and less variable the length of the tone group. In this way, for example, it is possible to compare a liturgical text with a sports review, both of which are contained in the SEC.

This kind of comparative analysis is particularly dependent upon large amounts of transcribed data, only provided by a corpus. It is not realistic to require learners or even teachers to collect and transcribe it first. The existence of a large corpus provides reliable data for detailed and large-scale prosodic analysis, which would otherwise simply not be possible.

3.2   Accent placement

Another important prosodic function is its accentual function. The rhythm of English, as a so-called stress-timed language, is remarkable for its alternation of weak and strong syllables. Strong syllables are said to be stressed, or, if there is pitch movement on them, accented. The SEC distinguishes these by marking with a dot those syllables which are stressed (but not accented) and with a tonetic stress mark (rise, fall, etc.) those which are accented. There seem to be two basic assumptions concerning accents, firstly concerning what they are and secondly concerning the choice of words or syllables which carry them. Both need to be addressed.

3.2.1   What are accents?

Before considering where accents are placed, it is necessary to define them. A crucial distinction to be made, besides the abstract phonological concept, is that between *perceptual salience* and the *physical events* which cause it. The written language provides a useful parallel here. Words that 'stand out' on the page are prominent or 'highlighted'. This is a question of visual perception. If we ask, however, *why* these words stand out, the answer could be, for example, because they are underlined, or in capitals, or in italics, or in bold type, or in a combination of these.

There is a common-sense assumption that accented syllables are perceived to be so because they are louder than the others. They may indeed be louder, but loudness is not considered to be the most important cue to salience. It is generally either pitch prominence (downward or upward excursion), or increased duration, or both, which cue a perception of salience. These issues can only be dealt with in depth in a more advanced course in acoustic phonetics.

Since the marking of accents is an important feature of prosodic annotation, it is important to make corpus users aware of the issues. A useful starting point seems to be to consider what is *subjectively* salient in a spoken utterance – in other words, which syllables sound prominent.

If we assume, as phonologists do, that a syllable is either strong or weak, then it should be easy to tell which is which – but it isn't. Unlike textbook examples, real utterances contain syllables on a scale of prominence which can baffle students (and not only students) listening for discrete categories of stressed or unstressed. One particular difficulty is judging the status of syllables which are salient, but do not carry a tone (marked with a dot in the corpus). Another is to identify accents which do not begin with a step *up* to the syllable. These include low rises and low falls, which generally start with a step down. These are often hard to explain since they are not so physically salient in terms of pitch prominence or loudness, but only in terms of increased duration.

Because of these difficulties, students' own transcriptions can be very misleading. It is pointless to base a discussion of accent placement on an inaccurate transcription. To have a reliable, professionally annotated text for such an analysis avoids this. At the same time, the attempt, however tentative, at practical analysis gives learners a better understanding of what the professional transcription represents.

3.2.2   Where do accents occur?

A common view expressed by students, and probably shared by others, is that accents occur on the 'important' words. This is a view which I find it exceptionally hard to eradicate (assuming of course that it is false). The main things students are asked to look for are:

- the relative frequency of accent assignment on lexical and grammatical words
- the number of accents in a tone group
- the position of the 'nucleus'. (I usually dispense with this term since it is theoretically controversial, but as it appears in most of the literature it needs to be referred to, at least in passing.)

Discussions are based around examples of accent assignment which do not fit the 'rule'; namely, that accents fall on the last lexical item in a tone group or utterance. Major issues are the de-accenting of given information, the setting up of parallelisms, and the stress patterning of compounds when written as two words (see Knowles 1987). Lexical stress, the dictionary-defined pattern of accentuation in polysyllabic words, can also be examined. The syllable assigned lexical stress in the dictionary is not always assigned stress or accent in connected speech.

3.3   Pitch movement

After dealing with phrasing, stress and accent placement, it is possible to consider the issue of 'tones' or pitch movement.

Recognizing the different tones is perhaps the most difficult aspect of intonation for the untrained. One difficulty is deciding on the basic distinction between down and up. Students can be distressed because of an apparent inability to tell the difference between a fall and a rise. As Roach (1991: 133) points out, the idea of up and down is in any case a metaphorical one. Fundamental frequency (what we perceive as pitch) is measured in time and not space. Vibrations can be faster and slower (i.e. there are more or fewer in a given time), but not higher and lower. None the less, the expression of more and less, or faster and slower, in spatial terms of up and down is a common metaphor. (Amounts of money go up and down; vehicles go at high and low speeds.)

Most students seem to be able to assign the terms high and low to notes of different pitch. The system of (nuclear) tones, however, is more difficult than just recognizing high and low; it is also a matter of recognizing and describing the direction of gradual pitch change, i.e. whether, for example, the tone starts high and then falls, or starts low and then rises. The distinction involves selecting from a number of audible phenomena those features which a phonologist regards as meaningful. A typical falling tone is given that term because the pitch begins to fall some way into a syllable, usually on the syllabic vowel; however, before the pitch can fall, it must first rise, resulting in a contour something like that in Figure 15.2.

It is purely a matter of convention that we call a syllable that goes up and then comes down a 'fall'. Unfortunately what students

Figure 15.2   Pitch contour of a typical falling tone

tend to hear first is the rise, and not the fall, and they are therefore very likely to say 'but I'm sure it goes up', when a more
skilled analyst has identified a fall. One possible solution is to
introduce the idea of tones by showing the f_0 contours created by
a prototypical fall (see Figure 15.2), rise and fall–rise, either with
a diagram or, if possible, instrumentally.

The symbols for the tones are then introduced as stylized representations of these patterns, and learners can observe that the
stylization of a fall ignores the initial rise to the peak before the
fall. Again this is to some extent a confidence-boosting procedure.
If one person thinks the pitch goes up when another says it goes
down, it may be that both are right. The system of tones pre-
supposes a selective processing of the overall contour, which is a
phonological rather than a phonetic issue.

Recognizing tones is largely a matter of training in a particular
system. I treat it here as I treat the recognition of stress: not so
much as training, but as a means of gaining insight into phenomena which others have been trained to observe reliably. Investigation of the way in which tones are used in speech is therefore
chiefly carried out using corpus texts. Although some people
ascribe meaning to individual tones, I distinguish simply between
final (fall) and non-final (rise, fall–rise, level), and regard any
other meaning as contextually determined. This allows simple
hypotheses to be set up such as: *all declarative sentences should end
in a fall, and all falls should occur at the end of declarative sentences.*
This can then easily be investigated (and falsified) using corpus
data. Other well-known issues can also be studied, such as the
intonation patterns of adverbs and sentence adverbials, and the
patterning of lists.

4   Student activity

Assessment is based on coursework. For this, students are required to analyse the prosodic transcription of a small section of the corpus. They are asked to comment on accent placement, looking specifically for the de-accentuation of given information and the accentuation pattern of compounds; also any examples of departure from normal word stress. They are then asked to comment on the choice of tone, concentrating on the last in each tone group (conventionally the nucleus, but not specifically marked as such in the corpus).

So why not simply start with the transcribed corpus, and spare the learners the attempts at transcribing? First, it is my experience, and that of others, that students learn more about the principles of prosodic analysis in trying to do it themselves than in many hours of lectures. In the same way, a few lessons in playing the piano (or painting, or judo, or juggling, etc.) make one appreciate the professional a little more. With just a little first-hand experience, the students have some idea of how the professional transcription is arrived at, its strengths and its limitations.

To allow students to exploit their practical experience, however limited, of transcription, they are also encouraged to collect similar data of their own – for example, a prepared speech by a professional speaker – for purposes of comparison. The students are usually confident enough to mark and comment on tone group boundaries in their own data. On the whole they tend to respond mainly to the most obvious boundaries and mark fewer than I would. However, they are still able to make useful comments on the acoustic signals which prompted their perception of boundaries and are convinced once and for all that there are far fewer pauses in connected speech than they had previously thought. Some students attempt to transcribe further, adding stress marks and sometimes indicating pitch movement, but this is not a requirement.

They usually choose news broadcasts which they record off air. Some find it interesting to ask a friend to read the same text and compare the differences. They are usually struck by the similarity in terms of tone grouping, but observe clearly that there is a big difference between professional and untrained readers. This wide variation in performance is rarely described in the literature. Experience with describing corpus data provides students with the tools to observe and describe this variation in a way that could never be gleaned from textbooks.

Students are encouraged to follow lines of investigation which interest them personally. One part-time student, for example, who is also a nursery nurse, recorded herself reading to small children, and examined the pattern of boundary placement, comparing it to a professional story reading from the corpus. The main difference actually appeared between different sections of her own performance. Since her reading was interspersed with spontaneous talk with the children she actually had data which combined the read with the spontaneous. The difference in tone grouping was considerable, as one might expect. The foundation for such observations, however, could not have been laid without access to large amounts of corpus data.

Other students display an interest in poetry reading, one of the text types included in the SEC. The main issue here is to observe how metre and line structure on the one hand, and natural speech rhythms on the other, place conflicting demands on a reader. This is not easy, but students have often been able to observe certain features such as the treatment of enjambment by 'good' and 'bad' readers.

Another area that interests some students is the comparison between the performances of native and non-native speakers of English. The differences are of course very complex, but some features such as stress patterns, both lexical stress and sentence stress (including the de-accenting and reduction of function words) repay analysis.

To a certain extent, the nature of the corpus limits the students' freedom of choice in data collection. Spontaneous conversation, for example, is a rich source of prosodic data, but very different from reading aloud. It contains many more performance-related prosodic features, such as hesitations and incomplete utterances. Preparation for this kind of analysis would more appropriately be based on a corpus of conversation, such as the CSAE or the LLC. Working on the principle that students should not be trained to analyse one kind of data and then assessed on something completely different, I ask them to be guided by the corpus available, while none the less drawing their attention to other kinds of speech.

The benefits of corpus analysis are evident in all these individual projects. Firstly, it engenders a confidence in the learners, not only to embark on their own analysis but also to admit to *not* being able to determine some things. Secondly, it brings a much increased awareness of the role of prosody in human communication and provides some of the tools to investigate this.

5   Benefits for teachers

Having attempted to describe the use of corpus data from the students' point of view, let me now take a look at it from the point of view of the teacher. The most obvious advantage lies in the quantity of data available in this way, and the reliability of the transcriptions, which can also be tested against the original recordings. In addition, it makes the process of assessment easier. It makes it possible to separate out the assessment of skills with the assessment of understanding and interpreting. It is frustrating to find a student desperately trying to explain the occurrence of a rise which is actually a fall. Conducting part of the assignment on the basis of a professional transcription avoids the pitfalls of students analysing their own errors or misjudgements.

One possible disadvantage of using corpus data, whether spoken or written, is the element of unpredictability which comes with real data. This is, of course, only a disadvantage if one expects – or is expected by the students – to be able to explain whatever the data throws up. Real data requires teachers to be prepared for the new, the odd, and the unexplainable.

6   Conclusion

The use of annotated speech corpora for teaching prosody is clearly of value to teachers and learners alike. And yet I have only exploited a fraction of what an annotated speech corpus can offer.

Firstly the kind of texts contained in the SEC dictates to a certain extent the prosodic features that are dealt with. If I were using a transcribed corpus of conversation, I might concentrate more, for example, on the distribution of pauses (silent or filled) than on structural boundaries. Similarly, I might deal more with speech rate and turn-taking cues than with the prosodic behaviour of sentence adverbials.

Secondly, I have so far only used printed copies of transcribed corpus texts. I have not yet exploited the corpus (for teaching) in its machine-readable form. The majority of chapters in this book deal with the advantages of having text in machine-readable form over the printed page. In that respect this account is a little behind the times. But perhaps the discrepancy is not as great as it might seem. Students who learn about written texts using concordances and other retrieval methods are already literate. In a sense, my students are not prosodically literate. Before we exploit the advantage of using the data in its machine-readable form, the students must first be taught to read.

Even at this elementary stage, however, there are valuable lessons to be learned from prosodic transcriptions. Clearly the unpredictability of real data is an issue not only in phonetics but in all analyses of linguistic data. For the students it may be part of a more general learning process – a developing awareness of the nature of theories, their empirical testability and their shortcomings. By arguing over what may or may not be a tone-group boundary, or over what may or may not be a falling tone, students acquire an awareness of the limits of descriptive 'categories'. This can lead to a discussion about linguistic categorization in general, comparing binary categories (as tone-group boundaries are assumed to be) and prototypes (which allow for more or less typical members of a category).

Finally, by not demanding from students what they cannot do, it is possible for prosody to lose its reputation as an intangible, frustratingly elusive dimension of speech, and, to a certain extent at least, be demystified. Annotated speech data provides a link between predictable and relatively simple textbook data, and the bewildering complexity of naturally occurring speech.

Notes

1 These, of course, are not the only exponents of these functions, nor the only functions of prosody.
2 Even professionally trained transcribers can be 'not sure', although this tends to be obscured by the usually binary choice available in most transcription systems. It would in fact be useful for researchers if information on degrees of determinacy were available in some way to the end user of the corpus.

16

Corpus and Concordance: Finding out about Style

HOWARD JACKSON

1 Introduction

Final-year students on the English Language and Literature degree course at the University of Central England are offered an option module entitled 'Computer-Aided Text Analysis' (CATA).[1] Students take four modules in a semester, and each module is allocated a notional 120 study hours. Students will have been taught word processing in their first year, so that they can be expected to come to the CATA module familiar with a PC and reasonably skilled in word processing. Some students, especially mature students, own their own PCs.

This chapter shows how students can undertake computer-based stylistic analysis of texts with relatively limited resources. At the time of writing students have available for use three 386 PCs and some thirty Amstrad 1640 XT PCs, with a hard disk containing the software, and a 3.5" (Double Density) floppy disk drive. Hardware has since been upgraded to 486 PCs running Windows 3.1.

The CATA module requires students to assemble a mini-corpus of texts, investigate aspects of the language of the texts by using appropriate software on a PC, and to write up their investigation as a project report. For most students, the literary aspects of English study are their chief interest and they choose literature texts for their corpus. However, undertaking a computer analysis requires students to focus on linguistic features of their chosen texts and to look for 'hard' linguistic evidence for their literary intuitions and interpretations. Students receive the following academic support: instruction on how to use the software at the beginning of the module; a scheduled weekly tutorial of up to 30 minutes; unscheduled advice as and when required.

In preparation for the module, students are expected to read the appropriate sections in at least one of: Butler (1992), Hockey (1980), Rudall and Corns (1987), Sinclair (1986, 1991), Burrows (1987), Potter (1989).

The following sections will outline the stages that students go through in undertaking their CATA project: assembling the corpus, learning the software, formulating questions and obtaining results, drawing conclusions and writing-up.

2 Assembling the corpus

The first two or three weeks of the module are devoted to assembling the corpus and learning to use the software. Students are advised to create a corpus of between 6000 and 8000 words, though a larger corpus may be appropriate for certain kinds of investigation. A corpus usually consists of a minimum of two texts or text extracts, since the basic approach is normally comparative. Students are advised to make their texts of approximately equal length, since this makes statistical comparison rather more straightforward.

The choice of texts may be determined by a number of routes. Students may have an interest in particular authors, whom they may be studying on one of their other modules and whose work they think could usefully be subjected to a computer-based analysis; for example, 'Does the style of the openings of Hardy's novels change from his early to his later works?'. Students may have particular questions that they think could be answered by a computer-based investigation; for example, 'Is there something about the language of a best-seller that makes it so popular, by comparison with a classic work of literature?' or 'What makes the Authorized Version of the Bible sound more "poetic" than modern translations?'. A student may be interested in looking at the linguistic differences in particular text genres; for example, of a particular author (the diaries and novels of Virginia Woolf), or addressed to different audiences (science textbooks and science journalism).

The choice of texts and the questions that students are interested in asking of those texts go hand in hand. At the same time students need to be encouraged to think of how the computer software can enable them to find answers to their questions. A few

1. Comparison of passages from Dylan Thomas's prose, poetry and 'Under Milk Wood'.
2. Sylvia Plath's life as reflected in her poetry from different periods.
3. Some stylistic features of Ezra Pound's cantos.
4. Relative pronouns in texts from the LOB Corpus.
5. A comparison of science texts with science fiction texts from the LOB Corpus.
6. Hemingway's journalism compared with his short stories.
7. What makes a bestseller: comparison of passages from Jackie Collins, Fay Wheldon and James Herbert.
8. Comparison of opening and closing of *The Color Purple*.
9. Women's magazine stories: *Woman's Realm* and *New Woman*.
10. The treatment of the 'crop circle' phenomenon in various newspapers.

Figure 16.1   Examples of previous CATA projects

recent examples will show the kinds of texts and questions that students choose (see Figure 16.1 for further examples). One student had an interest in the novels of Alan Sillitoe and wanted to investigate whether his style had changed over the course of his output: extracts from *Saturday Night and Sunday Morning* (1958) and *The Storyteller* (1979) formed this corpus. Another student, with an interest in detective fiction, wanted to investigate differences in style between a novel by a classic male author and a recent female author: extracts from Raymond Chandler's *The Big Sleep* (1939) and Sara Paretsky's *Guardian Angel* (1992) formed the corpus. The student interested in why the Authorized Version of the Bible seemed more poetic compared the 'Song of Songs' in that version (1611) with its rendering in the *Good News Bible* (1976). Another student wanted to find out whether the modern sequel to Jane Austen's *Pride and Prejudice* had succeeded in maintaining Austen's style: extracts from *Pride and Prejudice* (1813) and Emma Tennant's *Pemberley* (1993) formed this corpus.

Once the choice of texts has been decided, the corpus needs to be assembled in electronic form. Some texts can be made available in electronic form, either because they have been purchased (e.g. the OUP Electronic Editions of Chaucer and Jane Austen), or because they are available from the Oxford Text Archives or downloaded from the Internet,[2] or because they have been kept from projects undertaken by past students. Otherwise students key in their own texts, using a word-processing program with which they are familiar. The text analysis software requires texts to be in plain ASCII format. Each text in a corpus will be assigned to a separate file. All texts are then proofread and edited, with markers and reference tags inserted as appropriate.

3   Learning the software

Students are taught how to use three pieces of software: PC-Litstats, Longman Mini-Concordancer and TACT. More recently, MonoConc for Windows[3] has been used as the concordance programme.

3.1   PC-Litstats

PC-Litstats, 'A statistical package for literary study', was developed by Stephen Reimer[4] at the University of Alberta. It takes an ASCII text file as input and produces the following output either on the whole text or on a specified sample of the text:

1   Word frequency counts: the number of words occurring once, twice, three times, and so on.
2   Word lengths: the number of words with one letter, two letters, three letters, and so on.
3   Initial letter frequencies: the number of words beginning with 'a', 'b', 'c', and so on.
4   Sentence length frequencies: the number of sentences with one word, two words, three words, and so on.
5   Verbal segment frequencies: the number of verbal segments (i.e. parts of sentences between punctuation marks) with one word, two words, and so on.

PC-Litstats produces some useful basic data to contribute to the comparison of the styles of two or more texts. PC-Litstats comes with a further program, the χ^2 (chi-square) program, which applies the chi-square test of significant difference to the output of Litstats, as a crude test, for example, of the common authorship of a set of text samples.

Students need to run each of their texts once through Litstats and obtain the output, which is stored in a file that can then be printed. The other software will be used more extensively. Students may use either or both of the concordancing programs Longman Mini-Concordancer[5] (LMC) and TACT.[6]

3.2   Longman Mini-Concordancer

LMC takes files in ASCII format, with a '.TXT' extension, either from a floppy disk or from a hard disk. LMC accepts files with a limited number of 'tags', of up to 8 characters each, contained within angle brackets, e.g. <poem1>. On each occasion of use, LMC loads a file into memory and creates a wordlist. File size is limited by available memory, but it could be up to 50,000 words on a machine with 640 Kb of memory. This limit is well beyond the file size that CATA students will be handling.

LMC works with a menu bar of drop-down menus. The 'Info' menu gives access to some useful basic information about the text that has been loaded, including: number of words (tokens), number of types, the token/type ratio, number of punctuation types and occurrences, number of characters and number of lines, and any tags found in the text.

The 'Wordlist' menu gives access to the various forms in which the wordlist is available: ordinary (forwards) alphabetical order; reverse alphabetical order (i.e. from the ends of words), which is useful for identifying rhyming words; frequency order, with the most frequently occurring word first; a punctuation list, with frequencies; and a 'wildcard' option, allowing for the listing of words containing particular strings of letters, e.g. '?oo?' for four-letter words containing 'oo' or '*ing' for words ending in 'ing'.

From any of the wordlists, one or more items may be selected for a KWIC (Key Word in Context) concordance display. A KWIC display shows each occurrence of the key word on a separate line, with either the first or last letter of the key word in the centre of the line and context either side filling up the line. The key word may be either left aligned (with the first letter central and more context to the left than the right) or right aligned, with the last letter central and more context to the right). A full-text display is easily obtained for any line in the KWIC display. The KWIC display may be sorted in various ways (via the 'Sort' menu): the occurrences of the key word may be sorted in order of their appearance in the text; if there is more than one key word, the display may be listed in key-word order; and the context may be sorted in one of four ways: to the left or to the right of the key word, and letters in forward or reverse order.

A 'Concordance' menu allows for words, including wildcards, to be searched for, as well as phrases. For example, 'the * of' would find all three-word phrases such as 'the best of', 'the kind of', 'the middle of'. A 'Proximity' menu enables a search to be made of a word in the context of a key word, either within 3 words or within 8 words, to the left, to the right or on both sides of the key word. For example, if one wanted to find 'the' + 'of' expressions where more than one word intervenes, a proximity search of 'the' to the left of 'of' would be undertaken.

LMC has a versatile set of search tools, which can be imaginatively exploited to provide data on the linguistic features of the text, which may then be suitably interpreted to make judgements about the style of a text. Particularly useful are the various ways in which the wordlist can be ordered, the inclusion of a punctuation list, and the manipulation that is possible on the KWIC display. Moreover, any of the displays can be easily printed out for examination elsewhere, or saved in a file for future perusal on screen.

3.3   TACT

TACT is more complicated initially to use. It has some facilities that LMC does not, though it also lacks some of LMC's facilities. TACT does not work directly on an ASCII text file: the ASCII file must first be processed by the 'MAKBAS' program in the TACT suite, to produce a 'text database', which is an indexed version of the text. TACT allows a text to be extensively referenced, which is particularly useful if the text is drama, where each act, scene and character can be given an individual reference, or if the text is a collection of poems or articles, where each author, title, date, etc., can be referenced. These references can then be used in the concordance displays to indicate where a particular occurrence is located in the text. TACT, by means of MAKBAS, indexes a text (i.e. provides it with a wordlist) only once: when a text database (TDB) is activated in TACT, the wordlist is instantly available; it does not have to be created anew each time. However, if the text needs to be amended or a new reference category is added, the text database must be recreated with MAKBAS.

The opening screen of TACT gives the number of types and the number of tokens in the text that has been activated. Like LMC, TACT operates with a menu bar, containing drop-down menus. The 'Select' menu gives access to the wordlist, which contains frequency data for each word, but which is available in only one form: a straight alphabetical listing. There is no punctuation listing.

One or more words may be selected from the wordlist and their context displayed in one of four ways. The key words may be displayed as an 'Index', which gives a single line for each occurrence, equivalent to the KWIC display of LMC, except that in TACT each line is referenced. They may be displayed as KWIC, for which the default in TACT is the line in which the key word occurs and two lines of context before and after, giving a five-line display, with references. The context for a KWIC display may be varied via a 'Dialog box': the number of lines before and after the key word line can be varied separately, or the context can be specified as the number of words before and after the key word. A third type of display is 'Text', which gives a screenful of text, with the key word in the centre; the text can be scrolled up and down. The fourth type of display is 'Distribution', which provides a bar chart of the distribution of the selected word(s). The default bar chart divides the text into ten equal sections, but this may be modified: the number of sections may be increased or decreased, or the division may be by a reference category (e.g. poem title).

All four types of display may be active at the same time, either as full-screen displays or with the screen divided (panelled) between the active displays, either equally (the default) or according to choice. There is the possibility of switching between displays and they can be synchronized. No sorting of context is possible, but where there is more than one key word, they may be sequenced in a display either in key-word order or in (occurrence in) text order.

TACT has a highly sophisticated means of searching a text by means of its 'AutoSelection Dialog Box'. The context of the key words found can be adjusted: the default is five words before and after. The search is specified on the 'Rule' line, which allows almost any string to be searched for. Besides the usual wildcards, the rule may specify 'character classes'; for example, '*b[aei].*' searches for words containing the character string 'ba', 'be' or 'bi'; '*b[~aei]*' searches for words containing 'b' when it is not followed by 'a', 'e' or 'i'; '*b[a:e]*' searches for words containing 'b' followed by any letter in the range 'a' to 'e' inclusive. A word search will produce a list of words containing the string specified, as a subset of the wordlist. Every word will be prefixed by the selection symbol (>). At this stage a word may be deselected before proceeding to a concordance display.

The rule in an AutoSelection Dialog Box may also contain a phrase of any length; for example, 'the| |of' will select three-word phrases having *the* as the first word and *of* as the third. The phrase search will produce a list of 'text positions', with each phrase preceded by the selection symbol. Any of the phrases may be deselected at this stage, before a concordance display is activated. Also, any of the positions in the phrase may be designated the key word position by including the selection symbol at the appropriate point in the rule; for example, 'the|>|of' will make the second word in this phrase the key word. In a concordance display, the key word can then be sorted into alphabetical order, to bring all the occurrences of each key word together in the display.

The AutoSelection Dialog Box allows for further, non-string, types of search. The operator '&' in a rule allows for a search of two words 'in the vicinity' of each other, with 'vicinity' specified by the 'Configuration Context' in the Dialog Box, e.g. five words before and after; so, the rule 'to & the' searches for positions in the text where *to* and *the* occur within a specified number of words of each other. The operator '~' means 'not in the vicinity of'; so, the rule 'to ~ the' selects *to* where *the* does not occur within the specified number of words.

The operator 'span' selects all the words occurring in the span of a specified word, as defined in the 'Configuration Context'. For example, the rule 'page; span', with a Configuration Context of five words before and after, will select all the ten words either side of each occurrence of *page*. Displaying the results as an Index with 'Order' set as 'Word Only' will show for each word selected how many times it has been selected and how frequently it occurs in the text overall. It is one of the ways that TACT provides for investigating collocations. The '&' operator mentioned previously searches for the collocations of specified words. There is also a 'Collocate' option in one of the menus, which searches for the collocations, within a specified span, of words selected from the wordlist and then calculates their 'Z-scores' and displays them in rank order of Z-scores, from strongest to weakest collocates.

Returning to the AutoSelection Dialog Box, there are two further operators to mention. The 'freq' operator selects words on the basis of their frequency of occurrence: the rule 'freq 2' would select all words which occur twice in the text; 'freq >2' would select words that occur more than twice in the text; 'b.*; freq 2:4' would select all words that begin with 'b' and occur two, three or four times in the text. The 'simil %' operator searches for strings which have a similarity with a given string to at least the percentage specified; for example, the rule 'simil thorough 75' would select words that had at least a 75 per cent similarity with 'thorough', such as *although, thought, through.*

The operation of a rule in the AutoSelection Dialog Box may be restricted to particular parts of the text. A range of lines or words may be specified; e.g. 'when line=100:600' added to a rule will restrict the search to between lines 100 and 600 of the text; 'when word>1000' will begin a search after the thousandth word in the text. Alternatively, the search may be restricted to one or more reference categories; e.g. 'when Act=4' added to a rule will restrict the search to the fourth act; the rule 'blood; when Act=4 | character=Macbeth' selects the word *blood* only in Macbeth's speeches in the fourth act.

While TACT does not provide the variations in the wordlist that LMC has, nor the sorting of context in concordance displays, it does, through the AutoSelection Dialog Box, have a more subtle and sophisticated mechanism for searching, including the identification of collocations. Another advantage of TACT is that it allows you to save certain search procedures for use in later sessions. You can create a 'Personal Database' (PDB), containing lists of words or phrases arranged under 'categories': a list may be activated in a subsequent session by selecting the appropriate category name. You can, secondly, create a 'Rule Library File', in which to store rules from the AutoSelection Dialog Box for use in subsequent sessions, with the same or indeed with any text database. You can, thirdly, create a 'Script File', in which you can 'record' a series of keystrokes, which can be 'played back' on a subsequent occasion.

This review of the software presents a summary of the computational resources that are available to students as they undertake investigations of their corpus. Students are encouraged to explore the software and to exploit as many of the features of the software as they can, in an experimental and exploratory way, to see if some operation throws up data that could be of relevance to the questions they want to answer, or indeed to questions they may

not yet have thought about. Students need to realize that serendipity may play a significant part in such investigations.

4   Formulating questions and getting results

The choice of texts that students make may well be accompanied
by a question or a set of questions that they wish to ask of the
texts. Usually these are couched in fairly general terms: 'What
differences are there between Hemingway's journalism from the
Spanish Civil War and his fiction that draws on that experience?',
'Do the styles of the Canterbury Tales differ as a reflection of the
characters that Chaucer chooses to be their tellers?', 'Does Sillitoe's
style change between 1958 and 1979, as represented by a novel
from each of those years?'.

At the same time as learning to use the software, students are
encouraged to sharpen their questions into lines of investigation
that can be implemented computationally, taking account of what
analyses of the texts the software can perform and what they cannot. Subjective judgements – 'The Authorized Version of the Bible
is "more poetic" than modern versions' – need to be translated
into investigations that will be looking at features of the language
of the texts. Students need to ask themselves questions such as:
What kind of features might make a text sound more poetic?
What kind of linguistic items contribute to the characterization
of style? What specific linguistic features might an author use to
create character? By seeking the answers to such questions students
begin to operationalize their initial questions and decide where to
begin in the investigation of their chosen texts. Students must
submit a brief (750-word) progress report by Week 5 of the semester, in which they are required to report on the texts they have
chosen, the lines of investigation they are following, the questions
they have formulated, and how they plan to pursue their project.

The texts have been passed through PC-Litstats (see 3.2) and
basic data on token/type ratio, sentence and word lengths has
been obtained: some of this information can be checked against
the punctuation list and the text information given in LMC. Students are now concerned with using the concordancing software.
In the general analysis of style, it is usually fruitful to begin by
looking at grammatical words, such as pronouns (personal, relative,

etc.), conjunctions, prepositions and determiners. These usually constitute the words in the text with the highest frequency, so a simple comparison of the frequency of occurrence of such words, as found in the wordlists, can sometimes be revealing and perhaps indicate further lines of inquiry. For example, in a comparison between a first-person narrative and a third-person narrative, it would be comforting to find that the first-person narrative had more first-person pronouns and the third-person narrative more third-person pronouns. There may also be significance in the relative frequencies of third-person masculine and feminine pronouns, and among these between subject pronouns (*he, she*) as against object pronouns (*him, her*), with subject pronouns indicating actors and object pronouns indicating 'passive' participants. In this last case, a check would need to be made, via the concordance, that no instances of *her* were possessive. Indeed, it is often the case that checks of this kind need to be followed up with a look at the context: are all object pronouns in fact syntactic objects, or do some occur after prepositions?

In the case of conjunctions, a preponderance of coordinating conjunctions, especially *and*, may indicate a paratactic style, though *and* may join other than clauses or sentences: the context would need to be checked. An extensive use of subordinating conjunctions, and relative pronouns, may indicate a hypotactic style and a certain syntactic complexity in the text. Heavy use of particular conjunctions may be stylistically significant; for example, *if* and *unless* in setting conditions, *because* and *so that* in indicating reasons or purposes.

For some types of investigation, students may concentrate on the themes, images or motifs in a text. In this case, the investigation begins with a perusal of the wordlist to identify vocabulary items that could be thought to belong to the semantic field that reflects a particular theme or image. This is where the 'Personal Database' facility of TACT can be a useful mechanism. The items identified in the wordlist will need to be reviewed in context, both to check that they are being used to reflect the chosen theme or image, and to see if the context can add information useful to the investigation. A thematic study can be further enhanced by exploring the collocations of the lexical items identified, using one of TACT's facilities to do this. One example of a thematic investigation was a study undertaken by one student of imagery relating to 'mythology', 'love', 'politics' and 'supernatural' in W.B. Yeats's poetry, with the aim of charting changes in these images from one period to another in his poetic output.

Poetry lends itself to all kinds of interesting investigations. One student was comparing Keats's odes with his narrative poetry and discovered that Keats seemed to have a particular fondness for creating hyphenated compounds, uncovered while undertaking a concordance search of punctuation marks, including the hyphen. Another student was comparing three Elizabethan sonneteers (Wyatt, Surrey and Shakespeare) and became interested in the use of alliteration by these poets: using the phrase and wildcard features of TACT's 'rules' (e.g. b.* | b.*) this particular feature could be investigated and compared in the work of these poets.

In the investigation of novels, one feature that is often explored is dialogue. As a start, quotation marks can be found in the punctuation list of LMC, and a concordance of these can be displayed. Equally, TACT can be used to search for quotation marks, though with a little less ease than in LMC. Dialogue may then be further investigated by examining the speech verbs that are used (*say, reply, remark*, etc.) and the manner adverbs that may accompany them (*icily, passionately, nonchalantly*). The speech verbs will be identified in the wordlist, and a concordance will reveal the accompanying adverbs; alternatively a wildcard search of '*ly' will find all '-ly' adverbs (and some other words, like *only*, which will need to be excluded), which will enable the proportion of '-ly' adverbs used with speech verbs to be ascertained. Such an investigation revealed to one student that the popular fiction text being studied used a much narrower range of speech verbs – with a preponderance of *say*, perhaps with a manner adverb, or indeed no speech verb at all – than the classic work of literature that was being used as a comparator.

It will be clear from the examples cited that the approach students are encouraged to take is largely exploratory. The occasional student works out a detailed plan of investigations in advance, which is then systematically carried through. More often, however, some lines of inquiry become quickly established, which then lead on to others, and so on. Some lines of inquiry turn out to be dead-ends, producing no useful information for the analysis of the text or for answering the questions that have motivated the investigation. Other lines of inquiry prove fruitful, and some may suggest further avenues of investigation, or some more detailed analysis of the feature that is being examined. The most successful projects involve a combination of imagination and doggedness: imagination to open up new lines of inquiry and doggedness to pursue them systematically.

Students are also encouraged to use their corpus as a means of exploiting the software, by trying out as many facilities of the software as they can on their texts. Not only may this lead to the discovery of features of the texts that they had not thought about exploring, but it may also lead to the testing of the software itself and to an awareness of the limitations of such software for textual analysis. In the end, such programs only produce data which itself in turn needs to be interpreted.

The results are produced in a number of forms, including tables of frequencies of sets of words, phrases, punctuation marks, word and sentence lengths, as well as lists of words representing themes and images, and collocation tables. The results are an assemblage of data about the linguistic features of the texts being analysed. It is probably, for most students, the first time that they have paid such close attention to the language of texts or collected such a range of data about a single text. But what students now realize is that the results do not speak for themselves: they have to be interpreted and evaluated; conclusions have to be drawn; the results have to be related to the initial questions.

5   Drawing conclusions and writing-up

It is to be expected that conclusions will have been emerging as lines of inquiry were being explored and as data was accumulated to answer the question with which a student began the investigation. At this stage, all the data can be brought together, sifted, the relevant results retained, and the complete picture that has emerged can be contemplated, organized and written up. Now is the time to ascertain whether the weight of evidence accumulated provides a positive or a negative answer to the initial question, or whether the answer is uncertain. Are the literary intuitions that the student began with about the texts confirmed or called into question? Students not infrequently find that the data that they have teased out with the computer runs counter to their intuitions about a text. It can be a salutary lesson.

Students are required to produce a final 5000-word write-up of their CATA project, in which they are expected to include at least the following sections: aims of the investigation; method; results; analysis and interpretation; evaluation of the use of the computer. Under 'Aims', they are expected to justify the choice of texts for their corpus, and to outline the questions they wished to answer with their corpus. Under 'Method', these questions are elaborated into the lines of inquiry that were pursued, and how the computer software was used to explore the corpus in pursuing their investigations. Under 'Results', the data they have accumulated is presented, in an organized way, under linguistic features (e.g. conjunctions) or themes (e.g. portrayal of female characters). The 'Analysis and Interpretation' section then comments on the results, interprets their significance and relates them to the aims of the project. Finally, and in some ways the most difficult part of the report, the 'Evaluation' requires students to reflect on the project they have carried out and to comment on the advantages and limitations of a computer-aided text analysis.

In the evaluation, some acknowledgement is usually made of the small-scale nature of the project and the danger of generalizing from such a limited investigation. Comment is sometimes passed on the disadvantages of using 'bare' text, and how much more might be achieved with grammatically tagged texts. And some point is often made about the limitations of the data that a concordance program can produce and the fact that it cannot do the interpretation for you. At the same time, acknowledgement is made of the 'hard' evidence that such a program provides to either reinforce or to call into question some cherished interpretation of a text. Students who have fully exploited the software can often make some useful comments on the limits of the software's capabilities. Students begin to appreciate that computers and their software are but tools, but nevertheless tools that can enhance the analysis and interpretation of texts.

6   Conclusion

Students opt for the CATA module for a variety of reasons. A few admit to a 'computer phobia', which they expect to overcome by intensive and structured use of the computer for a purpose related to their studies. Some see the opportunity to make a further and more in-depth study of a chosen author's work, or to

study the work of an author whom they have not had the opportunity to study elsewhere on the course. Others are genuinely
interested in exploring the application of information technology
to the study of texts and particularly literary texts. For others, it
represents a welcome contrast to the other modules they are doing
in the semester, and the report style of assessment is attractive.

What do students gain from doing the CATA module? Firstly,
their IT skills are developed, which is of benefit in terms of their
subsequent employability. They also learn that computers and software have limitations as well as possibilities, and that what they
are dealing with is a tool that is open to exploitation. Secondly,
students develop further 'transferable skills': the management of
a self-initiated project, including the management of their time;
research and problem-solving skills, as they attempt to find answers
to questions and pursue lines of inquiry; report-writing skills, not
a noted skill of literature students, which requires organization
of material and the integration of text and non-textual material
(tables of results). Students also discover that the systematic exploration of some aspect of a text may sometimes reveal the unexpected:
the serendipity factor in research.

Thirdly, and perhaps surprisingly, students engage in cooperation with others in the pursuit of a goal. Students are working on
individual projects with their own corpus of texts: that is what they
'own' personally and there is no competition for it from other
students. What they share is common access to computers and to
software. That is the challenge they all face: how to make the software work for them. And it has been evident that this common
challenge engenders a large amount of mutual help and cooperation, as students show each other ways that they have found of
using the software or share with each other lines of inquiry that
they have found fruitful.

Lastly, students gain a new perspective on texts, and especially on literary texts. They find that intuitions about texts and
interpretations of texts can be supported by quantifiable evidence
gained from a computer analysis, or that they can be challenged
by such evidence. Using concordance software forces students to
pay attention to the linguistic features of the text and to examine
what it is in the language that engenders the impressions they
may have had from a superficial reading of the text. For a linguist,
that is perhaps the most satisfying outcome.

Notes

1   I am grateful to my colleague Judith Aldridge, who runs the Computer-Aided Text Analysis module with me, for commenting on a draft of this article. Computer-aided Text Analysis has been offered as a final-year (Level 3) option module on the BA Hons English Language and Literature degree at UCE (formerly Birmingham Polytechnic) since 1987/88, since when over 120 students have taken the module. For the first four years, students used the Oxford Concordance Program (Hockey and Marriott 1980) on a mainframe computer (Jackson 1990). Then, for 1991/92, TACT became available on PCs in the School of English (Jackson 1993), and Longman Mini-Concordancer was added in 1993–94. In 1996 MonoConc for Windows became the preferred concordance programme.

2   The Oxford Text Archive is part of Oxford University Computing Service. The Archive contains a large number of texts in a number of languages, with varying availability, including some that can be freely downloaded via FTP. For details see Appendix 2. The Oxford University Computing Service is also host to the CTI Centre for Textual Studies, which publishes a twice-yearly newsletter, *Computers and Texts*, as well as a very useful *Resources Guide* (Hughes and Lee 1994). The Centre holds copies of software relevant to textual computing and offers advice to academics. The address is the same as for the Oxford Text Archive.

3   MonoConc for Windows was developed by Michael Barlow at Rice University (USA). (See Appendix 4)

4   For details of PC-Litstats, see Appendix 4.

5   Longman Mini-Concordancer was developed by Brian Chandler and first published in 1989. The LMC was withdrawn from production while this book was in press. The editors feel, however, that the description here remains useful as it applies in large measure to other, similar programmes.

6   TACT was developed by John Bradley and Lidio Presutti at the University of Toronto. It was issued in Version 1.1 in 1989, with Version 1.2 following in 1990. TACT is freeware and has been widely used in humanities computing. See Appendix 4.

17

The Role of Corpora in Critical Literary Appreciation

BILL LOUW

1 Introduction

The opportunity for corpora to play a role in literary criticism has increased greatly over the last decade. Ironically, it has done so largely unnoticed either by critics or corpus linguists. During the period when corpora were limited both in terms of size and access, no claim could plausibly be made that a corpus might complement intuitive skills of literary appreciation. No matter how well sampled a corpus was, its total size at that time amounted to little more than the equivalent of a dozen or so novels.

Linguistic stylistic studies carried out during this period tended, without actually saying so, to treat each machine-readable literary work as a 'corpus' in its own right. True verification of the critic's intuitive responses during these early investigations was limited, because it was not possible to compare a particular work with the language as a whole. Where literary works were used computationally as a foil to one another, investigators were, in reality, dealing with two limited 'corpora', each written by a single author. The strongest critical statements which arose from computational analysis during this period, although powerful, were thus largely 'comparative'. Claims that they were truly stylistic findings foundered from a lack of evidence about the whole language.

A number of stylisticians were acutely aware of the developments necessary to allow a comparison of individual texts with a truly representative sample of texts in the whole language (Bally, Bloch, Riffaterre, Spitzer, etc.). However, even as late as the mid-1970s, both the computer technology and the willingness to use it as part of their *apparatus criticus* were signally absent from departments of literary studies. Linguists themselves had expressed pessimism concerning the viability of the descriptive goals of stylisticians.

> Another difficulty in the work of the 'style as deviation' school of linguistic stylistics is its definition of the norm from which an author's style is supposed to differ in certain ways. For example, Bernard Bloch defines style as 'the message carried by the frequency distributions and transitional probabilities of [a discourse's] linguistic features, especially as they differ from those of the same features in the language as a whole'. *This definition is a chimera. The 'frequency distributions and transitional probabilities' of natural language are not known and never will be, and even if they could be ascertained they would constitute no particularly revealing insight into either natural language or style.*
>
> (Freeman 1970: 6; my emphasis)

Some literary critics of distinction who were exposed to the early computational work of their colleagues saw in it no great potential for the provision of immediate access to large amounts of the whole language. The work of David Lodge is a case in point. There can be no doubt that he was exposed, as early as the 1960s, to the computational research of John Sinclair, for he makes a point of parodying it in his later writings. However, when he comes to think through the problems posed by Riffaterre concerning the subjectivity of literary critics, computers and corpora do not occur to Lodge as a potential source for verifying critical intuition.

> It is interesting to trace the logical stages of Riffaterre's pursuit of a science of literary styles. They may be set out as follows:
> (1) Style is the means by which a writer obtains certain effects in communication.
> *So*
> (2) One way of studying style would be to relate the writer's intentions to the verbal forms he uses.
> *But*
> (3) Intentions are not recoverable.
> *So*
> (4) We study the responses of readers.
> *But*
> (5) Readers' responses are distorted by subjective value judgments.
> *So*
> (6) We consider the readers' responses as mere indications of the presence of stylistic devices.
> *But*

(7) Readers' responses may be unreliable merely as indications of the presence of stylistic devices.

   So

(8) We shall control the evidence of readers' responses by the structural criteria of deviation from contextual norms.

   Then . . .

Then what? The style analyst has his *data*, a catalogue of all the stylistic devices in a given text (supposing, that is, that the method is practicable, which seems doubtful), but he is still confronted with the task of deciding whether (a) any particular Stylistic Device (SD) has worked, and (b) how it has worked in relation to all other SDs in the text. Is there any objective, 'scientific' way of answering such questions? I think not.   (Lodge 1966: 59)

It is worth noting that Lodge, in common with so many academics, falls victim to the 'bootstraps fallacy' by believing that, in some way, the determination of stylistic devices will be an event which is internal to the text under investigation. In writing '*Then* . . . Then what?' Lodge could have provided no better entry point for a reference to corpora. Riffaterre had exhausted the subjective end of the continuum which centred around writers' intentions and readers' responses. In (8) he makes the decision to look to the conventions of the language for objective evidence.

So what were stylisticians doing while corpora were growing two hundred times larger than what had, for two decades, come to be accepted as the 'standard' size of approximately 1 million words?

The movement towards the production of larger corpora was mainly motivated by attempts to improve lexicography. This culminated in the production of the world's first corpus-based dictionary at Cobuild in 1987. This work used a corpus of 21 million words of running text and its size at the time was unrivalled. But very little use was made of this material as an aid to literary appreciation. The literary critic has gained access to large amounts of text in the past few years only through CD-ROM technology. Open access (by subscription) to large corpora, came with the opening of the Bank of English at Cobuild in April 1994. The British National Corpus also plans, in cooperation with Lancaster University, to offer open access to its corpora.

2   Will critical appreciation become corpus-based?

Criticism is an ancient, prestigious and revered area of study in the humanities and one in which proficiency is only deemed to have been reached after many years of dedicated immersion in the canon of English literature. Any suggestion that the literature of popular culture might displace the canon is currently being fiercely resisted. Indeed, it may be confidently assumed that those who oppose Easthope's position believe that the canon has come into being through critical practice and that, without the canon, that which still purported to be critical practice would, in fact, be nothing of the sort.

Many scholars within the discipline of criticism also believe that critical ability will emerge spontaneously in a reader, and that if it fails to do so, the reader is best advised to abandon the pursuit of criticism. The possibility that the principles on which criticism operates might be derived via methods other than through the response of a gifted reader's intuition to a reading of literary works is rarely entertained.

However, the existence of corpora of over 200 million words (at which the Bank of English stood in the summer of 1994) will mean that critics and their students could have access, within a matter of seconds, to more text (the equivalent of about 3500 novels) than the average reader is exposed to in the space of a lifetime of dedicated reading. How can this huge resource be used?

2.1 Data-assisted literary appreciation: testing intuitions

Corpora will provide massive amounts of evidence for any query the critic would otherwise have to place before his or her intuition. Much of the recorded discourse of the literary criticism tutorial involves appeals such as: 'But do people actually say . . . ?' (followed by some quotation from the text under discussion). By appealing to the corpus rather than to the mind, such requests can be satisfied almost instantly. The investigator's intuition is either corroborated or revised by the evidence provided by the corpus. As will be demonstrated below, appeals to the corpus for verification of an intuitive insight, or (in the case of L2 learners) to compensate for the absence of native-speaker intuition, frequently result in the modification or displacement of the original insight.

One of the first questions which the nascent subject area of 'corpora and criticism' will need to answer is whether recourse to corpus data is a form of 'cheating'. Even colleagues who have for many years praised the notion of literary deviance from a norm, may shrink from consulting that norm. Yet there is general agreement that the difference between the norm and features of the text is responsible for many of the 'devices' which give the reader so much pleasure.

At first sight there would appear to be less of an 'ego-trip' involved in appealing to a corpus rather than to personal intuition. However, early trials suggest that students of literature derive at least as much satisfaction from the act of verification as they previously did from imposing dogmatic and authoritarian critical statements which were supported by intuitive evidence alone. It is worth offering some examples at this point.

2.1.1   Example 1

First-year university students at the University of Zimbabwe (for whom English is a second language) wished to appeal to the Bank of English for verification of their feeling that the last line of the first stanza of the poem 'Elvis Presley' by Thom Gunn (Figure 17.1) was intended ironically. They all made their predictions of what, in whole language, might be expected to follow the form '*wielding a*' and waited dutifully for Cobuild to provide an answer to fill the information gap (see Figure 17.2).

In the event, the spirited debate which ensued both before and after the results had arrived, produced a deeper and more satisfying critical response than would have been the case during a normal reading. Even though many students were gratified to find that *knife* was an especially prominent item in the Bank, there was a general consensus among them to the effect that a superordinate term like *weapon* would provide a better means of anticipating the sentiments of the last line of the poem.

But the process did not end there. There was further debate as to whether the many other ironic lines in the Bank of English could be dealt with by substituting a word like *knife* or *weapon* as a means of pre-drafting the wording of the critical statement. Hence, the businessman who '*wields* a wallet' is someone who is prepared to use money in the same way that other people would use a knife. The concordance was able to establish the profile of such a large number of amusing situations (line 4 was a particular source of amusement), that the instances of irony could be demonstrated

> Two minutes long it pitches through some bar;
> Unreeling from a corner box, the sigh
> Of this one, in his gangling finery
> And crawling sideburns, wielding a guitar.
>
> [Verses 2, 3 omitted]
>
> Whether he poses or is real, no cat
> Bothers to say: the pose held is a stance,
> Which, generation of the very chance
> It wars on, may be posture for combat.

Figure 17.1   'Elvis Presley' (Thom Gunn)

```
1 to grunt and hiss as though          wielding a bat four times the weight
2 ide door of the shop. She came out wielding a big red fire extinguisher
3 said he didn't care much for         wielding a budgetary axe. Anyway, he
4 Thatcher Attacked by a Woman         Wielding a Bunch of Daffodils. Er what
5 has demonstrated its dexterity by  wielding a chain saw to make cuts in a log
6 unit commander to the 19-year-old wielding a gun in the spotlight knew what
7 The youth, firing a pistol and       wielding a knife, was arrested immediately
8 He was confronted by one man         wielding a machete, another with a double-
9 inquisitor, a voluble gentleman      wielding a pint of beer which, no doubt
```

Figure 17.2   Sample concordance on 'wielding'

to outnumber what everyone had intuitively assumed would be the norm.

If there is any danger in such appeals to data for assistance, it probably lies in the possibility that some spontaneity may be lost. For example, this might occur where a reader seeks to verify a feature which does not lie at the heart of the concerns of the passage.

However, one should never underestimate what insights the corpus can prompt, and, on balance, students seem prepared to risk the effect of delays in the retrieval and processing of queries to the corpus in return for the startling insights which most of the searches reveal. Even those students who felt that the corpus had verified their intuition almost exactly, agreed that they had still added to their knowledge of what contributes to the *nature of literariness* in language. One student said:

> This data shows us that not all instances of irony are alike. The proportion of irony in a phrase like *wielding a* is much higher than I would have expected. Perhaps a form like this is moving so close to normal usage that it will soon not be a particularly powerful thing for a writer to say.

> One had a lovely face,
> And two or three had charm,
> But charm and face were in vain
> Because the mountain grass
> Cannot but keep the form
> Where the mountain hare has lain.

Figure 17.3 'Memory' (Yeats)

```
 1 left. My cries of anguish were      in vain. of course, I rue the day I denied
 2 New Order records in between were   in vain. I hate that, she snaps
 3 a day. But all her complaints were  in vain. It was no good her trying to
 4 to find some of those efforts were  in vain. The snow fell non-stop for nearly
 5 him. However, his efforts were      in vain. and he joked afterwards: I still
 6 but their efforts to save her were  in vain. Many of the same children form
 7 Sadly Sam's heroics were            in vain. Moments later Lanny Wadkins
 8 sacrifices of World War II were     in vain. that the countries that lost the
 9 as dishevelled. His insults were    in vain. Mr Justice Whitford awarded us the
10 of all horrors, nasty smells were   in vain. And at lunchtime yesterday the
```

Figure 17.4 Sample concordance on 'in vain'

2.1.2   Example 2

In an earlier seminar with a group of students reading English Honours, a woman student had been particularly vociferous in her condemnation of Yeats's '... sexism and conceitedness...' in the poem 'Memory' (see Figure 17.3).

She had been unable to provide textual evidence for her opinion. Most members of the class had concentrated their efforts on the image that the '... mountain grass cannot but hold the form where the mountain hare has lain'. However, the evidence she required to put her point came in a data-assisted query to the corpus regarding the earlier part of the poem which many other students had dismissed as more prosaic than the central image.

The term *efforts* as it appeared in the concordance for *were in vain* (see Figure 17.4) allowed her to rest her case.

> The persona was not prepared to make any effort himself but was still prepared to judge 'a pretty face' and 'charm' as having been 'in vain' as part of the attempts of the women to get him to show an interest in them. The suggestion that their faces and charm were their *efforts* is typical, male arrogance ...

she announced with scorn. Corpus data had empowered her with the evidence she needed in order to state the issue she had felt so keenly intuitively.

It could be argued that a form of data-assisted literary appreciation takes place every time a student of literature consults a dictionary. The *Collins Cobuild English Language Dictionary* offers a more authentic form of short cut to the experience of others than many other dictionaries do, but this is still mediated through the summary provided by the lexicographer. A corpus, on the other hand, by offering direct access to large numbers of authentic contexts, brings the reader into contact with what Firth regarded as repeatable events in both the text and the world.

2.2   Data-driven literary appreciation: new insights

The above examples show how corpus data can provide powerful support for a reader's intuition. In the next section I should like to argue that corpora have the potential to provide insights into aspects of 'literariness', in this case the importance of collocational meaning, which have hitherto not been thought of by critics.

At his address to the Leeds Conference on Phraseology in 1994, John Sinclair made the following statement:

> One hypothesis is that the notion of a linguistic item could be extended, at least for English, so that units of meaning were expected to be phrasal, and the idea of a word carrying meaning on its own was relegated to the margins of linguistic interest, in the enumeration of flora and fauna for example.

If something as fundamental to the *apparatus criticus* of literary scholars as word-meaning goes to the wall as a result of a better understanding of collocational phenomena such as delexicalization, and 'semantic prosodies' (see Louw, 1993), both of which can only be perceived using computers and corpora, neither the critics' traditional terminology nor any amount of rephrasing of it will be of assistance as these findings begin to penetrate the discipline of literary criticism.

3   The collocational basis of several literary devices: some examples

3.1   Collocation in the development of symbolism

Collocational studies within the works of particular authors are now well placed to show how symbols are developed systematically.

> 1 The *bald*, white tumuli of your eyes.
> 2 She may be *bald*, she may have no eyes, She's pink, she's a born midw
> 3 Nor leave me to set my small *bald* eye Skyward again, without hope, of
> 4 ed rocks sunning in rows, *Bald* eyes or petrified eggs, Grownups
> 5 estone The *bald* slots of his eyes stiffened wide open On the inc
> 6 ight around my bed, Mouthless, eyeless, with stitched *bald* head

Figure 17.5   Sample concordance on 'bald' in Sylvia Plath

This most frequently involves the removal from a form of its normal collocates and their replacement with a set of collocates which, within the body of a poet's work, consistently and gradually build up the new symbolic form. For example, in the case of Sylvia Plath the words *eyes* and *bald* collocate in ways which contribute to her symbolism. *Eyes* are normally associated with ways of reading the emotions of other people. However, for Plath they are rendered expressionless by the form *bald*, a collocate which nowhere appears near the form *eyes* in the entire Bank of English. The concordance in Figure 17.5 demonstrates the effect with almost alarming power. This symbol, as Plath has decided to develop it, has an obvious influence in establishing the strong sense in her work that relationships which purport to be close are, in reality, dysfunctional.

For symbols to work effectively, their creators cause them, systematically, to avoid any relationship with their normal collocates. Thus Yeats uses a form like *ladder* or *stair* or *dance* until they achieve symbolic status, but the effect would be utterly destroyed if the collocates of any of these terms appeared near them. Hence in 'The Circus Animals' Desertion', Yeats writes: 'Now that my ladder's gone I must lie down where all the ladders start: in the foul rag and bone shop of the heart.' If *ladder*'s most frequent collocates like *rungs*, *climb*, *social*, etc., were to be introduced, the symbol would degenerate into cliché. This phenomenon appears not to have been examined by literary critics and the computational evidence for it now needs to be laid before them.

3.2   Delexicalization

If the main task of the corpus in literary appreciation is likely to centre upon comparing literary texts with itself, it would be in a strong position to provide the reader with caveats of various kinds.

Standing under the fobbed
impendent belly of Time
Tell me the truth, I said,
Teach me the way things go.
All the other lads were there
Were itching to have a bash,
But I thought wanting unfair:
It and finding out clash.

So he patted my head, booming Boy,
There's no green in your eye:
Sit here, and watch the hail
Of occurrence clobber life out
To a shape no one sees –
Dare you look at that straight?
Oh thank you, I said, Oh yes please,
And sat down to wait.

Figure 17.6   'Send No Money' (Philip Larkin 1962)

If we consider the form *hail* in the poem by Philip Larkin (see Figure 17.6), a computational treatment of it would involve a number of activities.

1   It would discover that the form has the status of a hapax legomenon (i.e. it appears once only in all of Larkin's poetry).
2   This would rule out any treatment of *hail* as a potential symbol.
3   The form *hail* occurs in the poem in the environment immediately before *of* rather than in the company of collocates which would establish its full 'intuitive' meaning, such as *storms, cold* or *stones*.
4   The form with *of* would be recoverable within the computer's inventory of phraseological meanings.
5   The computer would alert the reader to the fact that on a balance of probabilities Larkin intended the more delexical meaning. This might serve to disarm any reader, especially a teacher, who might be bent on treating *hail* at the level of word-meaning.
6   The computer would offer the evidence for the idiomatic meaning in a KWIC concordance such as the one in Figure 17.7 from 37 million words of the book corpus at Cobuild.

In practice, 'reminders' of this kind by the corpus are likely to be extremely frequent and will provide constant evidence of

```
 1  he guerrillas poured a concentrated    hail of AK 47 fire towards them, ZG 1 Eputti
 2  ther side with our shields from the     hail of assorted missiles. The stairway up t
 3  oor she smiled deprecatingly as the     hail of barks continued from inside the house
 4  s. Finally he had gone down under a      hail of blank cartridge fire, and the force
 5  lts from front and flank. Beneath a      hail of bullets and grenades Brinson had bee
 6  he night of the outbreak, died in a      hail of bullets at three o'clock one morning
 7  ilm, The Eagle thought. A veritable      hail of bullets was coming straight at the r
 8  arrest Griffiths and were met by a       hail of bullets after a ZG 0 chase in which
 9  d. The police moved forward under a      hail of debris, their nightsticks drawn. Beh
10  ge of being flown by airship into a      hail of terrorist gunfire, looking for a nic
```

Figure 17.7   Sample concordance on 'hail'

readers' blindness not only to the presence of phraseological meaning within the language but also to an author's intention to invoke it in a specific instance.

4   Conclusion

If it can be demonstrated that certain forms of literary knowledge might never have been apprehended were it not for the use of computers and corpora, then it follows, probably to an extent yet to be determined, that our critical theory ought to provide a permanent role for corpora in criticism. Because the influence of corpora is likely to bring about forms of criticism which might never have emerged through normal critical readings, a stage will be reached where some acknowledgement of the role of corpora in arriving at those critical statements will become necessary. However, many critics may be reluctant to provide such acknowledgement because of the indictment of their intuitive critical skills which this would imply.

A key question in elucidating these issues will inevitably be: Could the forms of criticism which are prompted by data-assisted and data-driven literary appreciation not have come about spontaneously without recourse to corpora? The difficulty with such questions is that they are, of necessity, raised *after* the act of criticism has been carried out. The temptation will always be there to say of any critical insight which has been prompted by reference to the corpus: 'I felt it anyway!' Such reactions are instances of the phenomenon of '20 : 20 hindsight' (see Louw 1993) and ought to be dealt with very firmly indeed. In fact, one safeguard against this problem would almost certainly be the establishment of corpora of written criticism against which the new insights provided by data-assisted and data-driven criticism might be compared. Such an approach would prompt the aggressive but justified retort: 'If you felt it anyway, how do you explain the fact that the following critics who have commented on this text did not ...?'

If corpus-based research has demonstrated that linguists have been pursuing the illusion of 'word' meaning for several thousand years, the same must be true of literary scholars. If the orientation of literary studies has, in an equal, unwitting, and entirely excusable state of ignorance, relied on the spectre of word meaning for the provision of a description of literary phenomena, then this orientation must be as ripe for revaluation within literary criticism as it currently is in linguistics.

What then, in conclusion, do these developments require of literary critics? Firstly, we will need to acknowledge that, as far as it affects literary studies, the new 'knowledge', in whatever form it comes (and collocational meaning is just one instance of it), was never really fully recoverable in the mind. Secondly, we will need to accept that the new 'knowledge', because of its nature, has more right to remain within the domain of the corpus than the mind, and that the mind is now in an unspoken but none the less real partnership with corpora.

Section D

Practical Perspectives

Introduction

It is one thing to be convinced that there are good reasons for using corpora, but it is another thing to act on that conviction. As the chapters in this volume show, there are many ways in which corpora can be compiled, presented and explored. Nearly all require some interaction with the computer, for obvious reasons. Unfortunately, this simple fact probably serves to deter and even prevent many people from making active use of corpora, as, with the possible exception of the youngest generation, computer confidence, not to mention competence, is still far from universal within the teaching profession, and the same may of course be said (though to a decreasing degree) of access to appropriate computing facilities. In Chapter 18, Renouf points out that dealing with many of these practical issues is part and parcel of any serious effort to encourage and train teachers to use corpora in their work.

The chapters in this section seek to offer some encouragement and advice to those who are keen to put into practice ideas they may have regarding the use of corpora, but who have experienced, or would expect to experience, some difficulties as a direct consequence of having little practical experience in the field.

Two of the chapters take the form of case studies which introduce topics of wider relevance. Inkster describes a collaborative effort involving his students over a number of years to assemble a varied corpus of materials for teaching French at undergraduate level. In the process he considers the motivating and skill-enhancing effects of the students' participation, as well as providing an illuminating insight into the imaginative uses to which the Internet can be put by the teachers and students, and some concrete pointers to text sources for foreign language learning. King considers a set of problems which serve to make life harder for the specialist in languages written in non-Latin alphabets. Looking at the case of Cyrillic and Greek alphabets, King provides the reader with a useful overview of the resources which are currently available for handling such exotic corpora, but even more usefully attempts to explain the anatomy of the problems in order to enable the reader to understand the type of issues that need to be faced, even when the particular circumstances are different. He also offers some guarded optimism that in the not-too-distant future the problems will be alleviated by key developments in the handling of character sets.

Hughes offers an essentially non-technical overview of the computational and strategic issues that are raised when developing a computing infrastructure for the exploitation of corpus resources.

Copyright problems are endemic in corpus work. Because the inclusion of a text in a corpus is frequently an instance of re-publication, the question of who is licensed to reproduce the material and for what purpose cannot be as simple as in the case of an original publication. The issues are further complicated by the fact that corpus data may be captured from a source, such as the computer network, where the copyright status of the original material is itself a matter for discussion. Inkster provides answers to some of these questions. Although his answers only scratch the surface, we hope they will serve to orientate the reader in this difficult field.

18

Teaching Corpus Linguistics to Teachers of English

ANTOINETTE RENOUF

1 Background

This chapter draws on my experiences of teaching corpus linguistics to postgraduate students over the last decade and, until recently, at the University of Birmingham.[1] In the early to mid-1980s, while large textual corpora were already in existence (7 and then 20 million words within the Cobuild Project alone), the resources required to make them available to classes of students were generally lacking. Corpus data could be incorporated into teaching in the form of paper print-out, but direct access to computer screens for individualized work could not be offered in class strength. By the late 1980s, the situation was improving. My Unit was equipped with a suite of ten networked PCs in a dedicated teaching room, and I was able to introduce courses for groups of four students without bringing our research activities to a halt. This was a modest beginning, but useful as a pilot study, and the students benefited from exposure to the full Birmingham-Cobuild Corpus resources, and from close supervision.

2 Teachers as learners

Postgraduate students of applied linguistics in this country are typically non-native-speaking teachers of English from tertiary educational institutions abroad. They are therefore people who, on returning home, might wish to continue as corpus-based researchers themselves, but who, as teachers, might ultimately wish to introduce the teaching of corpus linguistics. An appropriate course for them will take this into account. As potential researchers, they need practical instruction and first-hand experience of corpus-based study; as teachers, the practical experience doubles as case-study material, around which an analytical and pedagogical framework can be built.

Fligelstone (1993) usefully identified three categories of teaching activity in this regard:

- Teaching about (i.e. the principles and theories of corpus linguistics)
- Teaching to exploit (i.e. the practical aspects of corpus study)
- Exploiting to teach (i.e. deriving language-teaching materials from corpora).

The first two of these apply where the students are also potential teachers of corpus linguistics. The third is an option which might be taken up: the course might just be aimed at giving teachers a first-hand taste of corpus-based research for its own sake, or the findings might in addition become the knowledge base from which teaching materials are constructed. The route taken is a theoretical and practical matter. Theoretical, because some approaches to corpus-based language teaching involve the language learner being an active researcher who interacts directly with the 'raw' corpus data to learn facts about a language, while others involve the intermediary preparation of corpus-derived materials as an aid to learning. Practical, because the course must have sufficient time and human resources to accommodate both meaningful study and materials development. Such dual-purpose courses have been successfully run at Birmingham on the basis of 15 hours of class time by us with Tim Johns, and by Johns alone (Johns 1991b), by keeping the scope of study within modest bounds.

I would add a fourth category of corpus-linguistic teaching activity to those of Fligelstone; namely:

- Teaching to establish resources.

The would-be teacher of corpus linguistics may well, on return home, first need to create the material conditions for the enterprise. The issue of corpus design and data acquisition will therefore need to be addressed.

3   Designing a course in corpus linguistics

In the light of the considerations that have been raised so far in this chapter, the design for a course would incorporate the following components:

- Introduction to corpus linguistics:
  - Definition of corpus
  - Definition of corpus linguistics
  - Demonstration of the benefits of corpus-based study
  - Contextualization of the course
- Negotiating the course programme
  - Planning individual mini-research projects
- Introduction to corpus-based study
  - Methodology
  - Constitution of the lexicon
- Introduction to computing resources
  - Managing the classes
- Advice on writing up research findings
- Course conclusion
  - Course feedback
  - Distance support
  - Aims and objectives

Some of these proposed course components outlined will now be discussed in some detail.

4   Introduction to corpus linguistics

The local conditions with respect to computing and computer-based study vary considerably from country to country. It may be assumed that teachers choosing to attend universities with a corpus-linguistic component in their postgraduate course will be acquainted with the basic notion, but they may well not have had first-hand experience of corpus-based research. One might proceed to introduce them to the field as follows.

4.1   Definition of corpus

It is useful to explain some basic assumptions of corpus linguistics, beginning with the fact that the term 'corpus' may be used to refer to a body of text which is intended to be representative of one or more aspects of the language as a whole. According to this view, while it is clear that the totality of language cannot be known and so the corpus will not (unless accidentally) be a perfect microcosm of the whole, the corpus must have some claim to authority in order to merit study. Accordingly, the most authoritative corpus will contain all works of a given writer, but otherwise, its authority will have to rest on such qualities as variety, scale or modernity. Such a corpus type is to be distinguished from the very large textual accumulations which now exist in many countries. The latter do not claim to be representative, but rather to be a resource which can furnish more than enough instances of particular textual phenomena, or from which a subcorpus may be drawn.

4.2   Definition of corpus linguistics

4.2.1   Text linguistics vs corpus linguistics

Teachers may have experience of text linguistics, and may need to understand that corpus linguistics differs from this in focusing not on the language within an individual text or texts but on language use common to some or all of the writers or speakers represented within the corpus. Text linguistics looks within, while corpus linguistics cuts across, a text.

4.2.2   Illustration vs evidence

It may not be obvious to the teachers at the outset that corpus-based study is essentially quantitative – i.e. its purpose is to identify the generalities of language use. A distinction needs to be made for them between attestation (or illustrative example) and evidence: language teachers are inveterate snippers of juicy instances of usage from newspapers, but these individual occurrences cannot be evaluated or relied on in terms of typicality. Indeed, that which attracts human attention in text is often the idiosyncrasy. Corpus linguistics entails the exhaustive study of chosen or all linguistic phenomena in a given corpus; only then can the data be regarded as providing evidence, albeit partial, for its existence.

4.2.3   Introspection and informant testing vs observation of text

The idea of observing textual data may be appealing to the teacher, but it may not be immediately clear what this approach offers that other methods of language description do not. A distinction needs to be drawn between it and, for example, introspection and informant testing. Corpus linguistics offers access to the actual language used by a cross-section of speakers of the language, whereas introspection yields insights into the mental lexicon of a single speaker. Corpus linguistics can provide unmediated access to language, revealing aspects which are otherwise inaccessible to the conscious mind; whereas in informant testing, it has traditionally been assumed that speakers will be able to introspect reliably about their own patterns of usage.

4.3   Demonstration of the benefits of corpus linguistics

A verbal introduction along the above lines will be accepted in principle by teachers, but is usefully followed up with a practical demonstration of the benefits peculiar to corpus linguistics. This can take the form of a series of questions about the typicalities and generalities of language use, on the one hand, and about the characteristics of language use of the individual teacher on the other. There are many questions that cannot really be answered without recourse to a corpus.

For example, in a course focusing primarily on lexis, one might pose such questions as:

1 What are the core or primary meanings of the words *keep* and *see*?
2 What would you regard as the main facts about the meaning and use of the word *listen*?
3 How much can you say about the meaning and use of the words *affirm* and *confirm*?
4 Give examples of how the following words are used in text: *axiomatic, synergy, symbiosis, serendipity.*
5 When do you use the word *which* and when *that* in text?
6 Do you split infinitives? In what circumstances?
7 Which words do you use most to express logical connection – in speech, in writing?

Questions 1–4 are chosen to highlight different aspects of the nature of the language use which are discovered by observation of corpus data. Here, Question 1 addresses the essentially phrasal role and dependent status of high-frequency words. Question 2 raises the issue of pragmatics, in that the word *listen* is used, among other things, to gain the floor in conversation. Question 3 focuses on the potential for overlap in use between two similar words, and the insecurity that can be associated with rarer or more formal lexis. Question 4 continues the theme of insecurity: this time with reference to the process of assimilation into general language of neologisms or, as in the given examples, of technical terms from specialized domains. Once teachers have decided that their intuitions are decidedly hazy with respect to the first four questions, relevant concordanced extracts can be circulated for inspection. Questions of the latter kind (5 to 7) enquire into the idiolect of the individual teachers, and are effective in demonstrating the limitations of introspection, and generally evoke surprise and amusement in the group. However, they could not be answered fully without recourse to the appropriate corpora.

4.4   Contextualization of the course

An initial delve into corpus data is enlightening, but budding corpus linguists also benefit from a greater perspective on the place of this activity in the field of corpus linguistic study as a whole. A session may be inserted at the beginning, or perhaps later, containing an outline of the various corpora worldwide, and associated research. Timid individuals are empowered by the sense of their contribution to the larger field.

5   Negotiating the course programme

Every group of MA postgraduates seems to be different. Some prefer to have extensive input on the facts surrounding the field of corpus linguistics. Others wish to get hands-on experience of the corpus data as soon as possible. A range of preferences is met on the number and timing of feedback sessions in the course. It is important to plan the course in the knowledge of the overall MA workload schedules: times of examinations and deadlines for other written assignments.

5.1   Planning individual mini-research projects

When offered the opportunity to study any aspect of language of interest or curiosity, teachers are typically nonplussed and can waste considerable time casting around for a research topic. To anticipate this, it is essential to have warned them weeks or months in advance of the need to arrive with a topic or topics in mind. Even so, several will not be so prepared, and it is useful to give a review of past or possible projects, discussing the corresponding procedures and outcomes.

The choice of mini-projects should take into account the teacher's level of language competence: it is not always wise, for example, to encourage those with a limited command of English to focus on features of collocation, idiom or metaphor, since they will not have the necessary intuitions to differentiate nonce or idiosyncratic formations from established ones, or to pick grammatical strings from true collocation behaviour. In fact, these areas are difficult for even the most proficient non-native-speaker. The selection of project topic should also take into consideration the nature of available corpus data. Small corpora, of the million-word variety, will support the study of individual word use, but studies above word level will only be satisfactory if they involve the higher-frequency ranges of lexis. A similar picture holds for the study of grammar. Obviously time is a consideration in relation to the scope of study.

It may be a good idea to encourage collaborative research. A mini-project based on around 12 hours of class-time is a modest little endeavour; combined efforts are heartening; they might lead to something substantial or publishable. Kirk (1994) has listed varied and ambitious mini-projects arising from his different course structures; some past topics chosen and tackled by teachers on our courses are listed below:

- 'Chopping the Hydra's Head': idioms involving *face* and other names of parts of the body
- *I mean* in English conversation
- Estimation of number in English
- *Market* – its meaning and collocation in contemporary journalistic text
- The difference between *recently* and *lately*
- A study of the words *range* and *scope*

- The use of adjectival forms of lexemes denoting religious denominations
- A comparison of the meaning and use of *try* and *try to*
- The different meanings of *dry*
- A study of the metaphors associated with *hand* and *hands*.

6   Introduction to corpus-based study

6.1   Methodology

Newcomers to corpus-based study begin by being overwhelmed by the data. It is mesmerizing, and they need to have possible methodologies suggested to them. Methodologies, because observations of lexicographer practice and preference over years in the Cobuild project show that individuals naturally vary in their approach. Corpus-based study involves the interaction between the intuition of the researcher and the evidence in the text. This can be a fairly simple affair where very little data is involved, but questions of judgement, interpretation and even selection come increasingly into play as the frequency or complexity of the language phenomenon increases.

One method is to begin by considering what one expects to find in the data, and then looking at the data to see how far the expectation is met. This can help some researchers to make sense more quickly of what they find, but they must be warned to remain sensitive to the data, or they will find only what they knew already. The expectation of what will occur in the data may come from personal intuition, or may be aided or even originate from a conventional lexicographic or grammatical account. Another method is simply to start at line 1 of a concordance, interpret it (of course with reference to one's own linguistic repertoire) and gradually develop a profile of use. A further method is to allow oneself some time to scan the entire concordance for an item in order to establish a general impression. The scanning procedure is, as expected, easier if each focus is limited to a single feature.

6.2   Constitution of the lexicon

Students are not generally aware of the way text is constructed or of the types of words within it. It is useful to give them a ranked word-frequency list from a single text, together with an extract from the top, middle and lower frequency ranges of word types from the corpus they will actually work with. From this information, it is possible to derive an understanding of the profile of lexis in any textual data. It can be seen that grammatical words (*be, has, up*) make up the majority of the running words in text, followed by 'universal' words such as the major verbs and nouns (*day, man, time*), then by discourse organizers (*thing, matter, way*) and technical (e.g. topic) words, then by a run of less frequent inflexions and lexical words, leading into the final 50 per cent or so of the type list in any corpus, consisting of *hapax legomena*.

This profile begins to make clear to the student the consequences of selecting concordance lines for a common as opposed to a less common word form: in the first case, thousands of instances may emerge for study; in the second, tens or hundreds. This is of practical importance to the student, since it is a guide to the likely success or feasibility of a certain topic.

7   Introduction to computing resources

The teachers will be introduced to the PC laboratory at this point, and initiated into the use of a machine and accessing corpus data. It is important to ensure that they are given clear, user-friendly instructions for the use of the computer and printer, and a simple but comprehensive set of commands relating to the access and manipulation of corpus data. Feedback from successive courses serves to refine the guidelines.

7.1   Managing the classes

The course may take the form of a series of ten contact sessions, in which the teacher(s) may be supervising ten individual research projects.

In this classroom model the material, that is the corpus via the computer, takes the primary role of language informant, with the tutor as manager or enabler. Two people are in fact needed to manage each session. One tutor is needed to manage the study event, facilitating the interaction between the student and the source of information. Another tutor, or individual with computing knowledge and communicative skills, is required to supervise the machine use. It is possible that teachers exist who have both these skills, but it is stressful to play two roles with a class of ten individual researchers who are inexperienced in the area. It is helpful if both people are linguistically trained.

There is a potential problem with ancillary resources, such as the printer, in terms of its servicing. It is usually one of the tutors who has to refill the printer and protect it from overuse. Students prefer to study output on paper, so that they can conveniently annotate it. However, if not educated otherwise, they will print off hundreds of pages without reflection.

The write-up period will probably extend well outside the contact hours. The course tutor must expect to spend considerable hours in individual tuition sessions.

8   Advice on writing up research findings

A short in-service course would not culminate in a final written assignment, but an MA course may entail a write-up, which could in turn form the basis of the degree dissertation. Teachers for whom the mini-project was their first experience of corpus-based study do not necessarily have an idea of how to convert their observations into a research report, and so an informal template is helpful. This would include an outline of the study objective, a description of the data and the steps taken to observe it, leading to an account of the findings, and some kind of conclusion (possibly implications for further research or other activity, for teaching, and so on).

9   Course conclusion

9.1   Course feedback

One or more sessions should have allowed the opportunity for teachers to give feedback on the course. Formative evaluation is useful in allowing improvements to come into effect in the remaining life of the course. Establishing a critical stance on the field is part of becoming a corpus linguist, and it is informative for the course tutor while being empowering for the teachers to identify the shortcomings in a corpus and in the corpus-based approach to language description.

9.2   Distance support

It is not possible in all cases to maintain contact with teachers once they have left. However, there are some corpus projects (Cobuild Ltd at Birmingham, BNC at Oxford) which do have the resources to support teachers with data and advice from a distance.

It is important to remember that the composition of teachers on a corpus linguistic course is varied, and not all will have institutionally funded access to corpus data or computing resources of the sophistication available during the course. Some will be individuals with very modest PC or other microcomputing facilities and no hope of institutional financing. In many continents, teachers are returning to fairly hopeless situations, lacking in corpus data, computers, or the conditions to allow them to function (such as air-conditioning, security, space, stationery, technical support or maintenance provision).

There is a certain responsibility on the part of the tutor, once having awakened interest and ambition, to discuss with teachers how they can continue to study textual data; to explore with them the possibilities of their becoming corpus creators and managers at their own institutions; and to provide information on the corpora that are available and how to buy access to them. There is a particular need to offer some hope to the less well-resourced participants. A self-help coda to the course is required. This would cover guidance in areas including the following:

- Principles of designing a corpus
- Acquisition of corpus data
- Textual data available commercially (e.g. CD-ROMs of newspaper data)
- Corpus data available to researchers (e.g. Cobuild, BNC)
- Annotating and processing corpus data
- Corpus analytical software packages available (public domain and commercial)
- Alternatives (e.g. Tim Johns offers hope to the teacher with one basic microcomputer and a classful of students ; see Johns (1986, 1988, 1991a, 1991b, 1993))
- Corpus linguistic reading lists (in addition to those provided for the course)
- Contact addresses for useful people and institutions (e.g. ICAME).

9.3 Aims and objectives

At the end of the course, if it has been successful, the teachers will be left with a series of lasting impressions. They will have had first-hand experience of corpus-based study, and gained confidence in carrying out basic text analytical operations on a microcomputer. Hopefully they will also have acquired a fascination with computers and data-based study, an awareness of the advantages, disadvantages and issues in corpus linguistics, and above all they will have gained new insight into a small aspect of the English language.

Note

I am indebted to my colleague Alex Collier who installed the facilities for corpus-based teaching at Birmingham and subsequently supervised the computational aspects of a series of 15-hour courses. From our experiences of this work, I have extrapolated the guidelines which shape the body of this chapter.

19

First Catch your Corpus: Building a French Undergraduate Corpus from Readily Available Textual Resources

GORDON INKSTER

1 Introduction

LANFRANC is a collection of French texts stored on computer. It was created with the help of undergraduates as part of their degree course and has been subsequently used as a research tool by themselves and others. The material it contains was drawn from a number of sources, including on-line archives, discussion lists and other documentary material accessible via the Internet. Its pedagogic value and the problems surrounding its construction are described below.

Lancaster's French-language text-bank was born of envy and poverty in the mid-1980s at a time when few foreign language machine-readable texts were available for language students in Britain. The LOB Corpus offered teachers and students of English a tool that could provide an immediate empirical response to queries about patterns of usage. French colleagues, lacking a similar resource, could only fall back on preformulated prescriptions, the limited examples provided by dictionaries and grammars, or spur-of-the-moment ad hoc 'rules'. It was hoped that LANFRANC would offer a sounder and richer range of data.

Offering students the opportunity to uncover linguistic fact by themselves allows them to participate actively in the induction of 'rules' for syntactic or stylistic linguistic variation, diachronic and synchronic. It empowers the learner, promotes learning by exploration and, potentially at least, frees them from the tyranny of set texts and syllabus.[1]

Misgivings about the artificiality and patronizing quality of the then existing CALL materials also presided over LANFRANC's inception. The tolerance of sceptical language students for the then-available drill-and-practice routines seemed limited once novelty had evaporated. Access to material distributed over the Internet, however, offers the impression of participating in a real-world activity. It requires learning a modest amount about accessing machine-readable data and text editing. Manipulating the same material thereafter offers students the highly motivating satisfaction of instant feedback that language-learners in a university context often feel they lack, quite apart from any other job-related skills they may acquire in the process.

It is hard to overstate the pedagogical benefits of urging upon language students the value of practical computer use, and especially of familiarization with networks. The latter constitute a major linguistic medium they will encounter throughout their later career. Searching them to locate, select and retrieve cognate extracts is a reading activity that can be adapted to the abilities of the learner. Learning how to do it all in French, moreover, brings diffident and sometimes unexpectedly inhibited language students into contact not only with computer scientists in their own institution, but also with native speakers overseas, to the mutual benefit of all and at times with unexpected consequences, sometimes even matrimonial.

Corpus building has none of the artificiality that can vitiate traditional CALL. It gives students at least the illusion of actual involvement in the 'language industry'. Moreover, encouraging e-mail contact with tutors, peer-group support and on-line course seminars using the Caucus conferencing system have all been part of the two courses that gave birth to LANFRANC and invite its exploitation.

The earliest of these was an optional course on literary concordancing using the Oxford Concordance Program (OCP). The absence of suitable machine-readable French text obliged students to create their own under guidance. This pioneering activity involved some in scanning a text of their choosing, others in downloading by FTP and other forms of data capture, and all of them in editing and 'marking up' according to simple local conventions described below. The students' familiarity with their own versions of the text thus acquired greatly facilitated their later development of OCP routines to explore them.

The satisfaction afforded by contributing in some measure to a collective corpus-building enterprise, together with the real-life benefits of computer literacy, have been appreciated by larger numbers of students in a more recent second-year unit initiating them into the same activities on a smaller scale and with more specifically linguistic goals.

In both cases the assessable outcome for university degree purposes has been a piece of small-scale personal research deriving from the material thus created. One hopes and suspects that the real benefits to the learners concerned have been quite different.

2 Copyright

An abiding difficulty in all such home-made projects is ensuring the lawfulness of materials made available to students, to which one may have access for personal use. No one wishes to confine study to the necessarily dated language of work that has come into the public domain, but copyright remains an impediment to encoding and storing modern literary and commercial material.

Documents accessible through the Internet are often of uncertain status. Some contain a specific prohibition, others a copyright disclaimer. Mailings to Usenet are assumed in the USA to carry an 'implied licence' to retransmit, and the use of anonymized extracts from mailing lists for study purposes within an institution falls within the realm of 'fair dealing'. Were this not so, obtaining varied samples of the most spontaneous varieties of contemporary written language would be difficult indeed.

In other cases the custodian of the data source will often grant limited permission to educational institutions, especially if that source is itself educational in character, or belongs to some other public body. It is also noteworthy that by agreement with the French newspaper and periodical publishers' association, non-Francophone universities are empowered to make copies of single articles for language-learning purposes without further specific approval.

A consequence of this is that most LANFRANC texts could not be made available outside the institution or put to commercial use.

3   Text encoding, storage and mark-up

The LANFRANC corpus is stored centrally on the university main-frame computer and backed-up on archival tapes. Year-round 24-hour access via the campus network ensures that students can indeed individualize their learning practices in exploiting it. Financial imperatives, however, mean that a campus network comprises heterogeneous equipment, some of it outmoded. A consequence of this has been the need to make use of a 'lowest-common-denominator' encoding system, to enable safe transmission of data across the different types of computer system connected to the global network.[2]

This has meant using the original, non-extended ASCII character set, which does not include diacritics or accented characters. A variety of encoding conventions for these are still in use for network transmission. The format chosen for LANFRANC was the one which involves the fewest key-depressions on a QWERTY keyboard when entering data by hand or editing (see Figure 19.1). This is in effect the French character set used by most printers, and offers the added advantage that hard copy can be output 'correctly' by switching the printer as required.

à	@	
ç	\	
é	{	
è	}	
ù	l	
â	a^	etc.
ï	i=	

Figure 19.1   LANFRANC French accent coding conventions

Some students find it briefly disconcerting to discover that the computer storage and representation of characters can usefully differ from their printed appearance, and are sometimes less easy to read on screen, but these, too, are valuable lessons.

Such a convention involves sacrificing some secondary punctuation symbols that do indeed have relevance to French practice. However, the purpose of the corpus and the disparate character of its sources meant that typographical precision had to be sacrificed in favour of 'plain-text' and verbal accuracy.

```
<T PHEDRE>
<A I>
<S 1>
<Pe HIPP, THER>
<C HIPP>
Le dessein en est pris: je pars, cher Th{ram}ne,
Et quitte le s{jour de l'aimable Tr{z}ne.
Dans le doute mortel dont je suis agit{
Je commence @ rougir de mon oisivet{.
Depuis plus de six mois {loign{ de mon p}re,
J'ignore le destin d'une te^te si ch}re;
J'ignore jusqu'aux lieux qui le peuvent cacher.
<C THER>
Et dans quels lieux, seigneur, l'allez-vous donc chercher?
D{j@ pour satisfaire @ votre juste crainte,
J'ai couru les deux mers qui s{pare Corinthe;
J'ai demande Th{s{e aux peuples de ces bords
O| l'on voit l'Ach{ron se perdre chez les morts;
```

Figure 19.2 Extract from the LANFRANC text of Racine's *Phèdre*

The original material, in some cases so old that it had been entered in upper-case only, contained numerous forms of encoding and sometimes 'marking-up' of varying degrees of richness. Creating a homogenized corpus meant editing each text into a standard format and including the same minimal level of mark-up in each. Figure 19.2 contains a short sample from the corpus.

Material procured from the Internet set particular problems, for until the advent of the World Wide Web much of this was not accented in the first place. This was initially true even of official publications, and does not seem to impede intelligibility among native speakers. Clearly, though, it is undesirable to put unaccented material at the disposal of undergraduate learners. UNIX tools were developed to speed up the accenting of such material, and separate lexica were created of forms (a) that must be accented, (b) that may be accented and (c) that may never be accented. Student assistance made a key contribution to such tedious chores, and offered at least some much-needed spelling reinforcement in return.

Integrating material drawn from the 'Net' presented other difficulties. Items from Usenet and mailing lists regularly include quoted elements that need to be excised, especially if frequencies are a concern (see Figure 19.3 (overleaf)). Yet doing so can also make such contributions barely comprehensible. Unmoderated contributions are also riddled with ill-formed language whose

En reponse a une demande emanant d'un participant americain qui
plaidait pour que l'on puisse continuer a communiquer sans accents
Denis Simard repondait:
>
>
> Il vient un temps cependant ou il faut forcer un peu les
> choses et faire pression sur les administrateurs pour
> qu'ils adaptent leur vieux systemes aux nouvelles
> realites socio-linguistiques de l'Internet. Ce n'est
> plus a nous a nous adapter
[. . .]
>
Je plaide pour la plus grande patience. Les administrateurs
americains, surtout ceux des grandes universites publiques, se
soucient fort peu d'accents. Les claviers US ne peuvent taper les
accents que grace a des traitements de texte, type Nota Bene, Word,
etc . . . qui ne marchent pour l'internet. Un message emis avec des
accents est recu dans une crypto langue penible a dechiffrer.

Figure 19.3   Extract from a mailing-list reply that uses no accents and
includes extensive citation of a previous contribution

inclusion in a learners' corpus is of debatable value. Whichever
principle one may adopt, such problems make the value of discrete corpora containing cognate material readily apparent.

Recent enhancements of our campus network have made it
possible to change the coding used to HTML and make a start on
upgrading text annotation to TEI standards.

4   Sources of machine-readable French

The initial kernel of LANFRANC materials was provided by the
Oxford Text Archive 'U' category French texts, which do not
require any special further copyright clearance to be used by
purchasers or under their supervision. These were all drawn from
literary sources, having been produced by their depositors for
essentially non-linguistic purposes.[3]

By a happy chance they included drama, poetry and prose from
the seventeenth to the twentieth century, making some types of
contrastive and diachronic exploration immediately possible. Here
too, however, very extensive re-editing was needed to replace whichever accented-character conventions had initially been used. In
some cases this unfortunately also meant removing additional

'marked-up' information not included elsewhere in the corpus, for example the tagging of proper names or typeface.

The literary character of these texts made the point of the exercise both more acceptable and accessible to more sceptical language-teaching colleagues, conscious of the peculiar nature of the British undergraduate language curriculum. It also enabled the unit based upon their exploitation to be related more directly to one or more of the various courses being followed by each individual student.

The need for a comparable volume of contemporary non-literary material, obviously more valuable for language-learning purposes and to appeal to 'non-literary' students, was pressing but harder to satisfy. The Internet provided an initial source of French journalistic material when the Washington embassy began to distribute the breakfast summary of overnight news and press headlines produced each weekday for overseas diplomats and other expatriate francophones by the Agence France-Presse. This was initially distributed by e-mail from Georgetown University, but has subsequently been made available by other missions.[4] The material is subject to a copyright that prevents it being redistributed, but it is legally archived at various sites. Six months of it enriched LANFRANC by a further half-million words.

More varied French language documents were already becoming accessible by gopher. The administrative register was initially catered for by university prospectuses, course regulations, rules and disciplinary procedures. One variety at least of technical language was amply available in computer science department instructional materials.

French-language mailing lists, now numerous, were slower to develop. The first of these, Frogtalk[5] and Frogjobs, also seem to have been conceived in Washington and were addressed to graduate and post-doctoral students in the USA but willingly mailed elsewhere. These also provided publicity for other newly launched 'Net' publications. Quebec, home of the highly literary Balzac-L and the student-orientated Causerie,[6] were other early sources. Subsequently selections from other regular lists have been added, most notably Biblio-Fr[7] and LN[8] (Langue Naturelle). Today, of course, the number of special interest group lists is very large.

Usenet FAQs and bulletins, especially those in the newsgroup alt.soc.cult, offered further material, often of a still more colloquial character, which can be downloaded to a file or mailed to the user. A small volume of dialogue logged from the IRC (Internet Relay Chat) channels #francais, #france and #paris has likewise been included. This world-wide real-time discussion medium is of great interest to students because so many participants are their peers. The conversational character of interactive computer discussion, together with the polyglot features of IRC French, makes such material less suitable for a corpus concerned essentially with written forms of a more traditional kind. Network time-lags also mean that IRC channels frequently carry several interwoven discussions, making threads of coherent discourse hard to unravel.

With the World Wide Web has come a profusion of easily accessible documents from most fields of activity. In particular the enthusiasm of Jacques Toubon, Ministre de la Culture et de la Francophonie since 1993, has laid open to all a wealth of French government materials and press releases, explicitly copyright-free. Quebec is likewise a fertile source of French.

More recently still, the Association des Bibliophiles Universels (ABU)[9] has set about emulating Project Gutenberg by producing and storing high-quality public-domain texts, available to all by FTP. These have routinely been added to the LANFRANC collection, and texts for which the latter owns the copyright offered in return.

5   Engaging student collaboration

Final-year option course students have been among the most enthusiastic contributors to the LANFRANC Corpus as well as its users. Necessity combined with a desire to pursue quasi-independent study led some to see merit in creating or collating their own materials that could be added to the corpus, if only to allow specific contrastive studies.

This has involved acquiring both editing and data acquisition skills, from the use of file transfer protocols to text scanning, and thereafter some minimal programming in OCP (see Figure 19.4 for a sample of OCP output). To some these seemed clerical or technical processes far removed from their degree discipline, but most found a creative satisfaction in the novelty of collaborating in what they could see to be a forward-looking venture.

Dissertations resulting from their work have ranged over syntactic, stylistic and even political concerns (the reporting of the

```
CONCORDANCE of 'âme' in Manon Lescaut

âme      18

  802        un peu de tranquillité à mon âme
  972                   désordre de mon âme   en entendant ce discours ne saura
 1222                       et de l'âme   sont accordées à ceux-ci, comme d
 1585                              âme,   que dans l'état où nous sommes r
 1901      la passion dominante de mon âme,   tait la honte et la confusion
 2151         corps est un bonheur pour l'âme   vous n'oseriez le dire, c'est un
 2521               Ce garçon avait l'âme   moins basse et moins dure que ses
 2716      de son bien! Il n'y a qu'une âme   lâche qui en soit capable, par un
 2861                     ma chère âme,   lui dis-je en arrivant, et recom
 2927           maîtresse de mon âme,   que je n'avais pas un seul petit
 3047      amour l'eût gravé dans votre âme,
 3764      mais c'est pour toi, ma chère âme   que mon coeur s'intéresse : quel
 4349          mouvements de son âme   semblaient se réunir dans ses yeu
 4561            division dans mon âme
 4602              Nous avons l'âme   trop belle, et le coeur trop bien
 4837      cesse dans ma mémoire, mon âme   semble se reculer d'horreur chaqu
 4856                    Mon âme   ne suivit pas la sienne
 4925      à renaître un peu dans mon âme,   ce changement fut suivi de près
```

Figure 19.4 Extract from a student's study of 'psychological' terms in Prévost's *Manon Lescaut*

American presidential election by AFP). Students have been able to relate their choice of topic to individual interests and other courses studied.

Today, of course, balanced and representative French corpora of many sorts are beginning to become available – usually at a price.[10] The advantages of engineering one's own, and in particular of engaging student collaboration in its development, remain.

Notes

1 A useful discussion of the benefits of self-access can be found in Barnett (1993).

2 An increasing number of mailers, terminals and networks are now able to accept data transmitted using ISO charset Latin1, which is the preferred character set for most European languages requiring diacritics.

3 An up-to-date list of holdings can be obtained via the Oxford University gopher or World Wide Web pages.

4 British subscriptions may be obtained on application to *scientec@brunel. ac.uk.*

5 Frogtalk subscriptions should be sent to *listproc@yukon.cren.org.*

6   Causerie is essentially student gossip of the bulletin board variety and can be obtained from *listerv@uquebec.ca*. Balzac-L is an impressive literary list also run from Canada (*balzac-l-request@umontreal.ca*).

7   Biblio-Fr is principally aimed at librarians but contains much of interest to all. It is run from Rennes by Hervé LeCrosnier. Subscriptions to *biblio-fr@univ-rennes1.fr*.

8   LN (Langue Naturelle), French equivalent of Linguist and Corpora. Subscriptions *to foucou@univ-mlv.fr*. Information also from web site: *http://www-ceril.univ-mlv.fr*.

9   ABU (Association des Bibliophiles Universels) Information from *cubaud@cnam.fr*. ABU also has a new web page (*http://WWW.abu.org/ABU/*).

10   The most important source of literary French is the great ARTFL (American and French Research on the Treasury of the French Language) collection held at Chicago and duplicating the original at Nancy. It can be found at the URL *http://tuna.uchicago.edu/ARTFL.html*. A selection of this material is also available on CD-ROM. More recently still, the European corpus initiative has made a large volume of extracts from *Le Monde* available to researchers on licence at very modest cost. Further details are found at the URL *http://www.cogsci.ed.ac.uk/elsnet/eci.html*.

20

Creating and Processing Corpora in Greek and Cyrillic Alphabets on the Personal Computer

PHILIP KING

1 Introduction

The purpose of this chapter is to provide a guide to the complexity of creating, managing and analysing a set of text files in languages using Greek and Cyrillic alphabets. It ought to be as easy to do this for Greek and Cyrillic as it is for English, since all the processes are in theory at least the same, and the only difference is the use of different alphabets. In fact the difference in the alphabets accounts for all the problems which justify this chapter.

The underlying reason for the complexity arises from the lack of standardization (or the existence of different standards) for the codes used to represent alphabetic characters. The DOS and Windows operating systems for PCs and many proprietary word-processing packages all have one or more of their own standards within each system, and there is an incompatibility across these systems. An individual user operating a self-contained package, and working only within one of these systems, may learn to handle Greek or Cyrillic texts quite adequately despite the variety, but problems can arise as soon as one attempts to exchange textual material with others working in the same field, or acquires a new package or upgrades one's hardware or software. In view of the growing use of computers and corpora in Cyrillic and Greek, and with the current situation likely to persist for some time to come, a guide to the maze becomes necessary.

This chapter examines problems of text entry (principally through the keyboard) and transferability across operating systems and word-processing packages. This will require some explanation of the various character-to-code mappings in use, and it is hoped that this will enable language researchers and teachers to trouble-shoot and find workable solutions to problems they may have encountered in this area. I will also consider briefly corpus-processing software (concordancers). This chapter assumes no programming ability on the part of the user. Programmers or colleagues with programming skills may often say 'that's easy to fix' and offer to create a small program which solves a problem; such help should never be turned down, but for many people who would like to make a start in corpus handling, such help is not available.

I will not deal with a number of points which might be thought relevant to this issue. These include the use of optical scanners to convert print into electronic text, the Text Encoding Initiative (TEI) and Standard Generalized Mark-Up Language (SGML) and the reasons why one might want to create corpora of these languages in the first place. The use of an optical scanner would certainly largely bypass one of the problems I deal with below – the keyboard – but texts entered in this way would still require proof-reading and correcting through a keyboard. The scanner would also assign a code number to each character on the basis of one of the mappings referred to above. TEI/SGML is simply beyond the scope of this chapter, since the decision whether to mark up is independent of the decision to create a corpus, and mark-up is not necessary for many kinds of handling. TEI/SGML would not simplify any of the problems dealt with here (it might make text interchange easier, but this is offset by the apparatus required to encode or mark up in the first place, and to decode). Finally, the arguments for the use of corpora in teaching and research are general rather than restricted to particular languages, and are addressed elsewhere in this volume.

In preparing this chapter I have investigated a variety of software programs and packages. These are of four types:

1   *Word-processing packages.* These include *LocoScript Professional* (which has its own operating system, but works under DOS or Windows), *WordPerfect* (DOS and Windows versions) and the multilingual packages *Accent* and *Gamma UniVerse.* These all offer languages in addition to Greek and Cyrillic; and all offer a range of Cyrillic languages.
2   Windows fonts for Cyrillic and Greek, including *WinGreek* and *WorldFont.*

3   Keymap and keymapping programs and facilities, including *WorldFont* and *LanguageLink*.
4   The Russian and Greek code pages supplied with versions of MS-DOS 6.22 and above.

This is not, however, intended as a comprehensive review of these packages, and mention of a package or program in connection with a problem or a solution is not intended to imply that only that package has the problem or offers the solution. One reason for not making it a review article is that packages change, and upgrading means that many specific detail points might be irrelevant or simply wrong in point of fact in a year from now. The other main reason is that needs are individual and various, and space does not allow for a comprehensive discussion of suitability for a wide range of purposes. The potential buyer or user does, however, need to become aware of the right questions to ask, and this chapter is offered as a means of working out what these are. The answers may differ in detail as time goes on, although they will remain the same in principle.

2   Two notes on terminology and scripts

Certain terms would benefit from clarification, since the senses in which they are used in the software mentioned above vary from those of general usage, and sometimes from package to package. 'Font', as used here, means a set of up to 255 alphabetic and other characters, used in a Windows application. The corresponding term for a DOS application is 'code page'. The traditional sense of a particular style of lettering may also apply, but is secondary. Fonts in Windows may be known by style names such as Courier, Bodoni, Times, etc., but fonts containing Greek or Cyrillic characters may be known simply by the alphabet or language name ('Cyrillic1', 'WinGreek', 'Serbian1') or by a combination of style name and alphabet set (Times Greek, Courier Greek). Some such fonts (e.g. some used by Gamma UniVerse) may contain both Latin and Greek or Cyrillic characters, while others will contain only one alphabet.

Another pair of words whose precise meaning varies from package to package is 'country' and 'language'. Occasionally one may be used in the sense of the other (as when one package gives the option of selecting 'Belgian' or 'Swiss' as a language). 'Country' may also be applied to (a) the keyboard configuration (so French means azerty rather than qwerty); (b) (in DOS) the convention for ordering the elements of the date known as country page – this is NOT the same as the code page (on which see below). A term like 'the English code page' (Microconcord manual, p. 76) refers to code page 437; this also contains the accented characters needed for French and German, for instance.

It is important to define one's own needs quite precisely, particularly in terms of the alphabet and diacritics which one wants to use. Terms used by software publishers may not mean what one expects them to mean in ordinary language. Thus, if you are working with Greek, you will need to be clear whether the software can handle only the modern form of the language with the single-accent (monotonic) system, or whether it can handle the full accent system. There is no consistency of naming here. While 'Classical' or 'Ancient' means that the full accent system can be handled, the term 'Modern' generally means that only the simple single-accent system is supported. The term 'Greek' alone needs investigating. Accent Greek supports only the single accent system; WordPerfect, Gamma UniVerse and LocoScript Professional support both. One of the IBM code pages (737, also known as 437Greek) does not support certain characters occasionally needed in Modern Greek.

The term Cyrillic can be even more confusing. WordPerfect for Windows and LocoScript support many characters used in non-Slavonic Cyrillic-script languages of the former Soviet Union such as Kazakh and Uzbek (in the case of LocoScript, this is part of the standard package); the Cyrillic font supplied in WorldFont supports Serbian (among other languages) but is missing two or three characters needed for Russian; some Russian/Cyrillic fonts support pre-revolutionary Russian, while others do not. It is important therefore to be as analytical and as specific as possible about one's needs in order to ensure that one is using the appropriate program or package. In some cases the problem may be relatively easy to rectify – if, for example, you have obtained the WorldFont package, then simply changing fonts from Cyrillic to Russian will enable you to work in Russian.

The result of this generally unsatisfactory state of affairs can all too often be seen, for example, in publications which use or quote Greek, where accents or certain characters have been entered by hand, or often-inconsistent Latin-alphabet transliterations of Greek are used.

3 Keyboards

If you want to key in text in Cyrillic or Greek with ease, then there are three desirable conditions: (i) it should be possible to access a character with a single keystroke; (ii) it should be possible to use a keyboard layout with which one is familiar; and (iii) it should be possible to have access to a reference facility, to see which key produces which character. These three points will be dealt with in turn.

3.1 Accessing characters

Since there are up to 255 characters in a character set, there are obviously more than can fit on a standard keyboard. It may also be necessary to use punctuation or other signs peculiar to a particular language (cf. Greek semi-colon, or Russian abbreviation for 'number', or varieties of inverted commas). Indirect access to any of the characters in a particular set is always possible, generally by entering the ASCII or the ANSI number to which that character is assigned (or by the appropriate code number in WordPerfect for example), or by calling up the character map for the font in question, and selecting and inserting the desired character using the mouse or the cursor keys. This, however, can require up to six keystrokes to produce a single character and a good memory (or constant reference to a table) for the values associated with the characters, and is clearly not an efficient way of creating electronic text, though it may be useful for the odd word or quotation in a basically Latin-alphabet text.

3.2 Keyboard layouts

Most packages create a keyboard layout that corresponds to a standard one for the language concerned. Thus some allow a choice of Cyrillic keyboards which may correspond to the regular layout for the actual language in which one is working. In most cases there is a fixed number of choices, but it is possible, for example in WordPerfect or using the WorldFont keymapper, to set up one's own configuration.

In dealing with mixed-alphabet text, it is necessary to be able to switch keyboards easily. There are two basic ways of doing this.

One is by using a particular combination of keypresses to flip from one keyboard to the other. This is generally the method used by DOS applications; for example the Greek and Cyrillic keyboards available with DOS 6.22 and above can be called up in this way, as can those within LocoScript. If you are using a Windows application, then selecting the appropriate 'font' or language will automatically reset the keyboard.

3.3   On-screen keyboard help

Keyboards available in Greece come with both Latin and Greek characters printed on the keys, but short of an appropriate keyboard overlay, most packages offer an on-screen display of the keyboard in use. This may in some cases be simply a reminder of the new keyboard values; in other cases, it is possible to select a sequence of keys from the on-screen keyboard and put the corresponding characters into the text. Again, this latter method is too slow to be suitable as a way of entering more than a few characters or words.

4   Transferability

Transferability is the big problem for those working in anything beyond the basic Latin alphabet. Anyone who has had the experience of getting a dollar sign or hash (#) sign in place of the £ will have had a small-scale experience of the problem. (Even now CD-ROMs of British newspapers do not reproduce on screen the £ sign in the text, which is usually rewritten as 'pounds'.) The problem arises because of the way the information about the characters is stored in the DOS or Windows files. Essentially, each character is assigned a number value lying in the range 1–255. The characters assigned to values from 1 to 127 are more or less fixed (generally in DOS, though not always in Windows), and include the (unaccented) Latin alphabet, numbers, and basic punctuation. Beyond this, there are different standards which have been set up by different bodies at different times. These are usually known as 'code pages' or 'ASCII code pages' (where ASCII = American Standard Code for Information Interchange) in DOS, and 'ANSI code pages' (where ANSI = American National Standards Institute) in Windows

Code page no.	Languages	Comments
737(437Greek)	Greek (monotonic)	Four rare characters missing (lower case iota and upsilon with diaeresis; capital iota and upsilon with diaeresis); common on Greek PCs; cannot handle initial accented capital vowels. Supported by DOS 6.22 and above as page 737.
851	Greek (monotonic)	Two rare characters missing (capital iota and upsilon with diaeresis); handles initial accented capital vowels. Handles guillemet inverted commas(«»). Supported by DOS 6.22 and above.
869	Greek (monotonic)	Has complete set including characters missing in 737 and 851. Same code values as 851. Supported by DOS 6.22 and above.
855	Cyrillic	Handles Russian, Ukrainian*, Ruthenian*, Belorussian, Serbian, Bulgarian, Macedonian. Supported by DOS 6.22 and above.
		*But not the hooked g (World Cyrillic font code nos 165 and 180 – see Appendix I, at the end of this chapter)
866	Russian	Exists in two varieties, the first a complete Russian character set, the other containing extra characters for Ukrainian and Belorussian. According to IBM, this is the page to use for Russian. The Russian character set version is supported by DOS 6.22 and above.

Figure 20.1 Outline of DOS code pages for Greek and Cyrillic

systems. ASCII code pages may also be known as IBM code pages. A single Greek or Cyrillic character will have a different number value on different DOS or Windows code pages: thus the Greek character lower-case alpha is coded as 152 on DOS code page 737 (also known as 437Greek), as 214 on DOS pages 851 and 869 (which are in fact almost identical as far as the Greek characters alone are concerned), as 226 in ISO 8859/7 (where ISO = International Standards Organization), as 225 in some Greek fonts for Windows, and as 97 in others. ASCII code pages do not handle the full range of accents of Greek, but only the monotonic system. Figures 20.1 and 20.2 contain a summary of DOS code pages and fonts, providing an overall guide to the possibilities.

Character set	Languages	Comments
ISO 8859/7	Latin/Greek	Contains full set of Greek characters (monotonic only), including inverted commas. Corresponds exactly to ELOT (Greek Standards Organization) standard 928.
Windows	Greek	Almost identical character values to ISO 8859/7, except for value of capital accented A. Offers more types of inverted commas.
WorldFont	Greek	(GREEK1 in Appendix I, at the end of this chapter). Many of the code values for Greek correspond to the code value for similar Latin characters. This means that it is possible to take a Latin-character Greek text, and by converting the font to Greek1, effectively transliterate into Greek, and vice versa. Some characters (particularly accented ones) may not transliterate directly.
ISO 8859/5	Latin/Cyrillic	Same range of characters as IBM code page 855
Windows	Cyrillic	Different values and range compared to 8859/5; contains second variety of g for emigré Ukrainian and Ruthenian (characters 165 and 180 – see Appendix II, at the end of this chapter). Does not cover Cyrillic diacritics and modified characters for non-Indo-European Cyrillic languages.
WorldFont	Russian	(See code values in Appendix II, at the end of this chapter). As the code values correspond to Latin-character values of other fonts, it is possible to effect a rough transliteration as above (WorldFont Greek). The accuracy of the transliteration will depend on the correspondences used.

Figure 20.2 Outline of Windows font features for certain Greek and Cyrillic fonts

Since what is stored in each textfile is simply the code number and not the actual character, clearly one of two things is necessary: either you must use the same code page when retrieving the textfile as when saving it (which is what happens when you use the same word-processing package each time you open a saved text), or if you are using a different package, you need to have some way of converting the code numbers to the new ones which will give you back the original characters. Fortunately, this is possible to a degree with most packages, though packages are generally limited in some ways in the conversions that they offer, because developments regularly leap-frog each other (the latest software will only convert to and from chronologically earlier versions of other software, and not to or from anything more recent). The facility is usually available when saving or when opening a file. A facility that does this is known as a translation table (though it only translates code numbers and not languages). Software exists which allows users to set up their own translation tables – TransLex is an example of one such package, designed principally for Cyrillic conversions, but with a user-define facility, which allows you to convert any code number to any other code number.

With Greek and Cyrillic text, it is as well to check some of the claims for convertibility; some packages which offer the option of converting into or out of Windows or WordPerfect, for example, may only effectively convert the standard codes in the range 1 to 127, leaving non-Latin text stranded. It should be noted that extended Cyrillic, i.e. Cyrillic characters required by non-Slavonic languages of the former Soviet Union, is not supported by DOS – there is no DOS code page which contains these characters. (Although a package like LocoScript operating under DOS does have these characters, this is also why so few packages are able to support Welsh fully, because no DOS page has the complete character set needed for it.) The same is true for the full accent system of Greek. Hence it is more difficult to convert these across different packages without losing a quantity of information.

To give two examples of the file conversion facility, Accent offers to convert files not only from the formats of many other word-processing packages, but also from 24 different code pages, of which seven are Cyrillic or Greek pages. Even so, my current version does not offer the option of converting Greek files which are saved on page 437Greek, which is widely used on PCs in Greece, since it was the first Greek code page to be developed. LocoScript Professional converts to and from three Cyrillic pages and two Greek pages, as well as many other Latin-alphabet pages.

Although this approach generally works, it none the less represents a second-best solution, a series of ad-hoc patches. At present it requires much more persistence on the part of the user to handle non-Latin textfiles successfully than is required by their Latin-using counterparts. (This is generally, but not always true: the more a Latin-alphabet language makes use of accents, the more similar its problems become.)

A solution has already passed through the initial planning stage, but is still a long way from general implementation. This is to set up a single code which will assign a unique value to each of the characters of all the languages in the world, on a range of values not from 1 to 255 but from 1 to 65535. The Unicode project which does this is supported by major computer and software manufacturers, and the codes have been agreed for Cyrillic and Greek. When in general use as a worldwide standard, this will make the transfer of texts in any language as easy as the transfer of English texts is now. General implementation is still some way off, since software manufacturers are only just beginning to exploit the potential. Gamma UniVerse is, to my knowledge, the only multilingual package which is already compatible with the Unicode consortium's proposal. It will also be a long time before many current users are able to afford to upgrade their hardware or software, and most existing packages can be expected to be in use for many years.

5   Corpora in Greek and Cyrillic

Corpora are in ever-wider use for language research and language-teaching purposes. The expanding power of PC machines means that it is easier than ever to build up one's own collection of texts, and a large-scale project is no longer the only repository for a text collection. Concordancing software suitable for small-scale work has been produced by OUP. For DOS systems *MicroConcord* is available, and for Windows Mike Smith's *WordSmith*. This can handle both DOS and Window texts in Cyrillic and Greek. WordCruncher also can be configured for any language.[1]

Figure 20.3 shows concordance output for Greek. The procedure used to obtain it illustrates many of the above points. The text was originally typed in using LocoScript Professional. A plain-text ASCII file was then created by exporting the file on code page 851. Then, switching to DOS and using code page 869 (which is almost identical to page 851 – see Figure 20.1) supplied in DOS 6.22, MicroConcord was run. DOS 6.22 allows for easy toggling of the keyboard between Latin and Greek alphabets. The search word was keyed in, and the resulting concordance file saved. I then exited MicroConcord, went into Windows, called up Accent and opened the saved file. The file was put into the Courier Greek font, which is not a proportional font, so that all letter widths remain the same and the keyword remains centred on the page.

This procedure was in fact more complex than it needs to be; the original Greek corpus was built up before Windows became

```
MicroConcord search SW: πάε ι 80 characters per entry Sort : 1L/2L shifted –
1 characters.
```
1 ε ιδέα από σύγχρονο πόλεμο.   – Αυτό πάει πια, τέλει ωσε. ποια βουνά θα πάρεις σή
2 της φωνάζω.   Μέσα στο ταξί που μας πάει σπίτι της κατάλαβα την απογοήτευσή της
3 τραβάει από το χέρι να σηκωθώ και με πάει κοντά στο παράθυρο. Ανοίγει τις βελούδ
4 που είναι κολλητό στο παράθυρο. Εχει πάει πέντε παρά τέταρτο κι ακόμα να φέξει.
5 για τα καλά, την τραβώ με το ζόρι να πάει να κοιμηθεί. Κουβαλάει όλα τα δώρα της
6 φό της, πότε από τη νύφη της. Η Λίζα πάει χειρότερα, αδυνάτισε, δεν γνωρίζεται.
7 α σου φέρουν τις 'μαθητριούλες'. Σου πάει το θαλασσί ταγιέρ. Εγώ έχω μια μικρή δ
8 σα χρόνια εδώ, μα βλέπω πως κάτι δεν πάει καλά με σένα . . . Δεν τον αφήνω να τελ
9 ραφίες της Κνωσού απέξω. Εγώ δεν έχω πάει ποτέ μου στην Κνωσό. πότε να πήγαινα
10 ου ο Πάνος με το γελάκι του, που όσο πάει γίνεται και πιο ξεκούρντιστο. – Μάθε
```
Data from the following files:
WBACHILL.CTX

**Figure 20.3**   Greek concordance lines

available. It would be possible to reduce the range of software used either by going back into LocoScript to open the saved file, or by using Accent to create the corpus.

Even relatively small corpora may be sufficient to make many points for teaching and research purposes, because most of the languages covered by this chapter have not by and large been deeply researched. It is instructive, for example, to compare concordance output with dictionary definitions for Greek words, to find that common senses of common words may not be represented at all in the dictionary. Analysis of authentic data thus can have a more important role in the teaching and learning of the less widely used languages, since the facts of the language may be less well or less accurately established. Such work has an importance which is in inverse relation to the ease of carrying it out.

## 6   Conclusion

This chapter is an attempt to unravel some of the additional complexity which experience has shown to be daunting of handling small corpora in Greek and Cyrillic. Creating, manipulating and interchanging textfiles in these alphabets will continue to be a complex task for some time to come. It is gradually being made easier by the increased user-friendliness of packages, and by a greater incorporation of file conversion facilities in these packages. The move to the single standard proposed by the Unicode consortium will take some time because (i) it needs to be supported by 32-bit
```

software development, and (ii) even as this develops, many users will continue to work with their existing hardware and software. In the past few years the situation has improved considerably, but there is still some way to go.

Note

1   Some of these products currently available for PCs running DOS will allow the use of characters in the high-ASCII range of 128 to 255. To be able to use these with Cyrillic or Greek texts, it is necessary to have the relevant DOS code pages available and set up. If you are operating an older version of DOS, then you will need to obtain an upgrade to the latest version. The relevant documentation on code pages has always tended to be obscure in the DOS manuals supplied with the software as well as in the guides available in bookshops. (Currently (February 1997), the information on how to set up the relevant code pages is contained in a file COUNTRY.TXT supplied with the upgrade or the latest version, which should be printed off and studied.)

Appendix I:

Table of values for selected Greek code pages and fonts

GREEK	437G/737	851/869	WINDOWS GREEK /ISO 8859/7	GREEK 1*
A	128	164	193	65
'A	234	134	162/182	
α	152	214	225	97
ά	225	155	220	163
B	129	165	194	66
β	153	215	226	98
Γ	130	166	195	70
γ	154	216	227	103
Δ	131	167	196	68
δ	155	221	228	100
E	132	168	197	69
'E	235	141	184	
ε	156	222	229	101
έ	226	157	221	154
Z	133	169	198	90
ζ	157	224	230	122
H	134	170	199	71
'H	236	143	185	
η	158	225	231	104
ή	227	158	222	187
Θ	135	172	200	81

GREEK	437G/737	851/869	WINDOWS GREEK /ISO 8859/7	GREEK 1*
θ	159	226	232	113
I	136	173	201	73
Ί	237	144	186	
Ϊ		145(869)	218	
ι	160	227	233	105
ί	229	159	223	133
ϊ	228	160	250	142
ΐ		161	192	143
K	137	181	202	75
κ	161	228	234	107
Λ	138	182	203	76
λ	162	229	235	108
M	139	183	204	77
μ	163	230	236	109
N	140	184	205	78
ν	164	231	237	110
Ξ	141	189	206	88
ξ	165	232	238	120
O	142	190	207	79
Ό	238	146	188	
o	166	233	239	111
ό	230	162	252	210
Π	143	198	208	80
π	167	234	240	112
P	144	199	209	82
ρ	168	235	241	114
Σ	145	207	211	83
σ	169	236	243	115
ς	170	237	242	106
T	146	208	212	84
τ	171	238	244	116
Y	147	209	213	85
Ύ	239	149	190	
Ϋ		150(869)	219	
υ	172	242	245	117
ύ	231	163	253	218
ϋ	232	251	251	27
ΰ		252	224	228
Φ	148	210	214	70
φ	173	243	246	102
X	149	211	215	67
χ	174	244	247	99
Ψ	150	212	216	89
ψ	175	246	248	121
Ω	151	213	217	87
Ώ	240	152	191	
ω	224	250	250	119
ώ	233	253	255	232

* This font does not contain Latin-alphabet characters, but has a range of classical Greek characters in addition to those given here.

Appendix II:

Sample cyrillic code values for ASCII code pages and selected windows fonts

	855	866	WORD PERFECT	WORLD CYRILLIC	RUSSIAN 1	CYRILLIC 1
А	161	128	33	192	65	70
а	160	160	34	224	97	102
Б	163	129	35	193	66	60
б	162	161	36	225	98	44
В	236	130	37	194	86	68
в	235	162	38	226	118	100
Г	173	131	39	195	71	85
г	172	163	40	227	103	117
Ґ			103	165	203	
ґ			104	180		
Д	167	132	41	196	68	76
д	166	164	42	228	100	108
Ѓ	131		101	129		
ѓ	130		102	131	219	
Ђ	129		107	128	212	77
ђ	128		108	144	163	
Е	169	133	43	197	69	84
е	168	165	44	229	101	116
Ё	133	240	45	168	63	
ё	132	241	46	184	47	
Є	135	242	111	170	215	
є	134	243	112	186		
Ж	234	134	47	198	34	58
ж	233	166	48	230	39	59
З	244	135	49	199	90	80
з	243	167	50	231	122	112
S	137		115	189	211	
s	136		116	190		
I	139		121	178	201	
i	138		122	179		
Ї	141		123	175	208	
ï	140		124	191		
И	184	136	51	200	73	
и	183	168	52	232	105	98
Ј	143		128	163	202	79
ј	142		129	188		111
Й	190	137	53	201	74	
й	189	169	54	233	106	
К	199	138	55	202	75	82
к	198	170	56	234	107	114
Л	209	139	57	203	76	75
л	208	171	58	235	108	107
Љ	145		138	138	198	125
љ	144		139	154		93
М	211	140	59	204	77	86
м	210	172	60	236	109	118
Н	213	141	61	205	78	89

	855	866	WORD PERFECT	WORLD CYRILLIC	RUSSIAN 1	CYRILLIC 1
Н	212	173	62	237	110	121
Њ	147		142	140	200	83
њ	146		143	156		115
О	215	142	63	206	79	74
о	214	174	64	238	111	106
П	221	143	65	207	80	71
п	216	175	66	239	112	103
Р	226	144	67	208	82	72
р	225	224	68	240	114	104
С	228	145	69	209	83	67
с	227	225	70	241	115	99
Т	230	146	71	210	84	78
т	229	226	72	242	116	110
Ќ	151		130	141	222	
ќ	150		131	157	223	
Ћ	149		148	142	204	63
ћ	148		149	158	164	47
У	232	147	73	211	85	69
у	231	227	74	243	117	101
Ў	153	246	150	161		
ў	152	247	151	162		
Ф	171	148	75	212	70	65
ф	170	228	76	244	102	97
Х	182	149	77	213	88	123
х	181	229	78	245	120	91
Ц	165	150	79	214	67	87
ц	164	230	80	246	99	119
Ч	252	151	81	215	72	88
ч	251	231	82	247	104	120
Џ	155		168	143	213	81
џ	154		169	159		113
Ш	246	152	83	216	87	73
ш	245	232	84	248	119	105
Щ	250	153	85	217	125	
щ	249	233	86	249	93	
Ъ	159	154	87	218	60	
ъ	158	234	88	250	44	
Ы	242	155	89	219	89	
ы	241	235	90	251		
Ь	238	156	91	220	58	
ь	237	236	92	252	59	
Э	248	157	93	221	62	34
э	247	237	94	253	46	39
Ю	157	158	95	222	123	62
ю	156	238	96	254	91	46
Я	224	159	97	223	81	90
я	222	239	98	255	113	122
№	239	252		185	33	33

Note: WordPerfect Cyrillic, Russian 1 and Cyrillic 1 contain other characters not included in this table.

21

Developing a Computing Infrastructure for Corpus-based Teaching

GRAEME HUGHES

1 Introduction

For the newcomer to corpus-based teaching, the first task is to grasp what can be done with the corpora themselves. But in order to implement a corpus-based teaching program, it is also necessary to develop an appropriate computing infrastructure. This chapter addresses the problems faced by someone who is required to make a bid for equipment funding without being quite sure exactly of what is required. It will also prove useful to someone who has funds available and seeks to enlist the assistance of technical specialists in developing appropriate resources. The discussion covers some of the possibilities that are already available, and highlights the main issues that have to be borne in mind when designing the infrastructure. The suggestions made here are based on experience gained in the Department of Linguistics and Modern English Language at Lancaster,[1] but they are presented as far as possible in general terms, and without assuming more than the most elementary knowledge of computer systems. The emphasis in this chapter is on *computing* resources, and not on *corpus* resources. Various sources of information regarding the latter are given elsewhere in this book. Readers in Britain are especially encouraged to contact the CTI (Computers in Teaching Initiative) Centre in Oxford for advice on what is available and how it may be obtained and used.

It is assumed that a person or group of persons will be in the position of main 'initiator(s)', and that such persons may well lack any significant knowledge of the technical issues involved.

It is important that such persons acquire at least a conceptual grasp of the technology and its applications, if they are to develop an appropriate plan and retain some measure of control over its implementation.

In setting up any computing facility it is imperative to plan carefully before implementing it. Decisions that are made at the beginning can affect the flexibility of the system, and its ability to expand and change in the future. As corpus resources are changing, both in the size of corpora and the variety of annotations available, flexibility must be seen as a key aim. The following sections deal with the problems of planning a system under four main headings:

- Networking
- Issues to consider
- Hardware
- Finance.

2 Networking

In the early years of corpus linguistics, it was normal to have a relatively small corpus on a single 'stand-alone' machine. For teaching purposes nowadays it is necessary to have several machines, and in order to exploit them efficiently and cost effectively it is important to link them together in a network. The first planning decision to be made is, therefore, how the computers in the system are to be networked.

One of the simplest forms of networking involves sharing a printer between a group of machines. This can be done by using a printer switch, which is simply a small box that connects a number of computers to one printer and avoids the need to physically connect then disconnect each computer in order to print. Printer switches vary in size and sophistication but generally have the same layout. One end of the switch is connected by a cable to the printer, and from the other end cables run to each computer on the network. This means that any machine connected to the network will be able to use the same printer. As it is not necessary to buy a separate printer for each machine, the cost saving on a large group of machines is clearly tremendous. For a given budget it is more cost effective to purchase a single high-quality printer rather than a number of lower quality ones. It is important, however, to obtain an efficient printer and printer switch for such a system, because printing jobs are queued, and a slow printer or switch can leave the users waiting an excessively long time for their print-outs.

Another advantage of networking is that the content of disks can be shared. This can be done relatively simply with software such as Microsoft's Windows 95 or IBM's OS/2 or with the Macintosh AppleTalk system. Software of this kind will enable the sharing of data, concordances and other retrieval packages, printers, CD-ROMs, backup devices, etc., to and from all the machines. This is called 'peer-to-peer' networking.

The ability to share data is of particular interest in the present context. Only one machine needs to hold the corpus data, and the other machines simply access the data across the network. To give an idea of the scale of the savings involved, consider the case of a million word corpus. The text alone occupies some 5–10 Mb of disk space, and tagging and indexing can easily quadruple that figure. This entire space is saved on all machines except one. Apart from the saving of space, the one version of the corpus can be made more secure. Other users can load the corpus data but not change it, so that the corpus remains secure from unwanted modifications.

It is important to organize the sharing of facilities on the network. One machine can be used to distribute the shared data, another to control the printer, another the CD-ROM drive, etc. This, however, is not an ideal situation from the point of view of support and cost. For example, if one machine is used to provide the shared filestore support for many users, all accessing the data on its hard disk, this machine may become a bottleneck for the whole system, and in effect unusable as a standard machine. Alternatively, if the shared filestore is distributed among several machines, it can be difficult to know where particular parts of the data are stored. The solution to the problems of a large peer-to-peer network is to dedicate one machine to the special task of running the network. Such a machine is called a 'server' and a network organized in this way is referred to as a 'client-server' network.

A large institution such as a university may already have a server or a number of servers and it may be possible for a department to obtain disk space and facilities on it. This is certainly an easy way of creating a shared resource and may prove to be ideal in the early stages, and an ideal stepping stone before a department can provide its own server and support a full network service. An institution-wide network also enhances the value of a single machine in cases where funds are not available for several machines.

If an existing server is not available, it is advisable to obtain advice and support from the institution's computer service or an outside agency to set up a new server. There is machine-specific server software available, such as Novell Netware or Microsoft NT. It is important to be aware that client-server technology is a complex area and requires a considerable amount of time and expertise in designing, implementing and, perhaps most importantly, *supporting* a networked system.

The advantage of a server is that you can concentrate your resources on a purpose-built machine with the ability to supply data rapidly to many computers or 'workstations' by the use of fast disks and network cards. Support, although essential, is in a sense easier as the system is more structured, and growth can be achieved simply by increasing the resources of the server and/or increasing the number of machines attached to it.

If a local network is in turn connected to an institution-wide network, and if this in turn is connected to wider academic or commercial networks, a much wider range of possibilities becomes available. One of these is electronic mail, or 'e-mail', which is a method of sending messages from one person to another via computer. Mail may be sent from one part of the world to another and arrive just a few seconds later. You may also have access to the Internet and the 'Information Super Highway' through a network, opening up large amounts of resources for your teaching and research.

Networking is rapidly impinging on computing of all types. Even the home computer is no longer stranded in isolation, but may be connected to computers at work, or elsewhere in the global network by means of a modem and a telephone line, or by the faster ISDN data connections which are starting to become popular and relatively inexpensive in some countries. The increasing reliance on network connections is certainly evident in the field of language corpora. We have already seen that sheer volume of data has resulted in a shift from 'stand-alone' to shared resources. The continuation of this trend is likely to mean that increasingly we will be working with data which is not stored locally at all, but which is accessed remotely across networks. This is not a distant prospect. Already it is possible for subscribers to carry out searches on the Cobuild 'Bank of English' (see Sinclair, this volume), and the British National Corpus (see Leech, this volume) is planned to be made generally available via the network. The way this will work is that when the user loads the retrieval program, or concordancer, program instructions will be sent via the network to a server that may be many miles away, where the data is centrally stored. In such cases the role of the network can be seen as incidental to the user. The user simply operates the program, and the network activity is carried on behind the scenes. Whether the data is stored on the workstation, on a local server, or on a machine in another city, or even another country, need not be of any concern to the user. In such cases we say that the network is 'transparent', though 'invisible' might be a more appropriate term. Through the increasing development of transparent applications, and, in any case, as people become more attuned to the customs and practices of 'exploring the Net', we can be fairly certain that the current trend towards networked computers will continue apace.

Thus, even though the intended system may have to be modest in the first instance, it is essential to consider what is likely to be needed in the future. If your facility is successful, then demand for new features will come quickly and will be great. The likely need for networking at some stage should not be overlooked.

3   Issues to consider

In view of the range and sheer size of corpora which are now becoming available and the different things people will want to do with them, it is impossible to cover all of the factors involved in the creation of a computer system relevant to the needs of all institutions. Not only will the needs of different departments and institutions vary, but the scope for developing and maintaining a computing infrastructure will in part be determined by the amount of funding and technical back-up available. Hence this chapter is best viewed as a skeleton outline of what a system might look like. In view of the rapid rate of change in computer technology, it is difficult to write anything that will not quickly become dated. However, although some of the technical details discussed in this chapter will inevitably change, the range of issues to be considered can be expected to remain substantially the same.

In this section I will outline the factors that should be considered when setting up either an individual or a group corpus exploitation facility. These include:

- analysis of needs
- institutional computing policy
- maximizing use
- technical and user support
- space.

To analyse your needs you have first to assess them and then find out how this can be achieved with available equipment. This means seeking not only technical computing advice but also the opinions and wishes of potential users of the systems you are to develop. This can generally produce a mix of answers, some of which will not be consistent. In some cases the requirements will conflict, e.g. in a group environment the users may want the ability to alter the systems yet the technical staff may want to keep the systems in a stable configuration by limiting the scope of users to effect changes. So it is necessary to follow this initial trawl for advice with a clarification stage, filtering the information gained and asking further questions where necessary. In the areas where conflict of requirements occur, these must be resolved. Many institutions have central computer support staff and these will prove invaluable in providing you with information about what is possible, what is available and what will soon be possible and available. But it is reasonable to exercise a degree of scepticism, and to be insistent on matters where you feel that what is on offer is not quite what you want. Ultimately, you might not get what you want, but successful computing infrastructure design does involve a certain amount of negotiation, and not just over money.

A common problem concerns communication between scholars and technical staff. While computer support staff will understand the intricacies of the network, they may not necessarily show an immediate appreciation of the specific issues involved in corpus exploitation. As initiator, it will be your role to explain in general terms what is required of the technology. Ultimately, someone must assume responsibility for designing the system. This is best carried out as a collaborative act between a technical specialist and someone acting on behalf of those who will be using the system. There is every reason even for the non-technical partner to take an interest in current technical developments by consulting computer magazines, relevant journals, computer specialists and colleagues in other departments, but at the same time it is important to keep in mind at all times the needs of those who will be using the system. The scenario outlined here assumes that, in the first instance, it will be someone with limited computing expertise who is responsible for initiating the project. An ambitious development plan might incorporate the eventual recruitment of technical staff dedicated to the administration of your systems and, if this happens, the dynamics of systems development will naturally change, as you will then have a proactive technical expert to take up your cause.

Your institution may already have a policy which will, to a large extent, determine your computing environment. Your institution may support a particular type of personal computer – e.g. Macintosh or IBM PC-compatible, or a particular type of network, e.g. modem access to a mainframe or dedicated cabling from your desk – and, of course, this provides a very strong influence on your choice of facilities. This will apply equally to groups and to individual users within an institution.

A further factor to consider is the role which you envisage for any machines purchased. Are they to be used solely for corpus-based teaching and study? If so, then a slightly different specification may best suit your needs over a more general-purpose computer set-up. For example, you may only require or envisage ever requiring small corpus-based programs. Thus you may not need large amounts of memory within each machine; you may also not need large amounts of disk space to be available. If, however, you require more general facilities such as word processors, spreadsheets and statistical programs to be available, then both memory and disk space may need to be larger than your corpus programs require. You will also, as the example above shows, need to take into account the different amounts of software required by, respectively, a general and specialized facility. This applies both to single and group users, though generally one would expect a single user to require a multipurpose machine. If a computing set-up is only required for corpus-based teaching then you will need to consider whether you are able to make full use of the facility. Equipment that is idle for significant periods of time may be viewed as an underused resource, and if corpus-based teaching cannot solely occupy the computing facilities then maybe access to the facilities should be widened to make more effective use of them.

A crucial part of any development plan is the measures that will be taken to ensure that the system, once created, is kept up and running, that it is periodically updated, and that people are trained to use it. Depending on the level of finance available, it may be necessary to make use of what skills are already available within the institution, but where a system of some size is concerned, serious thought should be given to the question of buying in help, or even of employing a technical staff. The kinds of support required break down into two broad categories: systems support, involving routine maintenance and a whole range of systems administration functions; and user support, which includes both training and reactive support – helping someone out when problems are encountered. Whatever the scale of your ambitions, it is vital to give serious thought to all of these issues, and be clear about who will be called upon to do what in a range of situations.

The final general issue to be considered is space. If you are setting up a lab you require a suitable amount of space that can be devoted to that purpose. If you are only setting up a single machine then you still need to make sure that enough suitable space is available. For a group facility in a single room you need to have appropriate furniture for the task, such as: tables with enough space so that users can work alongside their machine and with enough depth to enable users to rest their hands in front of the keyboard; adjustable chairs for working with computers; space for printers and other equipment you may require, such as transcribers,[2] tape recorders, videos, etc. Note that this may not be a matter in which you have much choice, and you may have to fulfil legal requirements. In EC countries, for instance, the furnishing of computer rooms is subject to legislation on health and safety at work.[3]

If the room is to be used for teaching purposes then you may need space to be available to teach, i.e. space to sit and work in a group; facilities to allow groups of students to see a computer demonstration; black/white board space, etc. For a single user facility you would require space for your computing equipment, including possibly a printer and also space in which to work next to your machine.

4 Hardware

When planning a facility, it is important to look at the present state of the hardware technology and take that into account. However, since it is constantly changing you will regularly need to review the state of it during setting up. Whatever level of equipment you specify in your bid for funds, you may well find that by the time you come to purchase, you can get better equipment for the same money. In general, the best advice is to buy the better equipment rather than save the money, as the rapid obsolescence cycle of computing equipment generally demands that you should buy the best equipment you can afford in order to maximize its useful working life.

For any facility, whether it be single or a group, you will need machines, furniture and backup, and for a group facility you may also need networking and servers.

At the time of writing, IBM PC compatible technology is based around the Pentium processor and Macintosh technology around the PowerPC. When setting up a facility that is to last you should be aiming for these processors or as close as you can get to them. The closer you can purchase to the present state-of-the-art equipment the longer your machine or machines are going to be serviceable as technology moves forward. You should also be looking to have a minimum of 16 Mb (megabytes) of RAM (memory) and preferably more; 16 Mb is the minimum reasonable memory to run such operating systems as Microsoft Windows and IBM OS/2. Machines are often marketed with less RAM than 16 Mb, but this is simply a ploy to keep down the headline price. The trend over time is for this minimum to grow and generally when software packages state that this is the minimum memory recommended it means that it will just about run with this amount of memory, but if you want it to be really usable you will need more. Very soon, amounts of RAM which may sound quite excessive at the moment will become normal, and increasing the RAM during the working life of the machine is a common method of remedying flagging performance.[4] It is therefore important to make sure at the outset that RAM expansion in the future is easy and cost effective. Memory generally comes on 'single inline memory modules' (SIMMs) of various sizes and speeds that fit into the memory slots of your machines. To expand the memory that you have you need to purchase more SIMMs. Because of the size and configuration of the original SIMMs and the restriction your computer places on possible configurations, it is sometimes necessary to replace (either trading in or throwing away) the original SIMMs. In order to reduce this redundancy, check that the SIMMs provided in your machines allow you to expand memory without having to throw the original SIMMs away.

Hard disk (storage) size is dependent upon how you intend to use the machine. In a server situation your client machines will not have to hold the corpus data and therefore do not need huge hard disks. You will, however, have to allow room for the system software and any other software packages you may want to add onto the machine throughout the machine's lifetime. In some server configurations the client machine may not need to have hard disks at all. This obviously provides a significant cost saving with a small cost in terms of speed of the software, since the system has to run across the network from the server disks and will therefore be slightly slower. When allowing disk space for corpora, allow space for any indexes that may be necessary for your corpus access software. The indexing can often take up more space than the corpus data itself. It is essential to take advice on the issue of 'diskless workstations' from someone familar with local network arrangements, where these are already in place.

To put the issue of disk size into perspective, in 1990, 40 Mb was considered a good size for a hard disk on a desktop PC, but by 1995 many machines were supplied with at least half a gigabyte, and currently 2 gigabytes is becoming the 'entry level'. At the same time, as software packages are developed, they tend to increase their storage requirements, so there is not necessarily a lot more space for data. However, the growth in disk size norms has been accompanied by a steady reduction in the unit cost of storage, which is good news for corpus linguists, who have always ranked among the 'greedier' types of computer user, where disk space is concerned.

For a single user facility or even a group facility where storage capacity is restricted, you may require only a small amount of corpus data to be available at any one time. In this case a backup device would enable you to store data on tape or disk until you needed it. In any case, it is advisable to have a method of backing up data as accidents will always happen. Various ways of backing up data exist and the one that best suits you depends upon the amount of data you have and the type of backups you require. You may use floppy disks and therefore not need to purchase anything other than floppy disks since nearly all machines come with a floppy disk drive. This would prove feasible for a single user system when backing up small amounts of data (but would be unsuitable for backing up the entire system). As system sizes and data sizes grow, or as the number of machines on your network increases, this sort of method becomes impossible. There are various types of tape backup system, including systems based upon Qic, Exabyte and DAT tapes. To decide which tape type to use it is necessary to analyse your situation, and to discuss the issue with local experts (some institutions actually have campus-wide backup services into which your new facilities could be integrated). Each tape type has a fixed capacity per tape and a speed at which data can be stored and retrieved. You need to select an appropriate tape size so that you are not constantly changing tapes and also an appropriate backup system with a suitable data rate. This will enable you to back up your system in a reasonable amount of time, e.g. if you carry out weekly backups then your backup system needs to be fast enough to complete the backup within the week, before the next backup is due. There are costs in terms of tapes to be taken into account. There are also various methods of connecting the tapes to your machine or network, including the ports on the back of your computer, proprietary interface cards and SCSI connections. If you are going to use backup tapes to exchange data with other sites or colleagues, then compatibility becomes an issue and you should check what the other parties are using before proceeding.

5   Finance

A point that cannot be emphasized too strongly is that a computing infrastructure is not a one-off cost, but a continuing financial commitment. It is an easy mistake – and a serious one – to obtain funding for a facility but to ignore or underestimate the recurring and support costs that are required to maintain that facility. There are four main parts of financial planning:

- purchasing policy
- maintenance
- upgrading and replacement
- support costs (see section 3).

At Lancaster we estimate the life of a computer at between three and four years. At the end of this period it has to be replaced. The cost of replacement can be spread by replacing a third or quarter of the whole system each year, and the best way of starting a rolling replacement plan is to phase in the initial purchase, building up over three or four years. This ensures a relatively flat expenditure curve. It is interesting to note that non-computer hardware, such as printers, scanners, tape drives, etc., have lower maintenance costs, and tend to have a longer life cycle. One still needs to budget for the replacement of these items in the long run, however.

Networking costs can be a significant amount. This depends upon what sort of local networking environment you are using. There are various methods of networking and many rely upon network cards[5] being fitted to your machine. This can add to the cost of your machine and you should seek whatever advice is available locally before purchasing networking facilities. The cabling and fitting of the cabling also adds costs and there may be other costs involved in connecting to your institution's network if one exists.

In purchasing a system cheapness is not the same as value for money. When purchasing a machine, or group of machines, it is very easy to try to buy the cheapest and to buy more of the cheapest machine available. With the recurring costs involved in maintaining the machines and enabling them to run new versions of the software, buying the cheapest machines at the bottom end of the technology does not always prove to be the most cost-effective solution, and will be much more likely to deliver unsatisfactory performance. It is often difficult to appreciate, but is true none the less, that a machine which is fast by today's standards will seem at best sluggish and, at worst, painfully slow by the time it is due for replacement just a few years hence. In large institutions, those who review bids for equipment funding will normally be well aware of this. A consequence of this is that they may be more impressed by a bid for top-end equipment than by one which appears to be 'penny-pinching'. They are likely to interpret a bid for too modest equipment levels as a sign of naivety, and have less confidence in the ability of the bidders to carry out their plans.

With a group facility you need also to consider the costs involved in networking, space, furniture, support and training. You may also need to consider costs in providing filestore servers, i.e. machines that store data, such as corpora, which other computers can access via the network.

In view of the recurring costs it is unwise to purchase a system in the first instance if funds for maintenance and modernization are not available or are unlikely to be available in the future. The trick is to determine the scale of system that can be sustained in the longer term, and work towards achieving that.

To give an example of the scale of the ongoing cost of computing equipment, at present a new personal computer costs around £700 upwards in the UK, but in order to obtain a level of technology that is not quickly obsolete the costs are more likely to be around £1500–£2000. Although the technology is changing rapidly, these figures seem to remain surprisingly consistent. The change with time is that the level of technology that can be purchased at these prices is constantly increasing. In one sense, purchasers get more for their money, but as we have seen, trends in software development mean that they need to do so!

Maintenance expenditure is essential to stop a system deteriorating to a level of unusability. The likelihood is that over a period of time your computers may develop faults. These may be simple faults such as a faulty mouse or more major faults such as the hard disk or power supply failing. For simple faults it may be possible to get the machine repaired within your institution. For more complex faults it may be necessary to approach the manufacturer for help. Some computer firms offer maintenance agreements, whereby for an annual fee they will repair any faults that develop with your machines. The terms of this agreement will vary and you will need to investigate this. In a large group facility you may find that the cost of such maintenance agreements is high and that it is cheaper to accept the costs of repairing each machine as it fails. There are risks in deciding on accepting the costs of repairing each fault as it happens since it is possible that many machines may develop faults at the same time leaving you with a huge bill. You should also remember that this does not only cover the computers but also any other devices such as printers, etc. It is worth noting that PCs tend to become much less reliable (and therefore expensive to repair) after about three years of intensive use. If you are able to sustain a relatively short replacement cycle, and especially if you have technicians available to carry out repairs, then the maintenance contract may be an expensive luxury, but in other cases it may actually save money and make life easier at the same time.

New versions of both corpus and general-purpose computing software such as word processors are constantly being produced. These new versions generally offer new or improved facilities over the old versions. Although it is not necessary to keep up with the new versions to run a facility, you may find that users want the new features of new versions and that interchange with other institutions and users is assisted by having newer versions since they may also have the newer version of software. In purchasing updates it is often possible to take advantage of bulk deals and site licences. Upgrading is not an unnecessary luxury. For the reasons mentioned above the pressures to maintain current versions of software in an institutional environment can prove irresistible.

As your facility gets used you may find that users require more corpora, bigger corpora and duplicate corpora in various formats. They may also want different sorts of programs to be added to the system. This will require extra disk space either on the server or the client machines. An unfortunate side effect of upgrading software is that the new versions generally require more disk space and memory, requiring upgrades to the hardware before it is due for replacement. You may also find that your facility is heavily used and that more computers, printers, etc., are required.

The above three cost areas can amount to a considerable percentage of the original purchase price. At Lancaster we estimated this to be 25 per cent of the original cost price per annum, that is, an overhead *in addition to* the cost of replacing a given proportion of the system each year.

6 Conclusion

It has been the aim of this chapter to outline the main areas that you may need to consider in developing a computing infrastructure, be it on a group or individual scale. It has been seen that it is necessary to obtain as much advice as possible from as many sources as possible and to keep reviewing that advice in the light of new information and the changing nature of the field of corpus linguistics and computing technology. If you lack specialist technical knowledge, then seek the collaboration of a suitable expert when drawing up your final plans.

It has also been seen that, although the task can be subdivided into broad areas of interest, each of these areas directly affects the others and an overall view of any development has to be taken at all times. This can be difficult when being bogged down in details and therefore you, as systems developer, must occasionally try to step back from the details and look at the overall picture, with particular emphasis on the measures for ensuring that the system will function smoothly once in place, and on the long-term cost implications.

From the point of view of the individual and group users it can be seen that in many most cases the difference is just one of scale, especially when both are sited within an institution that provides some networking facilities. It is, however, in the networking area that the biggest differences are seen. Setting up a group facility may require the development of servers and all the associated costs and considerations need to be taken into account, whereas an individual facility requires the system developer to place everything that is needed upon the desk of the individual user. Even in institutions where a highly integrated network arrangement is sought, colleagues with computers situated off-site are, for the present at least, effectively in a stand-alone situation, albeit perhaps with the benefit of a modem connection to some remote facilities. However, this can be expected to change in the years ahead.

Finally, this chapter is not a comprehensive guide to all the areas that you need to consider in developing the system but it will hopefully provide you with some food for thought if you find yourself with such a task.

Notes

1 The systems at Lancaster were originally developed by Gerry Knowles, as then Head of Department, and Steve Fligelstone, who took on the role of initiator. My direct experience dates from the time when, as part of their development plan, I was employed as Systems Support Manager, with responsibility for both user support and general systems administration and development. An earlier article relating their experiences is Fligelstone (1993) Gearing up – planning a computer system for use in teaching and research. *Computers and Texts*, **5**: 2–4.

2 A transcriber is a secretarial machine that allows audio to be listened to in small repeatable sections. This tool is useful in the entry of spoken corpora to machine.

3 In the UK, Health and Safety (display screen equipment) Regulation 1992, and the Health and Safety at Work Act 1994 implement the European Directive 90/270/EEC (1990).

4   The reason that performance flags is of course not the age or state of the machine itself, but the fact that software becomes more and more demanding of computing power with each new version that is released.

5   A network card is a device inserted into your computer that allows it to communicate with other similar computers via the cables attached to the network card.

Appendices

Appendix 1

Further Investigation:
A Brief Guide

The days have long since passed when it was possible to reproduce ICAME's postal address and mention one or two publications and a dozen or so corpora, and feel confident that the reader would have gained a comprehensive overview of the corpus community and its output. Important though these sources remain, the scale of involvement in corpus-related work has grown to such an unprecedented extent that a comprehensive overview of resources is nearly impossible (see Leech, this volume).

Surveys and readings

Possibly the last brave attempt to single-handedly carry out a survey of available corpus resources was that published in Edwards and Lampert (1993), available on the ICAME gopher server.[1]

Contemporary reading may be garnered from a variety of sources. The Linguistic Data Consortium has a newsletter which it mails free upon request to interested parties. The newsletter contains details of current and future LDC corpus holdings. ICAME has in the past been an important source of papers concerning corpus building and exploitation via the ICAME Journal, long the only corpus linguistics journal. Recently, however, a new journal, the *International Journal of Corpus Linguistics*, published by John Benjamins,[4] has appeared. This journal will undoubtedly be a further important source of information on corpora and their uses.

Resources

ICAME continues to serve as the main repository and distributor for a number of major corpora, and in addition to perform other useful functions such as maintaining a mailing list. An overview of its activities, and even details of its resources, can now be gained using the World Wide Web. For those with access to the Internet, surely an increasing number, there are many things to look forward to for corpus linguists (see Inkster, this volume).

ICAME was, and remains, an institution from which corpora are available to the general public at quite a low price. Some corpus distributors, however, do not issue corpora singly, but rather offer 'membership' of what amounts to a corpus collection and distribution club. This subscription-based access to language resources is becoming increasingly common. American organizations such as the Linguistic Data Consortium (LDC) are quickly being mirrored by European bodies, such as the European Language Resources Association (ELRA). Fees for these bodies can be prohibitively high for the individual teacher (ELRA charges individuals or companies between 1000 and 3000 ECUS per annum for access to corpus resources).

Access to corpora via the World Wide Web promises to be a major means of corpus distribution in the future. To give examples of what is currently available, one may connect to a directory to see what corpus holdings are offered by a particular corpus distributor, such as ELRA,[5] or one may even log onto a corpus server and actually browse corpora remotely, as is the case with the trilingual corpus held at Lancaster.[6]

Notes

1   gopher://nora.hd.uib.no/
2   As part of their *Trends in Linguistics* series.
3   As part of their *Language and Computers: Studies in Practical Linguistics* series.
4   For more information on the journal, e-mail kees.vaes@benjamins.nl
5   http://www.de.elra.research.ec.org
6   http://www.comp.lancs.ac.uk/linguistics/crater/corpus.html

Appendix 2

Sources of Information and Electronic Texts

Bibliography: Classroom Concordancing/Data Driven Learning
An up-to-date bibliography of relevant publications compiled by Tim Johns.
URL: http://web.bham.ac.uk/johnstf/biblio.htm

ICAME (International Computer Archive of Modern English)
Repository and distributor of a number of well-known corpora of the carefully constructed and crafted variety, such as LOB, Brown, ACE.

Address: ICAME
Norwegian Computing Centre for the Humanities
Harald Hårfagres gate 31
N-5007 Bergen
Norway

e-mail: icame@hd.uib.no
URL: http://www.hd.uib.no/icame.html

Oxford Text Archive
A general repository of texts. An especially good source for electronic versions of literary texts. Site of the British National Corpus, which is distributed for a low one-off payment within Europe.

Address: Oxford Text Archive
Oxford University Computing Services
13 Banbury Road
Oxford OX2 6NN

e-mail: archive@oucs.ox.ac.uk
URL: http://ota.ox.ac.uk

Project Gutenberg
A variety of electronic texts made available in plain ASCII format.
All of these are public domain texts, and consequently this is
another good site for literary texts.

Address: Michael S. Hart
             Executive Director of Project Gutenberg
             Illinois Benedictine College
             Lisle IL 60532
             USA

e-mail: dircompg@jg.cso.uiuc.edu
URL: http://www.promo.net/pg/

CHILDES
CHILDES is a primary source of corpus data on language acquisition. CHILDES also distributes tools to aid with the transcription
of child language data.

Address: CHILDES
             Department of Psychology
             Carnegie Melon University
             Pittsburgh PA 15213
             USA

e-mail: brian@andrew.cmu.edu
URL: http://poppy.psy.cmu.edu/childes/index.html

Georgetown University
Georgetown University has a couple of interesting text resource
sites. One deals with Mediaeval texts (site A), while another is an
electronic archive with the specific purpose of providing resources
for teaching American literature (site B).

Address (site A): Center for Electronic Projects in American
                          Studies
                          c/o Randy Bass
                          English Department
                          Georgetown University
                          Washington DC 20057
                          USA

Address (site B): Martin Irvine
                          English Department
                          Georgetown University

Washington DC 20057
USA

e-mail (Site A): labyrinth@gusun.georgetown.edu
e-mail (Site B): tamlit@gusun.georgetown.edu
URL (site A): http://www.georgetown.edu/labyrinth/
info_labyrinth/info.html
URL (site B): http://www.georgetown.edu/crossroads/asw/
lit.html

CETH

An archive of electronic texts, both SGML encoded and plain ASCII, covering a wide variety of text types, from literature to inscriptions.

Address: 169 College Avenue
New Brunswick NJ 08903
USA

e-mail: ceth@zodiac.rutgers.com
URL: http://www.ceth.rutgers.edu/

Trésor de la Langue Française (TLF)

A series of French language texts compiled in a collaboration between the French national research council (CNRS) and the University of Chicago.

Address: ARTFL Project
Department of Romance Language and Literature
1050 East 59th Street
University of Chicago
Chicago
IL 60637
USA

e-mail: marc@tuna.uchicago.edu
URL: http://www.bib.uqam.ca/ARTFL/ARTFL.html

Lancaster University

A parallel aligned trilingual corpus of part-of-speech annotated French, English and Spanish texts. On-line browsing available on the world-wide web.

Address: CRATER Project
Department of Linguistics

Lancaster University
Bailrigg
Lancaster LA1 4YT

email: mcenery@comp.lancs.ac.uk
URL: http://www.comp.lancs.ac.uk/linguistics/crater/
corpus.html

IDS (Institut für deutsche Sprache)
Source of several German language corpora, including Bonner
Zeitungskorpus, Freiburger Corpus, Mannheim Corpus, LIMAS
Corpus.

Address: Institut für deutsche Sprache
Universität Mannheim
Friedrich-Karl-Straße 12
Postfach 5409
D-68 Mannheim
Deutschland
URL: http://www.ids-mannheim.de

Cobuild
Site of the Bank of English and other corpus resources, access to
which is controlled by a subscription service.

Address: COBUILD
Westmere Mews
50 Edgbaston Park Road
Birmingham B15 2TT
e-mail: direct@cobuild.collins.co.uk
URL: http://titania.cobuild.collins.co.uk

Electronic Text Center, University of Virginia
An archive of SGML encoded texts, some of which are publicly
available.

Address: The Electronic Text Center
Alderman Library
University of Virginia
Charlottesville
Virginia 22903
USA
e-mail: etext@virginia.edu
URL: http://www.lib.virginia.edu/etext/ETC.html

ELRA (The European Language Resources Association)
A repository for corpora which has developed as a result of European Union research initiatives in the area of corpus linguistics. To have access to ELRA resources a 1000 ECU per year fee is payable. At the moment few corpora seem to be owned by ELRA, but more are promised.

Address: ELRA Membership Secretariat
          c/o CL International
          46 Grand Rue
          L-1660, Luxembourg

e-mail: 100126.1262@compuserve.com
ftp: de.elra.research.ec.org
URL: http:/www.icp.grenet.fr/ELRA/home.html

Appendix 3

Corpora Mentioned in this Book

- **ACCOR** An acoustic and articulatory database recorded as part of a project investigating cross-language acoustic-articulatory correlations in co-articulatory processes. For information contact the web site:
  http://www.icp.grenet.fr/Relator/multiling/euraccor.html

- **ACE** (Australian Corpus of English) One million words of Australian English (compiled to be comparable with the Brown Corpus). For information contact:
  P. Peters
  School of English
  Macquarie University
  2109 New South Wales
  Australia

- **Bank of English** (see Sinclair, this volume) More than 200 million words of English.

- **BNC** (British National Corpus) 100 million words of English (including 10 million words of transcribed spoken English). Part-of-speech tagged. To be accessible via network, and available on CD-ROM. Contact:
  British National Corpus
  Oxford University Computing Services
  13 Banbury Road
  Oxford OX2 6NN

- **Brown Corpus** Brown University Corpus of American English (1967). Brown University Press, Providence, Rhode Island. A balanced corpus of written American English from the middle of this century. Available from ICAME on its CD-ROM.

- **CSAE** (Corpus of Spoken American English)   One million words of spoken American English. For information contact:
  W. Chafe
  Department of Linguistics
  University of California
  Santa Barbara CA 93106
  USA

- **ICE** (International Corpus of English)   A corpus of national varieties of English, all gathered in the period 1990–94. The corpus covers spoken and written data. For further information contact the web site:
  http://www.ucl.ac.uk/~ucleseu/design.html
  e-mail ucleseu@ucl.ac.uk, or write to:
  Survey of English Usage
  University College London
  Gower Street
  London WC1E 6BT

- **LOB** (Lancaster-Oslo/Bergen Corpus)   Norwegian Computing Centre for the Humanities (1978). Similar to the Brown Corpus in terms of balance and sampling period. However, this is a corpus of written British English. Available from ICAME on its CD-ROM.

- **SEC** (Lancaster/IBM Spoken English Corpus)   52,000 transcribed words of prepared and semi-prepared speech. The corpus is available part-of-speech and prosodically annotated from the ICAME archive. Contact ICAME for further information. The prosodically transcribed version has been published as a book by Addison Wesley Longman (Knowles *et al.* 1996).

- **POW** (Polytechnic of Wales Corpus)   100,000 words of transcribed British English child-language data sampled from 6 to 12-year-olds. The corpus is balanced for sex, age, socio-economic status and strong second language influence. Available at cost from:
  Robin Fawcett
  Department of Behavioural and Communication Studies
  Polytechnic of Wales
  Treforest
  Cardiff CF37 1DL

- **LLC** (London–Lund Corpus)   A corpus of spoken British English. Available from ICAME on its CD ROM.

- **TIMIT**   Developed at MIT by DARPA (Defense Advanced Research Projects Agency), this is a corpus of five hours of transcribed speech. This has been automatically annotated with a phonetic transcription, then hand aligned against the segmented and labelled corpus.

Appendix 4

Software Mentioned in this Book

Concordancers

CLAN: Can be picked off the ICAME gopher site (gopher://
nora.hd.uib.no:70/11/Programs/pc). If you do not have access to
the World Wide Web, contact ICAME for further information.

OCP: OCP, Oxford University Computing Services, 13 Banbury
Road, Oxford OX2 6NN, UK. (Micro-OCP: Oxford University Press,
Electronic Publishing, Walton Street, Oxford OX2 6DP, UK)

TACT: Centre for Computing in the Humanities, Robarts Library,
Room 14297A, University of Toronto, Toronto, Ontario, Canada
M5S 1A5

MicroConcord: Oxford University Press, Electronic Publishing,
Walton Street, Oxford OX2 6DP, UK
  Corpus A: *The Independent* and *The Independent on Sunday*
  Corpus B: Academic texts

MonoConc for Windows was developed by Michael Barlow at Rice
University (USA). It is available from: Athelstn, 2476 Bolsover,
Suite 464, Houston TX 77005, USA. E-mail: athel@nol.net

WordCruncher: Johnston & Company, PO Box 6627, Bloomington
IN 47407, USA

WordSmith (1996) Oxford University Press, Electronic Publishing,
Walton Street, Oxford OX2 6DP, UK. The author is Mike Scott,
University of Liverpool. A demo version can be downloaded elec-
tronically from the OUP web page.

Computer-assisted language learning

Contexts (see Johns, this volume)

Other

PC-Litstats (see Jackson, this volume)

Caucus: Charles Roth, Camber-Roth, 3588 Plymouth Road #223, Ann Arbor, MI 48105–2603, USA

The Unicode Consortium: 1965 Charleston Road, Mountain View, CA 94043, USA

TransLex: contact Just Software, PO Box 1329, Angmering, West Sussex, BN16 4ZE

Accent: Accent Software International Ltd, PO Box 53063, Jerusalem, Israel; UK: PO Box 15, Bushey, Watford WD2 1AZ

Gamma UniVerse: Gamma Productions, Inc., 710 Wilshire Blvd, Suite 609, Santa Monica, California 90401, USA

LocoScript Professional: Locomotive Software Ltd, Dorking Business Park, Dorking, Surrey RH4 1YL

WorldFont for Windows: Data-Cal Corporation, 531 E. Elliot Rd, Chandler, AZ 85225-1152, USA

LanguageLink: Link & Link Software GmbH, Kaiserstr. 21–23, D-44135 Dortmund, Germany

Appendix 5

An Informal Glossary of Computing Terms

ASCII (American Standard Code for Information Interchange)   A numerical coding system for computerized text (see King, this volume). When people refer to a computer document being 'in ASCII', they usually mean that it consists only of the characters that fall within the near-universally adopted lower range of ASCII codes, 1–127, which cover unaccented Latin characters, roman numerals, and a basic range of punctuation. Such files, which may also be referred to as 'text only', present far fewer problems than formatted word-processor files when it comes to manipulating data with different types of software and on different computing 'platforms'.

CD-ROM (Compact Disk – Read-Only Memory)   In physical terms, the compact disks on which we store data, and those which we use in our stereo systems, are exactly the same, though the data formats used on a CD-ROM would not normally make much sense to a domestic CD player. Note that although most data-CDs are indeed 'read-only', writeable CDs are becoming more common. Note that this term may be used to describe the CD itself or to refer to the device which plays the CD.

Concordancer   A program which identifies a pattern (usually a word) within a text, and prints out instances of its occurrence along with a specified amount of context.

DOS (Disk-Operating System)   The most widely used operating system for personal computers. It was developed for use with the first IBM PC, which became an industry standard.

E-mail (Electronic Mail)   Increasingly part of everyday life for people using networked computers. E-mail allows simple text messages to be composed on the screen and sent rapidly to one or more other computer users. More complex documents and programs can be sent by e-mail where circumstances permit.

FAQ (Frequently Asked Question/s)   One widely attested characteristic to have emerged on many on-line mailing lists (*q.v.*) and bulletin boards is the regular occurrence of questions which have been asked just recently by another user. As people have grown weary of answering the same question time and time again, it has become common practice for the list administrator to assemble, and periodically circulate, the answers to a list of 'frequently asked questions'. This, of course, has led to a new FAQ: 'what is an FAQ?'

Filestore   An area where your data is kept. It can also be described as disk-space, though it is increasingly common for filestore to be held on items other than disks – CD-ROMs (*q.v.*) for instance.

FTP (File Transfer Protocol)   A program for 'downloading' or transmitting data from one computer to another. A device known as 'anonymous ftp' represents one of the commoner ways in which data which has been made generally available may be collected by the user from its site of origin. Note that while this is a piece of software, it tends to come as part of an operating system (*q.v.*).

Gigabyte   A gigabyte (Gb) is usually referred to as 1000 megabytes (*q.v.*). However, technically it is actually 1024 megabytes.

HTML (Hypertext Mark-up Language)   A simple way of marking up an electronic document so that it can be placed on the World Wide Web (*q.v.*). HTML documents (known as 'Web pages') appear to the reader as ordinary documents, but may contain 'links' (usually visible as highlighted text) which, when activated by the user, will open up a further 'Web page' which may be any other document or resource on the Web. Providing you are able to place things on the Web, it is possible to construct your own HTML documents containing links to any other resources on the Web, and thus create your own unique resources for others to explore.

Internet (The Net)   The name given to the ever-expanding computer network which covers most of the globe and to which all major academic networks and many commercial networks have easy access.

IRC (Internet Relay Chat)   A multi-user real-time communication device available to many users of the Internet.

KWIC (Key Word In Context)   The most common type of concordance output, in which the search item, or *key word* is presented with a single line of context. When several lines of output are presented the key word is aligned vertically giving the impression of a column (see examples in, e.g. Inkster and Gavioli (this volume)).

Local Area Network (LAN)   A collection of computers linked by cable, and sharing a central device or 'server'. A LAN can be set up in such a way that people can read each other's files, or so that a single set of data stored on the server can be made available to everyone as though it were on their own individual disks.

Macintosh   Used to refer to a range of desktop personal computers produced by the Apple Corporation. Macintosh computers were the first mainstream desktop computers to have a highly graphical user interface. Macintosh software will not, as a rule, run on IBM compatible personal computers (and vice versa). However, Macintosh computers which run IBM compatible PC software as well as Macintosh software are becoming more common.

Machine-readable   A term to describe textual resources which have been stored on computer. It refers specifically to text which has been encoded as characters, rather than images (such as a FAX) which is really just a picture that a human being can interpret as text.

Mailing List   A mailing list is an e-mail-based bulletin board. E-mails are sent to a particular site for inclusion in an electronic mailshot. When the administrator of the mailing list feels that a new mailshot is ready, the collected messages are posted to people who have specifically subscribed to the mailing list.

Megabyte   Often referred to as 'Mb'. A byte is the standard storage space required for one character. A kilobyte (Kb) is generally 1000 bytes and a megabyte is 1000 Kb. However, technically a 'Kb' is 1024 bytes, and hence a 'Mb' is technically 1024 Kb. (*See also* Gigabyte.)

Net, the   *See* Internet.

Newsgroup   The name given to each theme-oriented information channel distributed via the Usenet (*q.v.*)

OCR (Optical Character Reader)   The name for a combination of software and hardware that is capable of reading printed matter and representing the text electronically. With high-quality typed data, an OCR can achieve an impressive rate of accuracy (in some cases approaching perfection).

Operating System   The software which runs the computer and allows other programs to run on that computer.

PC   Although in reality standing for nothing more than 'personal computer', the term PC is almost synonymous with computers which are compatible with IBM manufactured personal computers, as opposed to the Macintosh (*q.v.*).

SCSI (Small Computer Systems Interface)   SCSI (pronounced 'scuzzy') is a standard method of connecting devices together. It is becoming common in desktop computers.

SGML (Standard Generalized Mark-Up Language)   A means of encoding information within machine-readable text. This information may be truly diverse, but is usually limited to representing formatting within the text.

Tagger   A program which assigns labels to words or other units in a machine-readable (*q.v.*) text. Currently the most common type of tagger is one which assigns part of speech labels, typically using a probabilistic algorithm, based on frequencies observed in previously tagged, or annotated, text corpora.

TEI (Text Encoding Initiative)   An international initiative started by the Association for Computing and the Humanities to ensure that texts were easily transferable between sites. The main focus of the TEI is to ensure that a set of conventions exists to encode information in texts. Its recommendations are based on the use of SGML (*q.v.*).

UNIX   An operating system frequently used in academic environments, both on mainframes and (to an increasing extent) on smaller 'workstations', powerful computers, typically supporting several users at once.

Usenet   A conferencing system that handles a number of themed newsgroups (*q.v.*) over the internet (*q.v.*). Usenet can often be accessed from mainframe computers using such commands as 'rn' (read-news) 'trn' (threaded read-news).

Windows   An operating system (*q.v.*) which uses a graphical user interface and a desktop metaphor to enable users to interact with a computer. Windows is a PC (*q.v.*) operating system, but similar operating systems exist for most computers now.

World Wide Web (W^3 or WWW)   Increasingly data on the Internet (*q.v.*) is being presented via viewers which allows a hypertext-like navigation of multimedia documents to take place. The World Wide Web is the forum on the Internet where resources are made available for browsing marked up in HTML (*q.v.*) to allow this form of interaction.

References

Dictionaries

1966 *Dictionary of American Homophones and Homographs*, ed. H. Whitford. Teachers College Press

1980 *Oxford American Dictionary*, ed. E. Ehrlich *et al.* Avon, New York

1984 *Duden Grammatik*. Duden, Mannheim

1960 [1986] *Dictionary of American Slang*, ed. H. Wentworth and S.B. Flexner. Harrap, London

1986 *New Dictionary of American Slang*, ed. R.L. Chapman. Harper & Row, New York

1986 *Y Geiriadur Mawr*, ed. H.M. Evans and W.O. Thomas. Gwasg Gomer, Llandysul

1987 *Collins Cobuild English Language Dictionary*. Collins, London

1987 *Longman Dictionary of Contemporary English [LDOCE]*. Longman, London

1987 *Geiriadur Prifysgol Cymru ['Dictionary of the University of Wales']*. University of Wales Press, Cardiff

1988 *Webster's Ninth New Collegiate Dictionary*. Merriam-Webster, Springfield, Massachusetts

1989 *Oxford Advanced Learner's Dictionary of Current English*. A.S. Hornby (4th edition)

1989 *Oxford English Dictionary*. Oxford University Press, Oxford

1990 *Bloomsbury Dictionary of Contemporary Slang*. Bloomsbury Publishing Ltd

1990 *Longman Pronunciation Dictionary*, ed. J. Wells. Longman, London

1991 *Macquarie Dictionary*. Macquarie Library, Macquarie

1991 *Collins English Dictionary*. Collins, London

1992 *American Heritage Dictionary [AHD]*
1992 *Dictionary of English Language and Culture.* Longman, London
1993 *Stora svensk-engelska ordboken [SSEO]* [*'Comprehensive Swedish-English Dictionary'*]. Norstedts, Stockholm
1993 *Webster's Tenth New Collegiate Dictionary.* Merriam-Webster, Springfield, Massachusetts
1995 *Longman Dictionary of Contemporary English* (3rd edition)

Primary sources

1960 *Y Caniedydd.* Cardiff
1980 *English in Action.* Langenscheidt-Longman, München
1989 *Learning English: Green Line 6.* Klett, Stuttgart

Newspapers

1990–92 *The New York Times.* UMI, Ann Arbor, Michigan. CDs
1991–92 *The Washington Post.* UMI, Ann Arbor, Michigan. CDs
1992 *The Times.* The Times Network Systems Ltd. CD
1992–94 *The Independent.* Chadwyck-Healey Ltd. CD

Books, papers and articles

Ahmad, K. and Davies, A. 1992a *Knowledge Processing 2: Terminology Management: a corpus-based approach to eliciting and elaborating specialist terms.* University of Surrey Computer Sciences Report 5, Guildford

Ahmad, K. and Davies, A. 1992b *Welsh: the Language and Requirements of its Users. A computer-based corpus-informed investigation.* University of Surrey Computer Sciences Report 16, Guildford

Aijmer, K. and Altenberg, B. (eds) 1991 *English Corpus Linguistics.* Longman, London

Alatis, J.E. (ed.) 1992 *Linguistics and Language Pedagogy: the State of the Art.* Georgetown University Press, Washington DC

Alderson, C. 1996 'Do Corpora have a role in language assessment?' in Thomas, J. and Short, M. *Using Corpora for Language Research.* Longman, London, pp. 248–59

Alexander, L.G. 1988 *Longman English Grammar.* Longman, London

Anderson, S. 1992 *A-morphous Morphology.* Cambridge University Press, Cambridge

Aston, G. 1988 *Learning Comity: an approach to the description and pedagogy of interactional speech.* Cooperativa Libraria Universitaria Editrice, Bologna

Aston, G. 1996 Involving learners in developing methods: exploiting text corpora in self-access. In Benson, P. and Voller, P. (eds) *Autonomy and Independence in Language Learning.* Longman, London

Awbery, G.M. 1976 *The Syntax of Welsh: a transformational study of the passive.* Cambridge University Press, Cambridge

Ball, M.J., Griffiths, T. and Jones, G.E. 1988 Broadcast Welsh. In Ball, M.J. (ed.) *The Use of Welsh.* Multilingual Matters Ltd, Clevedon, Philadelphia, pp. 182–99

Ball, M.J. (ed.) 1988 *The Use of Welsh: a contribution to sociolinguistics.* Multilingual Matters Ltd, Clevedon, Philadelphia

Barnett, L. 1993 Teacher off: computer technology, guidance and self-access. *System* **21**(3): 295–304

Bauer, L. 1994 *Watching Language Change.* Longman, London

Baugh, A.C. 1951 *A History of the English Language.* Routledge, London

Bell, R. 1991 *The Language of News Media.* Blackwell, Oxford

Biber, D., Conrad, S. and Reppen, R. 1994 Corpus-based approaches to issues in applied linguistics. *Applied Linguistics* **15**: 169–89

Bolinger, D. 1946 Visual morphemes. *Language* **22**

Bolinger, D. 1976 Meaning and memory. *Forum Linguisticum* **1**: 1–14

Bongaerts, T., de Haan, P., Lobbe, S. and Wekker, H. (eds) 1988 *Computer Applications in Language Learning.* Foris, Dordrecht

Bradley, J. and Presutti, L. 1989/90 *TACT.* University of Toronto Computing Services

Brill, E. 1993 *A corpus-based approach to language learning.* Dissertation to the University of Pennsylvania, distributed by ftp

Brown, R. 1973 *A First Language.* Harvard University Press, Cambridge, Mass.

Brumfit, C.J. 1984 *Communicative Methodology in Language Teaching.* Cambridge University Press, Cambridge

Burnley, D. 1992 *The History of the English Language.* Longman, London

Burrows, J.F. 1987 *Computation into Criticism.* Clarendon Press, Oxford

Burt, M. and Dulay, H. 1980 On acquisition orders. In Felix, S. (ed.) *Second Language Development.* Narr, Tübingen, pp. 265–327

Butler, C.S. 1992 *Computers and Written Texts.* Blackwell, Oxford

Carroll, J.B., Davies, P. and Richman, B. (eds) 1971 *The American Heritage Word Frequency Book.* Houghton Mifflin, Boston

Chafe, W. 1995 Adequacy, user-friendliness and practicality in transcribing. In Leech, G., Myers, G. and Thomas, J. (eds) *Spoken English on Computer: Transcription, Mark-up and Application.* Longman, London

Chandler, B. 1989 *Longman Mini-Concordancer.* Longman, London

Chomsky, N. 1965 *Aspects of the Theory of Syntax.* MIT Press, Massachusetts

Chomsky, N. 1981 Principles and parameters in syntactic theory. In Hornstein, N. and Lightfoot, D. (eds) *Explanations in Linguistics.* Longman, London, pp. 32–75

Chomsky, N. 1988 *Language and the Problems of Language.* MIT Press, Cambridge, Mass.

Cook, V. 1988 *Chomsky's Universal Grammar.* Blackwell, Oxford

Corder, S.P. 1986 Talking shop: language teaching and applied linguistics. *ELT Journal* **40**: 185–90

Di Concilio, E. 1993 *Citations of nursery rhymes in newspaper corpora.* Unpublished research paper. Scuola Superiore di Lingue Moderne per Interpreti e Traduttori, University of Bologna at Forlì

Doyle, P. 1992 *Could they be persuaded? A teacher's investigation of the value of concordances to second language learners.* Unpublished MA dissertation, University of Birmingham

Dulay, H., Burt, M. and Krashen, S. 1982 *Language Two.* Oxford University Press, Oxford

Durrell, M. 1991 *Hammer's German Grammar and Usage.* Revised edition. Edward Arnold, London

Durrell, M. 1992 *Using German.* Cambridge University Press, London

Edwards, J. 1993 Principles and contrasting systems of discourse transcription. In Edwards, J. and Lampert, M. (eds) *Talking Data.* Erlbaum, Hillsdale, pp. 3–32

Edwards, J. and Lampert, M. 1993 (eds) *Talking Data.* Erlbaum, Hillsdale, NJ

Evans, M. 1993 NICOLAS: Using hypercard with intermediate level French learners. *System* **21**(2): 231–44

Faerch, C. and Kasper, G. 1984 Pragmatic knowledge: rules and procedures. *Applied Linguistics* **5**: 214–25

Fawcett, H. 1988 *The User's Guide to Pat.* University of Waterloo

Felix, S. 1982 *Psycholinguistische Aspekte des Zweitsprachenerwerbs.* Narr, Tübingen

Fligelstone, S. 1993 Some reflections on the question of teaching, from a corpus linguistics perspective. *ICAME Journal* **17**: 97–109

Flowerdew, J. 1993 Concordancing as a tool in course design. *System* **21**(2): 213–29

Francis, W.N. and Kucera, H. 1989 *Manual of Information to accompany a Standard Corpus of Present-Day Educated American English.* Department of Linguistics, Brown University, Providence, Rhode Island

Freeborn, D. 1992 *From Old English to Standard English.* Macmillan, London

Freeman, D. 1970 *Linguistics and Literary Style.* Holt, Rinehart & Winston, New York

Fynes-Clinton, O.H. 1913 *The Welsh Vocabulary of the Bangor District.* Oxford University Press, Oxford

Garside, R., Leech, G. and Sampson, G. 1987 *The Computational Analysis of English: a corpus-based approach.* Longman, London

Grabowski, E. and Mindt, D. 1994 Die unregelmäßigen Verben des Englischen: eine Lernliste auf empirischer Grundlage. *Die Neueren Sprachen* **93**(4): 334–53

Grabowski, E. and Mindt, D. 1995 A corpus-based learning list of irregular verbs in English. *ICAME Journal* **19**: 5–22

Granger, S. 1993 International Corpus of Learner English, in Aarts, J., de Haan, P. and Oostdijk, N. (eds) *English Language Corpora: Design, Analysis and Exploitation.* Rodopi, Amsterdam, pp. 57–72

Green, E. and Peters, P. 1991 The Australian corpus project and Australian English. *ICAME Journal* **15**: 37–53

Grenfell, M. 1992 Process reading in the communicative classroom. *Language Learning Journal* **6**: 48–52

Grundy, P. 1993 *Newspapers.* Oxford University Press, Oxford

Gunning, R. 1952 *The Techniques of Clear Writing.* McGraw-Hill, New York

Halliday, M.A.K. 1985 *An Introduction to Functional Grammar.* Edward Arnold, London

Halliday, M.A.K. and Hasan, R. 1976 *Cohesion in English.* Longman, London

Hardisty, D. and Windeatt, S. 1989 *CALL*. Oxford University Press, Oxford

Haslerud, V. and Stenström, A-B. 1995 The Bergen Corpus of London Teenager Language (COLT). In Leech, G., Myers, G. and Thomas, J. (eds) *Spoken English on Computer: Transcription, Mark-up and Application*. Longman, London, pp. 235–42

Hatton, L. 1988 The development of the nasal mutation in the speech of schoolchildren. In Ball, M.J. (ed.) *The Use of Welsh*. Multilingual Matters Ltd, Clevedon, Philadelphia

Higgins, J. 1988 *Language, Learners and Computers*. Longman, London

Higgins, J. and Johns, T. 1984 *Computers in Language Learning*. Collins, London

Hockey, S. 1980 *A Guide to Computer Applications in the Humanities*. Duckworth, London

Hockey, S. and Marriott, I. 1980 *Oxford Concordance Program*. Oxford University Computing Service

Holmes-Higgin, P., Griffin, S., Hook, S. and Abidi, S.R. 1993 *System Quirk: User Guide*. University of Surrey, Guildford

Howatt, A. 1984 *A History of English Language Teaching*. Oxford University Press, Oxford

Hughes, L. and Lee, S. (eds) 1994 *Resources Guide 1994*. CTI Centre for Textual Studies, Oxford

Hult, S., Kalaja, M., Lassila, O. and Lehtisalo, T. 1990 Hyper-reader: an interactive course in reading comprehension. *System* 18: 189–98

Ide, N. and Véronis, J. 1994 Multext: multilingual text tools and corpora. *COLING 1994: Proceedings of the 15th International Conference on Computational Linguistics, August 5–9*, Vol 1, pp. 588–92

Jackson, H. 1990 OCP and the computer analysis of texts. *Literary and Linguistic Computing* 5(1): 86–8

Jackson, H. 1993 Computerized text analysis in teaching. *Computers and Texts* 5

Johansson, S. and Stenström, A-B. (eds) 1991 *English Computer Corpora: selected papers and research guide*. Mouton de Gruyter, Berlin

Johansson, S. and Hofland, K. 1989 *Frequency Analysis of English Vocabulary and Grammar*. Clarendon Press, Oxford

Johns, T. 1986 Micro-Concord, a language learner's research tool. *System* 14(2): 151–62

Johns, T. 1988 Whence and whither classroom concordancing? In Bongaerts, T., de Haan P., Lobbe, S. and Wekker, H. (eds)

Computer Applications in Language Learning. Foris, Dordrecht, pp. 9–27

Johns, T. 1991a Should you be persuaded – two samples of data-driven learning materials. In Johns, T. and King, P. (eds) *Classroom Concordancing*, pp. 1–16

Johns, T. 1991b From printout to handout: grammar and vocabulary teaching in the context of data-driven learning. In Johns, T. and King, P. (eds) *Classroom Concordancing*, pp. 27–45

Johns, T. 1993 Data-driven learning: an update. *TELL&CALL* **3**

Johns, T. and King, P. (eds) 1991 *Classroom Concordancing* **4**. English Language Research Journal, Birmingham University

Jones, J.R. 1985 *Cemegion Ymbelydrol – Datblygiadau Diweddar, Ddarlith Walter Idris Jones*. Coleg Prifysgol Cymru, Aberystwyth

Jones, M. and Thomas, A.R. 1977 *The Welsh Language: studies in its syntax and semantics*. University of Wales Press, Cardiff

Jordan, G. 1992 *Concordances: research findings and learner processes*. Unpublished MA dissertation. London Institute of Education

Karpf, A. 1991 Universal Grammar Needs Organization. *Folia Linguistica* **XXV**: 339–60

Kennedy, G. 1992 Preferred ways of putting things with implications for language teaching. In Svartvik, J. (ed.) *Directions in Corpus Linguistics: Proceedings of Nobel Symposium 82*. Mouton de Gruyter, Berlin, pp. 335–73

Kettemann, B., Gratze, C. and Mittendorfer, F. 1991 Computers in English language education and research. *ReCALL* **5**: 15–16

King, G. 1993 *Modern Welsh: A Comprehensive Grammar*. Routledge, London

Kirk, J. 1994 Teaching and language corpora: the Queens approach. In Wilson, A. and McEnery, A. (eds) *Corpora in Language Education and Research: a selection of papers from Talc94*. Lancaster University

Klapper, J. 1992 Reading in a foreign language: theoretical issues. *Language Learning Journal* **5**: 27–30

Knowles, G. 1987 *Patterns of Spoken English*. Longman, London

Knowles, G, 1990 The uses of spoken and written corpora in the teaching of language and linguistics, *Literary and Linguistic Computing* **5(1)**: 45–8

Knowles, G. 1991 Prosodic labelling: the problem of tone group boundaries. In Johansson, S. and Stenström, A-B. (eds) *English Computer Corpora: selected papers and research guide*. Mouton de Gruyter, Berlin

Knowles, G., Williams, B. and Taylor, L. (eds) 1996 *A Corpus of Formal British English Speech.* Longman, London

Krashen, S. 1982 *Principles and Practice in Second Language Acquisition.* Pergamon, Oxford

Krashen, S. 1985 *The Input Hypothesis: Issues and Implications.* Longman, New York

Larsen-Freeman, D. 1976 An explanation for the morpheme acquisition order of second language learners. *Language Learning* **26**: 125–34

Larsen-Freeman, D. and Long, M. 1991 *An Introduction to Second Language Acquisition Research.* Longman, London

Last, R. 1992 Computers and language learning: past, present and future? In Butler, C. (ed.) *Computers and Written Texts.* Blackwell, Oxford, pp. 227–245

Laurillard, D. 1993 *Rethinking University Teaching: a framework for the effective use of educational technology.* Routledge, London

Lavelle, T. and Minugh, D. (forthcoming) High Time: a corpus-based investigation of its high time constructions in current-day newspapers

Leech, G. 1993 100 million words of English, *English Today* **9(1)**: 9–15

Leech, G. and Candlin, C. (eds) 1986 *Computers in English Language Teaching and Research.* Longman, London

Leech, G. and Fallon, R. 1992 Computer corpora: what do they tell us about culture? *ICAME Journal* **16**: 29–50

Leech, G. and Fligelstone, S. 1992 Computers and corpus analysis. In Butler, C. (ed.) *Computers and Written Texts.* Blackwell, Oxford, pp. 115–40

Leith, D. 1983 *A Social History of English.* Routledge & Kegan Paul, London

Lewis, H. (ed.) 1955 *Yr argraffiad newydd o'r Beibl.* London

Lightbown, P. 1983 Exploring relationships between developmental and instructional sequences in L2 acquisition. In Seliger, H. and Long, M. (eds) *Classroom Oriented Research in Second Language Acquisition.* Newbury House, Rowley, Mass., pp. 217–43

Lightbown, P. and Spada, N. 1993 *How Languages are Learned.* Oxford University Press, Oxford

Ljung, M. 1990 *A Study of TEFL Vocabulary.* Almqvist & Wiksell International, Stockholm

Ljung, M. and Ohlander, S. 1992 *Gleerups Engelska Grammatik.* Gleerups, Malmö

Lodge, D. 1966 *Language of Fiction*. RKP, London

Long, M. 1981 Input, interaction and second language acquisition. *Native Language and Foreign Language Acquisition* **397**: 259–78

Louw, W.E. 1991 Classroom concordancing of delexical forms and the case for integrating language and literature. In King, P. and Johns, T.F. (eds) *Classroom Concordancing*.

Louw, W.E. 1993 Irony in the text or insincerity in the writer? The diagnostic potential of semantic prosodies. In Baker, M., Francis, G. and Tognini-Bonelli, E. (eds) *Text and Technology: in honour of John Sinclair*. Benjamin, Amsterdam, pp. 157–76

Ma, K.C. 1993 Small-corpora concordancing in ESL teaching and learning. *Hong Kong Papers in Linguistics and Language Teaching* **16**: 11–26

MacWhinney, B. and Snow, C. 1991 *The CHILDES Project: Tools for Analyzing Talk*. Lawrence Erlbaum, Hillsdale, NJ

Maioli, C., Bassi, B. and Biolcati-Rinaldi, M.L. 1991 Ipertesti e presentazione della conoscenza nella didattica delle lingue. In Favretti, R. (ed.) *Il computer nell'apprendimento e nell'autoapprendimento linguistico*. Monduzzi, Bologna, pp. 65–75

McCarthy, M. and Carter, R. 1993 *Language as Discourse*. Longman, London

McEnery, A., Oakes, M., Garside, R., Hutchinson, J. and Leech, G. 1994 The exploitation of parallel corpora in Projects ET 10–63 and CRATER. In *Proceedings of NewLAP*, UMIST, Manchester

McEnery, A.M. and Wilson, A. (1996) *Corpus Linguistics* Edinburgh University press, Edinburgh

McEnery, A.M., Baker, P. and Wilson, A. (1995) A statistical analysis of corpus-based computer vs human teaching methods of part-of-speech analysis. In: *Computer Assisted Language Learning*, **8**, Number 2–3

McKenna, P. and Seeve-McKenna, N. 1992 Hyperlanguage: to boldly go . . . ? *Language Learning Journal* **6**: 71–2

Merrill, M.D. 1993 Advances in instructional transaction theory. Presentation at International Conference on Computers in Education, Taipei

Mindt, D. 1986 Corpus, grammar and teaching English as a foreign language. In Leitner, G. (ed.) *The English Reference Grammar: Language and Linguistics, Writers and Readers*. Max Niemeyer Verlag, Tübingen, pp. 125–39

Mindt, D. 1987 *Sprache–Grammatik–Unterrichtsgrammatik: Futurischer Zeitbezug im Englischen I*. Diesterweg, Frankfurt am Main

Mindt, D. (ed.) 1988 *EDV in der Angewandten Linguistik: Ziele–Methoden–Ergebnisse.* Diesterweg, Frankfurt am Main

Mindt, D. 1989 Richtlinien und Lehrwerke für den Englischunterricht: Wie steht es mit den Grammatikkenntnissen der Kultusminister? *Praxis des neusprachlichen Unterrichts* **36**(4): 347–56

Mindt, D. 1992 *Zeitbezug im Englischen: Eine didaktische Grammatik des englischen Futurs.* Narr, Tübingen

Mindt, D. 1995 *An Empirical Grammar of the English Verb: Modal Verbs.* Cornelsen, Berlin

Mindt, D. and Tesch, F. 1991 Computergestützte Forschungen zu einer didaktischen Grammatik des Englischen. *Fremdsprachen Lehren und Lernen* **20**: 39–51

Munro, S.M. 1988 Phonological disorders in Welsh-speaking children. In Ball, M.J. (ed.) *The Use of Welsh.* Multilingual Matters Ltd, Clevedon, Philadelphia, pp. 258–86

Murison-Bowie, S. 1993 *MicroConcord Manual. An introduction to the practices and principles of concordancing in language teaching.* Oxford University Press, Oxford

Nielsen, J. 1990 *Hypertext and Hypermedia.* Academic Press, London

Pawley, A. and Syder, F. 1983 Two puzzles for linguistic theory: nativelike selection and nativelike fluency. In Richards, J. and Schmidt, R. (eds) *Language and Communication.* Longman, London

Pfeffer, J.A. 1970 *Basic (Spoken) German Dictionary for Everyday Use.* Prentice-Hall, Englewood Cliffs, NJ

Pfeffer, J.A. and Lohnes, W.F.W. 1984 *Textkorpora 1. Einführungs- und Registerband.* Max Niemeyer Verlag, Tübingen

Picken, C. 1991 *Translating and the Computer 12: Applying Technology to the Translation Process.* ASLIB Association for Information Management

Potter, R.G. 1989 *Literary Computing and Literary Criticism.* University of Pennsylvania Press

Prabhu, N.S. 1987 *Second Language Pedagogy.* Oxford University Press, Oxford

Pyles, T. 1971 *The Origins and Development of the English Language.* Harcourt, Brace & Jovanovich, New York

Quirk, R., Greenbaum, S., Leech, G. and Svartvik, J. 1972 *A Grammar of Contemporary English.* Longman, London

Quirk, R., Greenbaum, S., Leech, G. and Svartvik, J. 1985 *A Comprehensive Grammar of the English Language.* Longman, London

Reimer, S.R. 1989 *PC-Litstats: a statistical package for literary study.* University of Alberta Department of English

Renouf, A. 1987 Corpus development. In Sinclair, J. (ed.) *Looking Up*. Collins, London, pp. 1–40

Roach, P.J. 1991 *English Phonetics and Phonology*. Cambridge University Press, London

Rowland, T. 1876 *A Grammar of the Welsh Language*. Simpson Marshall, London

Rudall, B.H. and Corns, T.N. 1987 *Computers and Literature: a practical guide*. Abacus Press, Tunbridge Wells

Rundell, M. and Stock, P. 1992 The corpus revolution. *English Today* **8**(2): 9–14

Sampson, G.R. 1992 *The Susanne Corpus*. University of Sussex

Schank, R. 1980 Language and memory. *Cognitive Science* **4**: 243–84

Schank, R. and Abelson, P. 1975 Scripts, plans and knowledge. In Johnson-Laird, P. and Wason, P. (eds) *Thinking: Readings in Cognitive Science*. Cambridge University Press, Cambridge, pp. 421–32

Schmidt, R. 1990 The role of consciousness in second language learning. *Applied Linguistics* **11**: 129–58

Scott, M. and Johns, T. 1993 *MicroConcord ver. 1.0*. Oxford University Press, Oxford

Sinclair, J. 1986 Basic computer processing of long texts. In Leech, G. and Candlin, C.N. (eds) *Computers in English Language Teaching and Research*. Longman, London, pp. 185–203

Sinclair, J. 1990 *Collins Cobuild English Grammar*. Collins, London

Sinclair, J. 1991 *Corpus, Concordance, Collocation*. Oxford University Press, Oxford

Sinclair, J. 1992 Shared knowledge. In Alatis, J.E. (ed.) *Linguistics and Language Pedagogy: the State of the Art*. Georgetown University Press, Washington DC, pp. 489–500

Skehan, P. 1993 Second language acquisition strategies and task-based learning. In Scarpis, V.D., Innocenti, L., Marucci, F. and Pajalich, A. (eds) *Intrecci e contaminazioni*. Supernova, Venice

Soukhanov, A. 1993 Word watch. *The Atlantic* **272**(6): 148

Stenström, A-B. 1994 *An Introduction to Spoken Interaction*. Longman, London

Stevens, V. 1991 Concordance-based vocabulary exercises: a viable alternative to gap-fillers. In Johns, T. and King, P. (eds) *Classroom Concordancing* **4**: 47–61. English Language Research Journal, Birmingham University

Stubbs, M. and Gerbig, A. 1993 Human and inhuman geography: on the computer-assisted analysis of long texts. In Hoey, M.

(ed.) *Data, Description, Discourse: papers on the English language in honour of John McH Sinclair.* HarperCollins, London, pp. 64–85

Svartvik, J. (ed.) 1992 *Directions in Corpus Linguistics: Proceedings of Nobel Symposium 82.* Mouton de Gruyter, Berlin

Svartvik, J. 1966 *On Voice in the English Verb.* Mouton, The Hague

Svartvik, J. 1990 *The Lundon-Lund Corpus of Spoken English: Description and Research.* Lund Studies in English 82. Lund University Press, Lund

Svartvik, J. and Sager, O. 1975 *Modern engelsk grammatik.* Esselte, Stockholm

Svartvik, J. and Sager, O. 1985 *Modern engelsk grammatik* (3rd edition). Esselte, Stockholm

Taylor, J.R. 1989 *Linguistic Categorization: Prototypes in Linguistic Theory.* Clarendon Press, Oxford

Tesch, F. 1990 *Die Indefinitpronomina some und any im authentischen englischen Sprachgebrauch und in Lehrwerken: eine empirische Untersuchung.* Narr, Tübingen

Tottie, G. 1991 Conversational style in British and American English: the case of backchannels. In Aijmer, K. and Altenberg, B. (eds) *English Corpus Linguistics.* Longman, London

Townson, M. 1992 *Mother-tongue and Fatherland. Language and Politics.* Manchester University Press

Tribble, C.T. and Jones, G. 1990 *Concordances in the Classroom.* Longman, London

Ungerer, F., Meier, G.E.H., Schäfer, K. and Lechler, S.B. 1984 *A Grammar of Present-Day English.* Klett, Stuttgart

Van Els, T., Bongaerts, T., Extra, G., Van Os, C. and Janssen-Van Dieten, A-M. 1984 *Applied Linguistics and Teaching of Foreign Languages.* Edward Arnold, London

Waitzbauer, M. 1994 CONTEXTS: eine Vorschau. *TELL&CALL 1994* 1: 42–4

West, M. (ed.) 1953 *A General Service List of English Words.* Longman, London

Widdowson, H.G. 1979 *Explorations in Applied Linguistics.* Oxford University Press, Oxford

Widdowson, H.G. 1983 *Learning Purpose and Language Use.* Oxford University Press, Oxford

Widdowson, H.G. 1989 Knowledge of language and ability for use. *Applied Linguistics* 10: 128–37

Widdowson, H.G. 1991 The description and prescription of language. In Alatis, J.E. (ed.) *Linguistics and Language Pedagogy: the*

State of the Art. Georgetown University Press, Washington DC, pp. 11–24

Widdowson, H.G. 1992 The description and prescription of language. In *Linguistics and Language Pedagogy. Proceedings of the Georgetown University Round Table on Language and Linguistics 1991*

Widdowson, H.G. 1993 Communication, community, and the problem of appropriate use. In Alatis, J.E. (ed.) *Language, Communication and Social Meaning.* Georgetown University Press, Washington DC, pp. 305–15

Williams, S.J. 1980 *A Welsh Grammar.* University of Wales Press, Cardiff

Willis, J.D. 1990 *The Lexical Syllabus: a new approach to language teaching.* Collins, London

Willis, J.D. 1993 Syllabus, corpus and data-driven learning. *IATEFL 1993 Annual Conference Report*, pp. 25–32

Wilson, E. *et al.* 1992 CALLGUIDE: using programmable hypertext as a shell for CALL programs. In Tomek, L. (ed.) *Computer Assisted Learning.* Springer Verlag, Berlin

Wilson, E. 1993a The language learner and the computer: modes of interaction. *ACH/ALLC Joint International Conference*, Washington DC

Wilson, E. 1993b An intelligent interface for computer-assisted language learning. In Bass, L.J., Gornostaev, J. and Unger, C. (eds) *Human-Computer Interaction: EWHCI '93, Selected Papers. Lecture Notes in Computer Science* **753**: 357–70

Windeatt, S. 1987 Concordances in language teaching. *ReCALL* **3**

Winograd, T. 1977 A framework for understanding discourse. *Cognitive Processes in Comprehension.* Erlbaum, Hillsdale NJ

Yang, H. 1985 The JDEST computer corpus of texts in English for science and technology. *ICAME News* **9**: 24–5

Zanettin, F. 1994 Parallel words: designing a bilingual database for translation activities. *Corpora in Language Education and Research: A selection of papers from TALC '94* **4** (special issue): 99–111

Zhu, Q. 1989 A quantitative look at the Guangzhou Petroleum English Corpus. *ICAME Journal* **13**: 28–38

Zipf, G.K. 1935 *The Psychobiology of Language.* MIT Press, Cambridge, Mass.

Index